A VARIOUS ART

A VARIOUS ART

EDITED BY
ANDREW CROZIER & TIM LONGVILLE

CARCANET

First published in 1987 by
Carcanet Press Limited
208-212 Corn Exchange Buildings
Manchester M4 3BQ

and Carcanet
198 Sixth Avenue
New York, New York 10013

British Library Cataloguing in Publication Data

A Various Art : an anthology.
1. English poetre — 20th century
I. Title   II. Crozier, Andrew & Longville, Tim
821'.914'08   PR1225

ISBN 0-85635-698-0

The publisher acknowledges financial assistance
from the Arts Council of Great Britain

Typeset in 10pt Palatino by Bryan Williamson, Manchester
Printed in England by SRP Ltd, Exeter

Contents

Introduction   11

ANTHONY BARNETT
From *Blood Flow*   15
From *Titular*   19
From *Fear and Misadventure*   19
After   22
From *Mud Settles*   26
From *Report to the Working Party* . . .   28
Blake or Yeats Slept With You   32
A White Mess   33
From *North North, I Said* . . .   35

DAVID CHALONER
Twice   42
"fatigue creeps closer under the awning"   42
"the problem the grass under the saplings"   43
Doors   43
Cameo   44
The Strategy   44
Never Let It End   45
"the first restless flaws of morning"   47
Travelling   47
Interior: Morning   48
"sitting here how do they know where"   48
"how restless they are"   49
"there is enough for us all"   50
Today Backwards   50
Incredible Vistas   51
Theory   52
Just Deserts   52
Now and Then   54
Inspiration is Just a Guy Called Art   55
Hotel Zingo   56
Pact and Impact   57
Here Today Here Tomorrow   57
Rain   58
Caption Block   63

ANDREW CROZIER
The Source   69
February Evenings   69

Two Robin Croft   70
Birds in Sunlight   70
The Veil Poem   71
The Life Class   76
From *Pleats*   77
Local Colour   83
Light in the Air   83
From *High Zero*   84
Forsythia   89
Utamaro Variations   90
Swoon   92
Winter Intimacies   92
Humiliation in its Disguises   93
Clouds and Windows   94
Evaporation of a Dream   94
White Launch   95
Fifth Variation   95

         ROY FISHER
From *City*   96
From *Interiors with Various Figures*   97
After Working   98
For Realism   99
From an English Sensibility   100
107 Poems   101
At Once   104
Some Loss   104
From *Handsworth Liberties*   105
The Trace   107
Wonders of Obligation   109

         VERONICA FORREST-THOMSON
Pastoral   117
The Lady of Shalott: Ode   118
The Garden of Proserpine   118
Cordelia   121
Richard II   126

         JOHN HALL
Couch Grass   128
Meaning Insomnia   133
Reeves Timber Yard   134

RALPH HAWKINS
"Easter Monday" 135
But It May Be So 136
No Head for Heights 143

JOHN JAMES
Exultation 145
"...or as we wheel" 147
On Leaving the Footpath 148
Written on Beginning Georg Büchner's *Lenz* & While
    Waiting a Return 148
Side Window 149
"This to be done" 150
"for the snow" 151
"a complete innocence" 152
Rough 152
"the day writhes in an immense crater" 153
The Dragon House 154
Good Old Harry 156
Inaugural Address 158
Craven Images 160
Bye Bye Blackbird 166
After Christopher Wood 167
Sister Midnight 168

TIM LONGVILLE
Epitaph 170
Pigeons 170
Grave Stone 171
Heavy as Ever 171
Going Off 172
Poem of Apology 173
Airs and Distance 174
Mine 174
Strict and Particular Old Lady 175
Company Figures 175
Apple and Cloth 176
One Leg and Peers 176
En Attendant 177
Poem on these Poems 177
Prospects 177
Pavane for a Dead Cat 178
Blue 179
Dogs 179

7

Graph 181
Homage to William Bronk 182
Music to Live By 182
Melancholy Speech of Bluebell the Bogomil Dog 183
The Verge of Speech 184
Between the River and the Sea 186
Conversations Among Poems 193
The Language of Delight 195

DOUGLAS OLIVER
When I Was in Bridport 197
The Furnaces 198
Ordnance Survey Map 178 199
Mongol in the Woods 200
Remember Stortford, Birthplace of Rhodes 201
Picnic 202
You're Julia 203
Not in Another Photo 204
Love in the Dark Valley 205
From *In the Cave of Suicession* 206
From *The Diagram Poems* 214
Bonis Avibus 219
From *The Infant and the Pearl* 220

PETER PHILPOTT
Like an Aerolith 225
Nine Men's Morris 225
"It's that we're identical" 226
What Was Shown 227
From *Some Action Upon the World* 229

J.H. PRYNNE
Sketch for a Financial Theory of the Self 233
If There is a Station Master at Stamford S.D. Hardly So 235
Against Hurt 236
Love in the Air 237
From End to End 239
First Notes on Daylight 240
Frost and Snow, Falling 241
Shadow Songs 243
Concerning Quality, Again 244
The Common Gain, Reverted 245
Thoughts on the Esterházy Court Uniform 246
A Dream of Retained Colour 248

One Way at Any Time	250
Love	251
As It Were an Attendant	252
The Bee Target on His Shoulder	253
The Ideal Star-Fighter	257
Es Lebe der König	258
From *Into the Day*	260
Treatment in the Field	261
Of Movement Towards a Natural Place	262
Again in the Black Cloud	263
From *High Pink on Chrome*	265
From *News of Warring Clans*	267
From *Down where changed*	269
From *The Oval Window*	271

JOHN RILEY

Views of Where One Is	273
Pentecost	273
Second Fragment	274
After the Music	274
From *A Sequence*	275
"I shall not weary you with poems"	275
The World Itself, the Long Poem Foundered	276
The Poem as Light	277
Poem on these Poems	278
in memoriam	279
Prelude	279
Poem	283
Czargrad	283
"waves lap against rock"	292
summer seeming	293
compound air	294
Chronographia Continuata	295
"quiet, willows and petunias are growing"	296
"ghostly fingers, gravitatio mundi"	297
"autumn winds are getting a move on"	297
"quiet birds fly"	298

PETER RILEY

"I am from language and will return to language"	299
"if it might be possible"	299
From *One Day*	300
From *The Linear Journal*	303
Birth-Prospectus. The End of Us.	310

From *The Musicians, the Instruments*   315
From *Lines on the Liver*   316
From *Tracts and Mineshafts*   321

JOHN SEED
Lindisfarne : Dole   330
After Time   330
Into What Depth Thou Seest From What Height Fallen   331
Lines in Wasdale Head   331
Nightshift   332
During War, the Timeless Air   333
"History teaches, but it has no pupils"   334
In the Sweet Dark   335

IAIN SINCLAIR
We Are Green, Then Grey, Then Nothing in This World   336
Oak Chrome   336
Mother Glacier   337
Book of Invader   338
From *Lud Heat*   343
From *Suicide Bridge*   350
Locale   356
Crossing the Morning   356
Spirit Levels   357
Flesh Eggs   358
A Hat Thrown in the Air, a Leg that's Lost   359
Autistic Poses   360
Serpent to Zymurgy   361
Kristallnacht   362

NICK TOTTON
Arms Which Articulate Nothing   363
If I Had to Do it All Over Again, I'd Do it All Over You   364
The Contours of Indifference   364
Influencing Machines   365
Not Slipping into Something More Comfortable   367
This Song is Dedicated to the One Eye Love   369

Bibliography   375

Introduction

This anthology represents our joint view of what is most interesting, valuable, and distinguished in the work of a generation of English poets now entering its maturity, but it is not an anthology of English, let alone British poetry. We did not begin with this distinction in mind; indeed, had we done so it might have appeared that there were no operative criteria by which to proceed. We knew this was not the case. Why, then, make such a distinction, as though the work of English or British poets did not belong to the general category of their national poetry?

The answer to this question will refer to culture rather than art, and must draw attention to the history of perceptions of English and British poetry since the 1950s. It is helpful to bear in mind, for instance, that polemic anthologies during this time, while laying claim to pre-eminent achievement, have done so within the inclusive reference of national representation. As in the phrase 'the best of British', the frame of reference of national culture and the notion of quality have been brought into uncomplicated mutual alignment, as though the prestige of national origin constituted a claim on the world's attention or, at any rate, was seal of approval enough for us. Successive anthologies of this type have also asserted their contemporary novelty of style and taste. Here the inclusiveness of national poetry, in the possessive embrace of a sectional view of change and difference, takes on the exclusivity of fashion. The longer this show runs the less it exhibits the organicism implicit in the notion of a national poetry (however complex and dividedly other the nation has become) and the more it bespeaks new Imperial suitings. Pre-war anthologies, for some reason, had no need of such clothes, and maintained a less complacent style of polemic, as though some cultural positions still remained to be stormed.

Most of the poets in this anthology began to publish in the 1960s. Most of them were university educated, many in departments of English. Their social formation, in other words, had much in common with that of the poets who generated and were the beneficiaries of the shift in taste in the 1950s, but this did not enable them to see the position thus publicly secured for poetry as a point of reference. Instead, in various places, in Birmingham, Bristol, Cambridge, London, and Manchester for example, several of them became aware of one another's presence and a shared reaction to current taste. The notion of reaction does not itself, of course, explain the event it describes, but one or two motives can be suggested in hindsight.

For one thing, poetry, if it is an art, is an art in relation to language in general; its artifice is various, and its rules apply to specific rather than to general occasions. But the poets who altered taste in the 1950s did so by means of a common rhetoric that foreclosed the possibilities of poetic language within its own devices: varieties of tone, of rhythm, of form, of image, were narrowly limited, as were conceptions of the scope and character of poetic discourse, its relation to the self, to knowledge, to history, and to the world. Poetry was seen as an art in relation to its own conventions – and a pusillanimous set of conventions at that. It was not to be ambitious, or to seek to articulate ambition through the complex deployment of its technical means: imagery was either suspect or merely clinched an argument; the verse line should not, by the pressure its energy or shape might exert on syntax, intervene in meaning; language was always to be grounded in the presence of a legitimating voice – and that voice took on an impersonally collective tone. To its owners' satisfaction the signs of art had been subsumed within a closed cultural programme.

But in addition, the redefinition of taste in the 1950s had had to be enacted by means of a wholesale rewriting of and reorientation towards the history of modern poetry, and this included the virtual suppression of parts of it. When they began to write, therefore, many of the poets in this anthology, confronted with such a depthless version of the past, found that as English poets the ground had been pretty well cut from beneath their feet. To accept the version of English poetry then sanctioned would be to become like a fly on a wall that had just been built. The general character of this moment and the types of choice it provoked cannot be separated from the wider context of English interest in the 1960s in American music, painting, and writing. Certainly, at the time, one of the means by which many of the poets in this anthology were identifiable to one another was an interest in a particular aspect of post-war American poetry, and the tradition that lay behind it – not that of Pound and Eliot but that of Pound and Williams. But more immediately important than this, perhaps, American examples provided lessons in the organisation and conduct of a poet's public life, indicating how poets might take matters of publication and the definition of a readership into their own hands by establishing their own publishing houses and journals. Most of the work collected here was published under such auspices. In the 1960s, as well, the publishing of poetry did not command much prestige in the media, let alone represent significant turnover; what little prestige it had, it appeared, attached to the publisher's privilege in being able to afford to subsidise a small portion of high culture.

We do not refer to the 1960s in order to invoke the spirit of a regretted golden age. Nor do we assert the claims of some speculative counter-culture, alternative or underground, an Albion in place of England perhaps. Our views concerning the constructed totalities that represent national culture, however defined, forestall temptation of that sort. Most of the poems collected here were, in fact, written in the 1970s and 1980s, and bear witness, in a way that sets questions or reaction or influence beside the point, to a developed confidence in the poets' own creative resources. But reference to the 1960s serves several purposes nonetheless. It indicates the time-span we have in mind when we speak of a generation of English poets. It defines a formative moment. And it draws attention to the decade in which an attitude to writing not represented here both reached its apotheosis and lost its vitality.

The last point is of curious interest because current constructions of British poetry, to our amusement though not to our chagrin, persevere with the stylistic remnants of that attitude. The poetry generally on offer is either provincial or parasitically metropolitan, and furnishes the pleasures of either a happy nostalgia or a frisson of daring and disgust. Or so we find. Our comment is not intended, however, to be harsh so much as cautionary. The poets represented here are, we suppose, unlikely to be familiar names to many readers of anthologies – those imaginary beings at whom we aim, and to whom we hope to introduce a range of poetry that has not easily been accessible. For this reason we provide a more than usually full bibliography. We have not attempted to provide a polemic apology or manifesto because no claim is advanced here for the existence of anything amounting to a school. Many of the poets represented have read and responded to one another's writing, but what impressed us most, while we made our selections, was the degree of difference that existed between individual poets, and the extent to which each poet had accomplished a characteristic and integral body of work, with its own field of interest and attention. What we claim is both the possibility and presence of such variety, a poetry deployed towards the complex and multiple experience in language of all of us. This is by no means, of course, ever one and the same thing, and the poets collected here will be seen to set their writing towards a range of languages, ordinary, scientific, traditional, demotic, liturgical, and so on. These denote topical and intellectual reference of different sorts, different procedures and affective states of language, but their variety and mixture equally point to the important common characteristic of these poets, commitment to the discovery of meaning and form in language itself.

As editors we have not, we hope it is clear, set ourselves the task of charting a general poetic milieu or recording its history. In order to make what seemed to us the best use of the space available we have had to make some difficult decisions and, in some instances, to agree to differ; had we been left to our separate devices each of us, no doubt, would have made a somewhat different choice. But we have, nevertheless, made an anthology of poems we could agree to admire.

A.C.

ANTHONY BARNETT

From BLOOD FLOW

THE BOOK OF MYSTERIES

Here, in the
book
of the what?

What foolishness.

How?

In rock and tree,
and, soundlessly,

what can I ask from you?

I told you,
I told you,

I formed you, the anger and the nothing that would
hold you; I, on you, hold.

DROPS

White
of the Northern bird –

What white?

White ice,
crystals,

besides, the
black lake, blue-gray lake,

because of the water-dark,
May sun.

Speech-like,
beside
bleak prayers of ice
breaks, before morning;

the morning
where your voice is transmitted

is silenced.

WITH YOU

Loss.

Thank you.
Your absence. For your absence.

Thank you for your absence.

Word.

Of stone.

HABEAS CORPUS

My behaviour,
barely perceptible,
was corrected.
I
did not

know
whether to tremble
or be still.

CROSSING

Germanic.

Irreligious.

You blaspheme. You utter your God.
You are renewed
in mountains where you were lost.
You sluice
yourself with water,
untouched. You are baptised.
You remain
with
your Jewishness.

At times
you await your dying,
your adoration and birth
of another; but you remain
with your Jewishness.

DEATH

Hearse
you carry
within.

You are
feather-like
pæan,

You do not
carry
sufficient ink.

You were
young.
– You were bequeathed.

I pleaded
companionhood.

You were
white

Hearse
you carry
me
within.

You are twice
defiled.

Within
me.

APODAL STRIDE (CURSIVE)

As the mower
commences, I

jar, disrupting
empty breast.

You were sweet
enough
with rose breasts enough
to stow my curse

I am forgiven,
blood flow,
I am forgiven.

From TITULAR

SOME SCANDAL THAT HAS FLOATED DOWN
FROM HIGHER CIRCLES

By the twilight
the airy insects arrive
gathering low
so that the wagtail
appears beside me.
Likewise, the
lake-lily is hardly
permitted to remain
flat on this surface.
It is tugged at,
bowled to the dining-
table. Prematurely,
the flat leaf
will be joined by
the bud. The paraph
caught on a filament,
the pleasure cannot
be denied.

From FEAR AND MISADVENTURE

I am abstract
quality
I am the large fern
fanning the wood,
with no more temporal movement.

True voices
in this vastness
speak to me at twilight.
They speak to me with a blackish
look and a black pen.
True voices,
easy to lose,
yours and mine,
in this vastness.

In Green and Blue
the day is over.
Memory is fresh as eye water.
In front of no one
I am tyrant and martyr.

The history of theatre
is that of absence.
It is unsound.
It is not wanted in this,
where climate would be displaced.

I walk from day to day
under an immensity
that escapes me, that I do not escape.
You command resources that I do not command
but you are not resourceful.
I exaggerate as you do not.
I smart with you.
I am stopped with you.
I mix up
I go to pieces.

You are the last frame
of light, picture light,
in the dusk
in the corner of my eye
as I doze off.
I do not know what happens
in you or in me.
When I awake
nothing has changed except
appearances.

The ferry boat comes out of the mist fast.
It is made fast to the bollard at the quay
and rocked by the wash of a liner.
The gangplank shifts
and people about to get off are held fast
in the mist.

Snow falls everyday,
and does not fall.
It is neither winter
nor summer.
I listen to your every sound.
What I think is all right
and what imperils me.
There, a falling away.
Surely, I am grown nearly,
am answerable.

How close is this wound,
that I thought would fall,
when I fell on my knee,
when I was afraid
– of vastness.
Lasting, because of my answer,

a retort,
out of place
in this between Green and Blue.
How suddenly the wound closes.
A flower would feel it so.
I got up.
I was no longer there.

AFTER

I

I am after, but not before;
I am unsure how life is after life before.

There are wild, there are garden:
no fact comes to life

but one lifeless.
Silent em: now where are you?

I cannot find you so easily
in this garden or this wild

because you are variable
and only beginning is invariable

and because you are moveable
and beginning is perhaps immoveable.

Talk, be silent, but respond.
I am like clinker.

I am consciousness of every and.
I think we make it so.

I get up. I lie down. I get up.
An impassible position.

But what do I think I have lost?
What do I think?

On seven days
God is lies, also Marx, Freud,

and the Saints, smaller saints, who had half-eyes.
It is true for you, me, and the rose,

whose half-eyes open –
and open eyes half closed.

So I cover up. It is in the sun's angle.
I think we make it so.

A polar rose modified by long shadows.
The Russian me eternal as a cat.

I swam.
I could not think of anything else.

I was definitely afraid.
Where are my toes? I wondered. Where was there shade

for digging in to? A fine gap
for getting through

as in a hedgerow? Oh, I love you so.
But there are limits to this.

II

How lovely is the smell of my love's annulus:
solar rose, lovelier than the past.

Sparrows build nests under the eaves.
Their droppings wash the woodwork.

I nuzzle close to the grass.
I do not know what I have done.

Sparrows twitter below the eaves
and beneath the reed of my chalumeau.

Roses grow in the sun.
They are coloured ordinals.

The fragrance of close mown grass
is as lasting.

She is undone. I am undone.
We head for Africa.

It is not how it is.
It is and it is not.

Levels of dirt become cleanness.
Man does what man has to.

Woman is all exposed.
Fuck this, and fuck this.

It is like love
and it is not love.

Quietly, I sit squinting at the sun.
Is it a veranda or a terrace?

It is covered, a platform
at ground level, with the front entrance

and the ground floor.
Yet it is a level area cut from a slope.

Is it a veranda and a terrace?
Is it a meaningful question?

The flagstaff has splintered.
The mouthpiece of my chalumeau is shattered.

Snow is melting on the ground
and ice on the water.

I left my love long ago
when I was asked to go.

It was hard. I left ignobly.
I am sure she has not looked for me.

III

There, is a stake, I see it, now,
    which is likened to the object.

It is not true. It does not pass for it.
    But, still, is a common growth,

by not leaning on a birch,
    as in going up and coming down, is

being – supported on a leaf slope.
    I am the lizard and the belied step.

I am quite harmless, and I am dry.
    My stone is at rest.

I am not historical enough.
    I am the splayed blossom.

I finger it.
    My crystalline lens is wet.

O lizard stay!
    I am grown fond.

Holding women's babes as blacks' music,
    historicity, was, before, and, is, beside.

Thus reflexion is least expected,
    but is not defective in the object,

but in judgement.
    It must not be symbolist.

I think of the whole caste,
    and how it sticks.

How it lasts out,
    how it is reduced.

In spring we set the grass to fire.
    We wonder if small beasts scurry

into ditches.
    They do. We want them to.

They scurry across badly prepared roads,
    badly signed.

We see that now;
    that they break up under ice

and metal parts of winter tyres.
    It is like simony.

We are smoked out.
    And work not hard enough.

From MUD SETTLES

I wish you would
warm to it,
like the rock face
and the water below,
be not forthright,
not devious,
but the rest.
I am not *wish*ful.
How watery my eyes are.

Here, roughly,
the wickers.
The size and shape deficient.
But they are built in.
They are serious, at risk.

Far off
(not actually so far)
a couple waving. It burrs.
No, it is the winter wild oat
irresolute at the edge.

The night stares out
dissolving
that which the night star doubts.

Why do I fear the symbol
of a night's gambol?

Look at the warmth of my bed.

Why should I doubt that?

With all the care in the world
I feel things draw to a close,
though they are really far away.

If they were around us.

Where does this language
really come from?

A wise man would seek it
close to home.

From REPORT TO THE WORKING PARTY...

THE SEVENTEENTH OF MAY

Art has not made our life
but it provides a shift

of unacceptable
truths derived from trouble.

An example: how touched
on tragedy and vouched

for by such behaviour,
unexplained, and referred

to the authorities.
Suddenly, the police.

FROZEN

I would like to walk over
again the city river

not alone, as I write this,
but quietly, with you, the least

revered of my rational
dreams. Oh yes, a miracle.

QUEST

That was an accident.
In dreams responsibilities begin,
interrupted by a cat's meow.
And where did that come from?
Whatever we have meant,
to each other, with repeated words, and in
dreams, singular and repeated, how
shall we know this is home.

JANUARY

What is credible?

I have said all this before.

Many things have lost meaning,
not everything.

TRUE MEANING

What do you insist on?

Reasons, reasons.

Incisions.

Whatever happened,
this is my true meaning.

FELL

I know that voice, tiny
in love. Try to rest.

We are not connected.
Now you are their guest,

and they are concerned at
the hotel, distressed.

And up in the mountains
the theatre sets.

YOU

You would like to go back
to Russia

because clarity
has nothing to do with

your heart
or happiness.

I BELIEVE YOU

I turn out the light
and turn to the wall.

I am worn out.
I am warm here.

I will address myself to you.
I will disappear with my mistake
and you with yours.

FAR

You draw aside the curtain.

The window is not clear.

You no longer know what you are saying.
You no longer know what to say.

You know your life will be difficult
though once you thought otherwise.

PHRASAL

I turn away from you
whom I no longer know.

I turn towards you
whom I do not know.

We were gentle.

You were one and the same.

BLAKE OR YEATS SLEPT WITH YOU

The story is wrong. Lies
were told and therefor' intended.
Polygamic, but admiring. The

colour of the sky changed: strong, strange;
weak, warm; later uniformed
indifference glossed as friendship.

Blake or Yeats slept with you nervously
wrecked but
tired and departed.

This may change.
                        If not
it is a dying race against
guillotines, a late

gittern, computing to *home*.
The colours change,
accompanyment is out, the knuckles

bare in the hills, is this
denied? Only, you, may, write
well.

Your striking hand *is* life
& death. Fidelity is expended, not dog-like.
And the kitten plays with the mouse.

A WHITE MESS

In the revolutionary shout
is the shoot
burning in her garden
under summer skies.

In March you greeted me
with raised eyes and
fanned tail.

Soon you sang often.

As I leave the house
your eye follows me, drives out,
and eyes me closely
from the fence as I pause
an eye-draught through the window.

I was bewildered
and did not stand
at the appointed place.

I wonder at what
has become
this water
flowing into oblivion.

This clear circular oblivion.

I see, in the light
of the following year
what is now.

Nature has freed me
in touching me with thorn
straw, sting and myriads
of things.

But I cannot go outside
this Nature.

So late the year
the flowers open

the tree curves in blue space.

And leans over the worker.

The blue
now incandescent
I cannot see at the moment
(was it green)
62½ plus or minus 2
(I went blind) horizons screen
(they are blue).
But over the horizon
falling snow,
and beyond the horizon
fallen snow
and nowhere the light of your upward glance
and nowhere petulance.

My voice nothing to you
but a perfect *Digitalis purpurea*.

From NORTH NORTH, I SAID...

Flying
Away and
away
with the
rough and
unshaven appearance
swept by the winds
of the earth's
multiple appearances.

How
I longed for
the surrounding arms
to surround
you with
the thoughts
of flickering the light
and the shallows
of the leaves.

Silvery
Light on the
different species of tree
drawn through the
cloudy sky
changed the green.
If you do not know
what I write
or like
walk out into
the light,
there.

Not
To call up
the demons
who imitate you.
Not to travel
distances
where you get nowhere.
Or remain
in a place
where you are given
to feel
or at least feel
you are
somewhere.

Lost
Face awaiting
nothing yet
attending
everything.
Placated
image of the
world.

Broad
Scapes from everything
to nothing
and back to
everything again.
Bound and released
the moving plant
elevates there
in the forest
and defies
the keeper.

When
The language
is stretched
to the last limit
of irreverences
then this is the time
when last needs turn
to latest and
through a few leaves
a last fruit
falls.

What
Lies between
the narrow
beams
depends
on conditions
of plight,
magnificence,
stacking and
proximity.

I
Cannot hide
behind what
I do or
disappear into
thick air.

    Dispersed
Between the
leaves and
the realization
that some distractions
rise straight
from the stem
and warm embarrassed
feelings.

    The
Rock over
the cliff
over the sea
poised
and the prophecy.

    It
Is easy
to stay here
beside the yellowing
ticket
and stones bridging
the water
and behold the
truth of those
fantasies
about which you
keep quiet and
in which you
are kept.

You
Press the
earth of
these images
here, and in
saying it
you think you
have an image
but
only the leaf
of an age.

The
Sudden change
of the weather
when travelling
or staying quiet –
warnings or no
warnings, but
now nowhere near where
is home for the
present, the silver
rains – yesterday
still, between the emblems
of the railings.

Cool
I was cool
as I never
was anywhere
except by the winter lakes
and summer lakes.
Spruce and fir
stepping down
there, reeds
improvising, the
unexpected
wave sounding.

Then
In naming
these arguments
stealthy with
the paws of
the shadow
furry with
the paws of
the shadow
of a leopard, then held
with the flow
of for and against.

I
Stayed to
watch the sun's
movement and
microscopic change.
I saw how
pure chance
explains
nothing at all.
I honour the
unexpected
calm I feel
rising
in me.

Also
Now no
knowing what
she will do.
Sucker into
strange, sullen
looks.

The
Sound carries
across this
expanse of
beach and sea
voices flying like
gulls and
broken resonances
fulfilling the promises
of broken shells
and silica.

What
Brought you here
in such elegiac
memory and splendid
elegance. You were
both mythic and
contemporary with
your presence
in the moment. In
both ways there were
teachers whose lessons
to mislead you
finally fell to
deaf ears. This was the
moment when you
established yourself
and disappeared
forever and forever.

Some
Brilliance
like a bird of prey
above the white
beam.

DAVID CHALONER

TWICE

the fresh bread and the smile
there is always the unexpected
proving that density of presence exists
her charms sail proudly the waves of my scrutiny
crimson lips stain the edge
of the facial expression
the lazy smile again   nudging her cheeks
questions line up at the margin
well lubricated machinery carries the situation
to a conclusion of words
she mentions the angularity of the music
the slippery distortion of breathing
the dilemma of a current response
the excellence of anticipation

---

fatigue creeps closer under the awning
the grey landscape describes nothing
that is not also provocative when exposed
the grim visage of understatement
does not eliminate the implicit sense of
continuity   one thing merges into the next
and the differences escape interpretation

the problem the grass under the saplings
the form the adaptable
grid structure the depth the russian
salad the present whereabouts the point
of entry the relative the termination
the working range the yet to be established
the master of assemblies
the loose and public afternoon the regarding
colour the paint will turn the edges
of the idea
the geometric disturbances the optical
trickery that exists the design
a hinge facilitates the altered
direction and angle the nervously
aware the problems extend to shake the glass
of water placed below the panel
the problems lounge about miserably like a wet morning
waiting for the sudden jolt or spongey push
and the lines go right on by them
sparkling with success
towards the charming innocence of a wall

DOORS

held open by a small wedge pushed between
the lower edge and the floor

when you leave it presses against you
unwilling to allow the passage you intend
until your monster hand exerts a specific
force and respect for your urgency
takes it the other way

contrary to accepted political notions
not being a barrier is an important function
in the life of a door

numerous sensations are available
relief   the footsteps reversed
foreboding   a block of darkness standing
in the porch
delight   a company of smiling strangers
apprehension   the reversed relief of footsteps
a question answered with a question
the keyhole of the sky the lock and bolt
of a waving hand

CAMEO

the radio excuses our dawdling
a plastic alibi protects dreaming statuary
tonight you feel you may never talk again
that sense of self-indulgent excess
the notion strikes you as real
although improper
just because it's late and the lights are turned
off and we're not out
on the streets
being deserted by intention
staring avidly at the huge and godless prickle of stars
at work with the irreconcilable adversary
we are to ourselves

THE STRATEGY

More and more the meaning of what is now taking place forms as
a tangible unit, achieving substance and purpose, proposing further
episodes, recording what occurs with brilliant and accurate detail.
The unification of fiction and daily events, the response of one to
the other, a homage to all who tread their span with feet placed
firmly in each realm, who step at will through either state, or both.

    It ought to come true. The position seems obscured by a know-
ledge of all that has become necessary in order to encourage the

experiments in their endeavours. An arm pressed back against the chair, and jumpy with cramp, deters the pen. Closely followed by lack of purpose, or an inability to decide where attention shall rest for the few remaining minutes. Interchange. The name seems familiar and does eventually tell you all you want to know. This is forgotten. The mind is a lost property centre, filled with confusion and variety, an uneasy repose, a sensational lack of strategy. The keeper wakens to your knock and consults your request with an inquisitive glance at the ledger in order to determine its worth, and such action as may be deemed pertinent.

However, the chance find leads to further discoveries and illuminations. Consider my reaction when the parcels arrive intact and secure, bound with that hairy string I never save, but is invariably seen around such large packages. Some popularity must influence its continued use. When the storm breaks the air divides, saturated with rain. The torn wrapping flattens on the path, the fibres falling apart. When you gather its pieces and place them in the bin a strange indifference stakes a claim. The storm should lack for nothing, should advise you of the possible change, of a new arrival.

Now great determination is called for, and there is time for other reasoning. Have we simply laid waste our idea of the ultimate statement, knowing our foundation on such precepts comes not from a willing desire to participate, but from the further stance of inheritance? That is, set back quite distinctly as an altar-like structure, where we find a vacuum in place of a god. And knowing this rely on our island sense of being vulnerable, which takes on the black look of great continents, and applies the bleach of parody to remove the uncomprehending stain. Or more simply, and effectively, convert the element of bigotry into work.

Recycling the politics of your own smile you look up from your studies and are struck by the emptiness of the room described. Is being here an alibi? This is what you are returning to when time seems to stand, poised and perfectly balanced, between that which is yet to materialize, and the recent past, as you dream the cross-reference of a remote and distorted existence.

NEVER LET IT END

When the first part made its presence known we were not prepared, although somehow remained calm, but anxious, until it seemed this was what all previous signs must have been indicating, and the positive side acted as a kind of stabilizer to the fact of our not really having been aware of anything we might seriously have assumed to be a sign. Nonetheless the matter seemed clearer if viewed in this way, and we settled back with our knowledge, to begin the process of interpretation. On good days the work seemed total and quite singular, glittering with a richly hued originality, but this naive and unrealistic view of things was always diluted by the bad days. No particular direction and page after page torn slowly and depressingly into strips. However! And that was no sure antidote. Briefly, our work was divided into sections and handed out at random for a personal interpretation. The most common method was that of the three-dimensional grid, where no system was fixed, and the operator chose according to his own requirement, whether the move should be vertical or horizontal, forward or the reverse.

He watched from the window, observed the garden colour slowly in the dawn, the idea pushing light into the room behind him, and over the table where the work lay, waiting. The journey back. They had followed the most direct route. Certainly the urgency had been largely dispelled, allowing the event's bizarre direction to filter through his awareness of it. The window filled with immense demonstrations of gleaming sunlight. Between sentences he pauses to sketch in a detail of the landscape drawn on the page, intermingling with words and punctuation, a room expands in such a way that the view is enclosed by the frame of the window above the table on which he works. In the sketch the table-top is clear of obstructions. Several lines later more detail is filled in: an open note book, papers in an uneven pile, a small reading lamp with flexible arm and fluted metal cowl, a glass ashtray, a pen. All on the page on the table in the room where he works, by the window.

Various avenues to explore. We work on several levels simultaneously. He is unable to maintain a continuity, disintegrating into the facets of the day and night that swarm in his head, exposing a series of startling alternatives on the page where the ink, changing colour, implies that a modification has occurred in the quality of the light. Once before the dawn had grown into his understanding of such a situation, but no memory is certain to contain the entire assemblage of detail when later recalled, or compel with quite the same intense ardour such avid response. The narrow encrusted footpath as far as the roses. A spangle of moisture along the edges of the leathery leaves. The neglected mansions are bleached slowly by the process of age, shrinking under the burden of their experiences. The silenced rooms become dense with waiting. When the doors are opened a sigh chokes hoarsely from the cranked hinges.

The sudden attention to catch the slightest impression of former dealings. A panorama of images drifting sedately through the haze, intent on decorating the view from the page.

---

the first restless flaws of morning
wipe darkness from the window
a deliberate gesture
that rewards your attention
with unhindered eloquence

here a line that seemed to stifle
the purpose has been deleted
and now the idea you had departs
slamming the day in your face

TRAVELLING

the wilderness turns up again
and you turn away

having embarked on a journey
you arrive at its sequel

the sun swings overhead
dazzling your eyes

when you admit "I am lost"
we take it to mean you feel immune

and the days absorb that remoteness

INTERIOR : MORNING

for Patrick Caulfield

you cannot tell the time by the grey light
in the window
the frame outlines a response
tempting permutations of coincidence
it would seem that some one has forgotten
to switch off the light
the underside of the yellow lampshade
a white ellipse of proof

in order to belong to what exists
both elements
light, therefore lampshade, and window
thus time, extend the dimension
that is our sense of dawn anticipated
an uneasy not working, but content
you observe the static lucidity of crystal sky
cool air pressed flat against the eye

a fixed point will also express variables
and you pass into that portion of yourself
which entertains the idea of duality
although the window is distinct and isolate
existing on an independent level of values
the present night and your unending morning
coexist with a hint of studied calm
as the sun breaks through to summarise

---

sitting here how do they know where
you are   or care   or why
how easy it all seemed   how trackless
if it was hope   it was a vague commodity
and lethal
we know this   and continue

around the periphery of the floor
a draft creeps disarmingly
you step from the door and continue
where the previous line left off
never so convinced as now
placed alongside the tattered remnants
I forget which afternoon
the arrangement   that was another year
who did you think you were anyway
certainly not convincing
or else alarmed and totally beside yourself
with dreams of empty fields
and the breath of travellers arriving
meanwhile your thoughts take off
for the spent passions of the west

---

how restless they are
mending their moments
who has experienced such a construction
without prior notification

close to affection
but getting further from the location preferred

whilst stairs make mountaineers
and curtains drawn back travellers
the image is its surroundings
plus various accoutrements

put out the last cigarette
put out the light

there is enough for us all
and the days
maybe a little wearier a little less buoyant
settle to their business
as before, and yet a touch revives you
fresh, cool
the perfect example of itself
as though in lasting long enough it qualifies
for a place in your confidence, which it does
but later
and an hour has passed already
because you check
the spongey air arranged in layers
illuminating a scrupulous display of truths
that mask the names we use

TODAY BACKWARDS

for John James

friday takes a step in the right direction
towards saturday
but first its cool evening of pleasurable dusk
house-martins swooping and turning for their perpetual dinner
and the stimulating cessation after the first
drowsy heat of summer

an hour reading lying in the sun
then I harden my heart loosen my bowels
and set to work

it is 2.00pm and gloriously fluttering green on blue
first from the window
and then across the paper
placing foliage that it might breathe
above the still and sparkling water
bearing its open surface like the glazed look

of one transfixed
that reaches you in the air above
and arranges the view reversed at your feet

an empty place is possessed by figures
only their conversations remain illusive
and we quickly occupy the lack with our imaginings

nowhere else was quite the same as today
floating between us on the gluey breeze

INCREDIBLE VISTAS

1
it was summer and thoughtfully calm
all gesture appeared stilled, superficial
at the corner of a green area the wavy line
descending across white, betrayed the stroke
claiming this mark as a forfeit for indiscretion
where harmony and history contrive
to assemble and dispatch their messages

2
the same wrist wearing a different time
protrudes from a fraying cuff
the hand sets out to relieve and relive
a burden of misplaced ideals
lifting the curtain that risks the tremor
of a drenching gush as rain peels back
a racing layer exposed by an immodest
and explicit sky sprawled wilfully and wide

3
the elbows of the age wear thin
and what we have learned celebrates our confusion
for we are sensibly rising to the occasion
as it seeks out what remains of our vanity
because it is here, in this room
whose window reveals the distortion
of an invented view that retreats
we settle for the renewal of risk

THEORY

Awake between times and now
it is later, out in the streets
breathing common air
spiced with an abundance of exhalations.
Voices adjoining distort the silence
of events following a spiral
firmly located in the after hours.
One of the pleasures of our days
hisses to a stop.
Low altitude cover rolls
back across the allotments off
the fire-station tower,
away from the white clock
tower of the garage, decked out
with red neon letters and border
outlines, off the fuzz of trees,
up and over my head replaced
by an evening blue fade.
Now we are irritable and vicious,
part of another occasion
that circumscribes the subjectivity
of a mirror. That worth equated with
striving results in satisfactory
solutions, is a popular misconception
seen repeatedly where barren wastes
deny their own proliferation, in arriving
at nothing but the familiar trappings
of achievement.

JUST DESERTS

The morning's mask of cool
moist light ascends
to modernist blue, meshed by green.

Shards and particles and words
press down and forwards

like a best foot. The sense
of their capability materializes
from the thin air undiluted.
Praise be to the continuing
independence of language.

And whoever says labour is noble
when not a constant delight,
or imbued with glorious velocity,
deserves a kick in the head.

Resentment of particulars
is a cargo jettisoned in the wake
of the advance. Returning possesses
no value, except to nudge the edge
of something we recall
from the vantage point of here
and now.

And now it is raining,
with a gentle hiss, through
tall grass and stiffening leaves.

The sun appears when least expected,
shedding explanatory light
on the letter abandoned mid
sentence. Even the clearing sky,
ransacked by testy air,
interrogates the secretive reckoning
by which the transactions are reviewed
and marked accordingly.

And marked accordingly the quickened
stroke abuses preferential choice.

NOW AND THEN

for John Riley

According to the impeccable calibrations
of my Boots Diary, nineteen seventy two edition,
the month in question was July, the day
was saturday, and I am doing my utmost
to remember, now you are not here to respond
and your last letter requires no answer,
which is what this is.
The weather was too warm for comfort,
unlike that is today,
which bears resplendent
your inimitable style despite the fog
that fails to obscure the essential process
as it burns away the rigmarole from meaning.
That evening never was completed
to our satisfaction.
Now it is late, according to the not so impeccable
calibrations on my wrist-watch dial,
and the air outside carries itself
aloof and cold through combinations of time
and place, searching the narrative
for a simple and provoking epigraph.
Wednesday is the day in question
as tomorrow approaches and the light
recedes, constant and rational;
will serve the purpose,
in the hope that nothing will be forgotten,
that no part will be ignored, and that
the thoughts of the few will encourage
the recall of many to your
"sixth sense
                    of the invisible"
whose progress continues
beyond us all.

INSPIRATION IS JUST A GUY CALLED ART

Recently I read, "pain is a great incentive
to art."
Which proves two things;
I've been reading again,
and you can not trust the printed word
until you have experienced that which it proposes.
Meanwhile treat it like it does not exist.

Pain *is* a great incentive,
but present understanding suggests
that it prevents more than is promised,
rather than being prelude
to a blinding exposure to insight and wisdom.

We should be thankful that the age of innocence
will never exist, dreamed by confectioners.
Do not get in the way of too much
spongey optimism, a sure hazard of the repressive kind.
Two jumps ahead,
so look what reading has done for us,
cutely gliding
over and beyond the obstacle.

But no easy landing, although daily training
prevents a complete breakdown of the balance mechanism.
Standing here,
two feet diverting from an intended course, free
to speculate on surrounding productions of serious air.

All the time in the world,
who counts the minutes spends the hours extravagantly.
The attractions of a chance remark
put you at ease when all around
an obsessive dismantling of language
expands and vibrates like a swarm
of voracious insects, darkening the cycle
of empty light.

HOTEL ZINGO

Today lacks the conviction of my feelings,
and my feelings lack the heart
of the matter. The cold drink
from the vending machine
is a weak sizzling potion
of remote origin, saturated with
carbon-dioxide zest.
Enough is enough before the second sip,
in a strange country, with a different tongue.
I'm getting sick;
the light has turned a nasty and peculiar colour,
tasting of oranges and vodka.
If you arrive now I will be out
in the streets, averting my eyes, stumbling
moodily into crowded bars,
looking for a way to the future,
with a lump in my throat from too many peanuts
and too many cigarettes.
Is this a combination that will delight
the audience of contemporary verse?
And where are you?

There is something odd
about sitting in such a remote place,
curtains open to the world, wanting to be
somewhere else as though that might be
the answer, while people pass below the window,
getting on with the day and its variations
on a theme.
If I am moved I am moving now
in the prepared direction, reprieved
and curiously at ease with the travel arrangements.

My bag is packed, my bill is paid,
my foot is through the door,
and the morning air is the air you breathe
that crumbles the words I have to say
to you, when we meet.
The solid body of natural desire,
the pliable substance of disastrous thought.

PACT AND IMPACT

The uncomfortable facts of verisimilitude,
the malaise of miles away, the window

and the walls; again a familiar landmark,
again the evidence of living in,

of leaving out, of letting go.
The evidence of your interest as it falls,

like a clear day falls through cloud,
exposing the distant infiltration

of stunning blue. Exposing the conflagration
of personal dilemma, adorned with the real

and the imaginary products of fallibility.
The fundamental ease of a firm line

meticulously detailed, perfectly terminated,
existing within the boundaries of shrinking days.

HERE TODAY HERE TOMORROW

It is nine o'clock where you are breakfasting,
and I have eaten a late lunch here.

The morning paper lies unread on the floor,
and the present facts of our lives are beginning
to sound like a news item. This and nausea
combine with intermittent bursts of activity
to occupy my time today.

The telephone rang twice, and each time I spoke
the receiver went dead
with a disturbing buzz and click. Who is out
there trying to make contact? Is it you?
Is it me they want to talk to anyway?

There was no answer then, there is
no answer now.

Mr Lyons calls to ask if I have any knives
that need sharpening, or scissors. I don't,
I am indisposed, they are in the drawer
dulled by boredom. I give him some cigarettes
and money, and he leaves feigning satisfaction,
wishing me luck.

I return to the work in hand, it is taking shape
like a knife,
but it is in my back.

RAIN

The rain stopped the clouds dissolved
the sun set in cool peach undemanding blue
and horrid orange. The wet pavements dried
in patches and pools of sparkling water,
bright and snappy as pain.
The taxi was abandoned.
The way back was abandoned, poor light
abandoned the street, poor visibility
assumed control. The circuit was interrupted,
contact broken.

Expressions of regret were abandoned; the next
day was abandoned. The past was passed
and abandoned to a non-aligned future.
A careless detour to avoid care.

The Northern Line was abandoned; the seven minute
walk and the flying ants were abandoned.
The sticky leaves and low branches
of the Lime trees were abandoned.
The corporate web was abandoned, together
with the basic understanding of most forms
of communication and response.

The books, papers and green typewriter,
were abandoned. The effects and affects
of post-modernist theories and manipulations,

the letters arriving, and the letters
departing, the phone calls and invitations,
abandoned.
The cloak and dagger of intention abandoned.
The make-shift make-up department, smudged
and smeared, and abandoned. The struggle
against uncivil conflict abandoned.
The right to accomplish the right
to accomplish, abandoned. In the first place
and subsequent places abandoned to thoughts
of fading into brilliance
one last one final time.

The majority of consequences abandoned.
The requirements of fear, and the demands
of loss, abandoned, or thought to have been.
The dark form in the dream of prospects
clinched in a cliché and abandoned
for waking in a cold room, with forgotten moments
of loss, persisting still, and nothing obviously
missing, abandoned. Lack of sleep
finally abandoned in the recognition of insomnia.
The yard below, filled with abandoned car wrecks,
abandoned. The dread of saturday, renewed
and impossible to abandon.

The bitter taste of vomit abandoned
to cold porcelain, with tears and mucus
sliding into the drain.

Direction abandoned for journeys without
destination.
Destination abandoned at the moment it can be
recognised. The birthday celebration, abandoned.
The lost afternoon forsaken for the streets
between us, followed by potential but invisible
assailants, projecting their violence, abandoned.
The ruined house crippled by neglect,
abandoned by a previous occupant, as we crush
a path of weeds to and from the door

in order to abandon it in turn.
The concert and the party in honour of
someone I do not know, abandoned.
The view of a face, a stranger, abandoned.

The view from the steps, and from the hillside
vantage point, and from the road around the peninsula,
abandoned. The gallery abandoned to a quiet
that inhabits the area despite our presence.
Was I ever there, abandoned?
A costly alternative and a cheap option
abandoned for no further action.

No further action abandoned.
The leak in the lean-to roof, abandoned.
The cracks in the ceiling that spread while
you are away, and I'm not looking, defying
the plasticity of vinyl paint, abandoned.

The impression of too many late nights,
abandoned for too many late nights and the difficulty
of getting back at such an hour, abandoned.
The proportion of the next page, landscape
or portrait, abandoned. The problem of curious regrets
and their history, abandoned.
Further contact with arbitrary limits abandoned.
Having to cease from efforts to locate,
and having made a connection, swiftly
to abandon it. This knowledge abandoned.

The green fading of the park, and the grey sky
becoming blue again abandoned. The wind
late at night striking the leaves that abandon
their stems, as the season abandons and is abandoned
in turn. The people I abandoned, who I need but
cannot approach. The fake reaction abandoned.
The airport abandoned, departing and returning;
the station and the bus-stop, by request only.
The problem of temporal emphasis and styles of being,
nudging towards the perilous assumption, abandoned.

The restricting and mundane abandoned for the merely
ordinary. The questions and their answers.
The questions and the answers instantly abandoned.

The shards of a broken cup, scattered across the floor,
abandoned in gathering dust. Unpleasant image.
The diminishing and alarming alibi,
no longer appropriate, abandoned.

So this is how the pace changes.
Washing socks after walking all day
in search of entertainment, and what was escaped from.
Clumsy and sweating, like an awkward phrase.
It cannot be explained, it does not apply,
there is no further use for that particular type
of reactionary accusation. The water is tepid
and avoids the requirement of thirst.
The despair of the morning rises before me,
I give in and carry on.
Sunlight melts the frost. My new second-hand coat
resisting the cold wind.
Simple facts are a by-product of events
of insufficient intensity, that is the heart
of the matter. Hints, suggestions, redundant devices.
Such are the contents of imagination abandoned.

This flexibility of random days we acquire
by default; where are you, you ask I ask,
speaking through wires and clattering exchanges.
Static. Interference.
All the lives in all the buildings lit by theories
and propositions.
If I speak am I real?
If you answer are you there?
If you speak will I hear?
If you listen will I see?

It is time to continue and question accordingly.
Time to repair the force of circumstance. Time
to imitate the preparations of migrants
busily dismantling an evolutionary shift.
Time to catch the last train back before the take
away closes, the lights go out, and the night stuns
us with sleep. Time to catch the train
of thought, so unbearable
and demanding, so unpredictable
and serious.

We left the house at first light. The kind that
precedes dawn. Recent events had curiously
transpired into one of those mystifying contortions
of the expected; abandoned like a sign of the times.

The neat phrase abandoned.
False information, presented in good faith, abandoned
The truth : enough of that, abandoned.
Redressing the balance, abandoned.
Clothing that precarious and diverse apparatus,
abandoned. The conversation you overhear,
eavesdropping at the edge of a precipice.
One step wrong that could be the foot in the door
of that sinking feeling.

The sense that changes to sensation,
and the tense to tension.
The problem is knowing what the problem is.

Then comes the probable breach, the ensuing rage,
the oblique ownership of credit,
this golden sunlight that could be mythical
if ill-used, taken as easy option,
is best abandoned.
Late rays carousing in the corners.
All we ever said, are saying now, and will say,
to the pure invention of tomorrow.
Nothing better than having the odds stacked
against you. This way you can feel
the pressure, sense the reverberations of risk.
If you change your parting, have you changed
your mind? If you change your mind,
why wear your hair that way? Why
confuse the circumstances with vagueness?

The feeling is like walking along a parapet,
without the benefit of a safety rail,
several storeys above street level.
Wearing shiny leather shoes to increase
the paranoia.
Attention to detail at the moment the telephone rings,
a cigarette drops into a cup of tea
and the incident is recorded, and abandoned.

Another call from the unexpected.
It is darker earlier now it is autumn.
It is colder in the bus shelter where I wait
for a connection.
I am not ready but it will not stop.

Impossible to say enough about such pedestrian matters.
The curious conditions appropriate to natural disasters.
The uses to which we put the obvious dereliction
of historic remains. Abandoned.
Symbolic trickery of the times. The contrite
and self-fulfilling prophecies of the past.
The matter of "good taste" we allude to
by rising each morning, crumpled from a restless sleep,
hopping around on cold linoleum, filling the kettle
and searching for something sweet to eat.
Why not stay in bed and discuss the spectacle of damp fog
swaying outside the window.
Leisure without guilt until three, when the afternoon
has all its bright and grandiose details
fading elaborately,
and it is too late for most intentions
to be accomplished, except for the one that allows
such plans to be abandoned,
as if the action, the potential, and the day
stop right here.

CAPTION BLOCK

There had to be a context, a route,
some gift wrapping, a scene or two
short on monopoly. Too awkward,
too secular. Too dubious.

This street fills with people and cars.
A speciality of glossy remains, permitted
their lingering dilemmas.

The day passes along, provisionally exact.
There is hardly time to compose an insult.

Locks draw back
to comfortable repose. Time
has some interesting aspects. Its duration
for instance,

your presence, the plans translated into
thwarted actions, the leisure
of political expediencies.

You may recall your presence there,
inspired and envied by knowing
no limit, like a bad dream,
a system of invitations and rebuttals,
the texture of the breakfast
at the beginning of your day off.

It does not resemble living in a caravan,
or any other familiar aspect
of your life style. There is no
conviction, without first having prepared
for drastic action, of a kind
that becomes an endless example
to us all.

And to us all the last echo of its
wailing lament, the crisp reigning of
an imminent spiritual exposure.
When it's tough outside tend to the right
and get some religion.
The role is crystal clear, it's a simple life,
but pays a handsome dividend in
conscience cushioning.

If the resultant space bears a caption block
it will read according to your needs.
Subjective to the last, that distant
glittering refinery of ideas,
the embodiment of opinion,
of uncorrupted facts. And the estuary beyond
flashes signals with the sun. I urge you, task,
reveal yourself. He stands in silt,
translated by upbringing
into a version.

Programmed responses jammed on a re-learning
mode. Today it was easy, but I don't expect
further conclusions, and I have someone to see
out there. Later it will be a work of sustained
effort and concentration, a labour required
by the spirit, whatever its taste.
Tradition wears a tight-lipped smile on
a mean mouth.

"I needed that holiday, but it went
without me." A demon timetable served only
to confuse the connections.
Where a hotel provides dubious comforts,
cost is abstract, until your money runs out,
and a dismissive air won't even get you
to the revolving door. My advice would be,
protect yourself against one way traffic,
refuse to answer questions, think logically
and with enthusiasm of the future, then go out
and find one. Distract yourself by taking a
walk. The sea front. The bilious sky.
Tennis in a sheltered court around the back.
If it is not your game allow the repetitive
"thwack" of the ball to lull you to sleep.

At breakfast the sea view accorded some
nourishment to his flagging spirit.
It waved too high, and for too long.
Proud possessor of an attractive narrative,
let it go. Your desires are preposterous,
pitiful and ultimately pedestrian. You wanted
to be a painter and now you are not.
Something warned him not to turn around;
he did, but they had gone. Stubborn
extravagance. Try anything once. Try
shorter sentences for their music, and
their charm. Try nothing more to say.

The water was cold and cloudy. The sky
was cloudy and wet. The family divided.
A day later the sun shone. The status
of the fugitive, with surrounding fiction, is
questionable, but politically desirable.

Stubborn extravagance preferred to "good" advice.
There is another version that seeks
to present itself.
"That's no laughing matter"; we joked and smiled
about its curious structure, the mechanism
of muscular interaction, tensions and reflexes.

We grow a little older each time
"New Art" hits the fan.
I have a question for you,
in the future, beyond reasonable doubt.
In the attic he existed on a diet
of noodles and soup, using the bath
to wash the dishes in.
Your destination then, is now, is a belief
in progress principles via disruption,
a foray through the margins of
an "underworld", and out,
like a gesture incapable of being
misinterpreted. But in England,
in the rural provinces, what hope
of leading anything but an aimless,
entirely safe and convivial existence.

A surfeit of ill health, death, drastic
measures, conservative association and church
jumble sales, amateur dramatic society
farces. Activate the humour valves.
Turn the tap of the tea urn. An anthropology
of rural sentiment.

An object, falling through space,
meets an object falling through space.
They greet as fellow travellers
in the dip and swell of past infringements.

Every form employed. The spread, like
paint, applied in masterful strokes.
When, finally, he discovered he had
the knowledge that he was not a painter,
he relaxed.
It took time but; but he probably
clarified a point or two in the intermission;
intermission signing off.

In the Favourite Café for breakfast,
long before the owner is shot in a family feud.
The mellow drama of chipped formica and
processed peas, Saturday afternoons and
second-hand bargains.

One version was overpowering with threat.
I never rose to that occasion. A list
of names as token knowledge of the
event, but that was all.
No use in labouring to create dissatisfaction.
To do away with numbers, colour references,
and doltish imitations of false witness.

Preposterous desires in an attractive narrative.
Proud possessor of such a faculty.
No nonsense activists and wishful thinkers.
"You think I should return," he said.
This was a version. I know its dimensions.
They lived by a river.
The meadow's dispersal of golden yellow
marigolds; the car wrecks across the ditch,
stacked three high, blood-stained interiors
decomposing in weather changes.

Cross country runners
struggle up the muddied slope, following
the trail of coloured paper strands.
Weekend exercise in landscapes of loss,
beneath shabby skies, defying the
bickering wind.
Rare migrant birds land provocatively
in the next field.
Mentioned brightness, speaking of colours.

They kicked in the door, ran crouching
against a rubble wall, armalites
tucked under armpits.
We passed the check point, on other business,
observing scenes from daily life.

"We lost our windows three times,
but the target is the housing department
across the street."

"A man I know has lost a leg, and his
doctor warns, the other is in danger, if he
continues to smoke. We drink in the same bar."
Two patrol vehicles, monstrous with mesh guards,
rumble across a waste ground of flattened
houses. Speaking of colours we wait for
silence. The insignia of intent.
The small change of serious comment. The question
of what you wear on your sleeve.

The condition of the city.
Education, commerce, social exchanges,
law and order violence, terrorist violence.
A death threat loiters with intent. A concealed weapon.
But you are from somewhere else and plan
to leave, remember? And the hill and
the mist and the housing schemes and
the real sense of foreboding and pain
along the two Roads; and the one bright
warm sunny day when it was necessary
to report an appalling sense of unease
drifting in the streets.

Droll correspondent, this is a case for a revival.
Wit rescue, come to our aid. Amusing twist,
turn your hand to smart comment.
All the protagonists threaten you with their
ultimate weapon, your own conditioning.
Feeling what, at the sound of laughter?
Check it. Progress report by way of under
cover agencies. Consider yourself to be convinced.
But by whose smile, aspirations, obsessions,
displacement, commemorative celebration?

ANDREW CROZIER

THE SOURCE

You are in the unlit area of the world
the mind doesn't see where the roots of trees
grip and twine in privacy, and the stars shine
with clear uninterrupted light. The play of
those surfaces is as real as the black top
of this table where you sat
just now, strong in itself which has not changed
since you got up, and somehow my elbow is
firmly supported. The windows resist the radiance
of the electric light with equal resource. I could not
approach you any closer were I to climb the stairs
and lie beside you without waking you. A false sense
of illumination creeps towards us inexorably as the sun
consumes itself, until I rejoice at the horizon for what is hidden.

FEBRUARY EVENINGS

I begin with a name. It isn't you
profiled against an orange skyline.
Nor the light that dazzled me when I opened a door
and realised after, I don't know how long
I stood there holding on to the doorknob, I faced
due west. It is early morning in March
which is the name of nothing I might hold to
since I can speak only from my temporary place
in the solar system. It is a February evening
the nights are drawing out and I love you
driving your car so attentive to the hazards of traffic
while I observe the passing skyline which so exactly
defines the way your hair falls onto your shoulders
alert to whatever should show up next.

Where were we going? I don't remember arriving
till I enter a room to see the sun setting
framed in the window and know that I still love
while you are elsewhere in its presence there is only
the light it sheds about us as I step into the area
where I can speak your name into a silence
which answers me.

TWO ROBIN CROFT

Jars with pussy-willow in them stand around the
Exhalation of a careful mind the fragments of
An afternoon's walk in a sharp wind
Now it is warm inside the buds are opening

Married to you I wish to prepare an
Anniversary for us a fragrance we may
Return to which will return to us each
Year as the sign we recognise it

Announces its own fiction about Spring
Nothing is more surprising than this
Deathless persistence yet even so your hand
Responded and broke off a few twigs
Everything that might be said comes into this
We need no other sign than this branch gives

BIRDS IN SUNLIGHT

In and out the open window
the light sonata flickers a drenched shadow
of its coming glory one sharp note
the swinging of a squeaky gate

again and again scattered on the grass
in shining crumbs of patience which pass

smokily upwards thickening the colour
of daylight to a descending glimmer

sustained by sound as each wet lens
contracts a throat to the point which bends
air into a tuneful concourse
of schemes of time a momentary pause

before everything stiffens and sets
into a shape a curtain suddenly floats
out on the breeze from an opened door
through which that glorious music now returns.

THE VEIL POEM

0.   *(left unfinished*

The garden clenched like a root, bare branches
evergreens, dry leaves, winter grass
quiet and still apart from the activity of birdlife
blackbird on the crazy paving, thrushes under the
hedge, two pigeons taken up in space
sparrows on every bush and twig

                    The light these days lasts
for a few hours, though here is no
yellow candle-light, and the storm I hear wind and rain
raging is an effect of bathwater
emptying into the drain outside or an electric motor
turning in the railway cutting down the road
the train that will take you into the city
through morning twilight and damp mists

1.

In the dark there is a fretwork
that reveals a lightness beside it, gradually
a tree stands out from the hedge and
the rest of the garden, the sky lightens

and bleeds off at the edges, quite sharp
but not definite, the blueness has the frequency
of space and there is nothing else but whatever
has brought this tree here, quite taut
but flowing smoothly through its changes
I know it again and again and see how
set in one place as it is and small and
fragile I cannot dominate it, in the dark
or with my eyelids closed it will score
my face. Along a bright corridor the way
turns or is transected and is lost
in shadow, framed by a black latticed screen
its light foreshortened, lacking
depth. There is no radiant source within
these walls, they hold the sunlight to
define their intricate arcing.

2.

What hides in darkness and what truths
it veils. Which side of these doors am I?
This arch might be the sky that bends over us
beneath which is our home, it is a wall
and outer skin beyond which we expire
like the breeze at evening. Let the wall be outside
for a change, my mind strangely free
amid this darkness. It has placed me
within these doors, they can have no secrets
from me any more. Though my judgement may falter
my feet are firmly placed and I can
walk with certainty, the cuts on my forehead will
heal easily, leaving no scars.

3.

In nature everything, we suppose, connects up
with everything else, yet this garden
is no natural symbol but one of a series
a complex system displaying a process
which is its own symbol when the people
off the train come out their back doors
to potter about. They do this

at weekends or in the evening when it begins
to draw out, the struggle of what is light and
what dark seen thus to advantage in a
domestic, backyard setting. How nature
disguises herself, how like a woman, she has
turned from her solitary way, withholding
a unique gift of truth. For the hermetic
correspondence of forms hidden beneath appearance
we substitute the ideal market of ecology
gross and substantial. Though we would rob nature
of her profusion this arch the roof of the world
echoes prodigally down the corridor, its facings rendered
an exactly repeated tracery of magic in
cardinal numbers, at each diurnal arc
a hanging lamp mimics our sun.

4.

Bend back the edges and pull what you see
into a circle. The ground you stand on
becomes an arc, the horizon another
each straight line swells out
leaving no single point at rest except
where the pitch of your very uprightness
bisects the projection of your focal plane.
Here at the centre of every intersecting circle
each infinite yet wholly itself
whichever way you turn a way is offered
for you to carry yourself, its knowledge
will inundate you unless it is held
along every inch of your skin, shaped as
the grace you make for yourself. The starlings
are all in place on the lawn, scattering
up and down for little things, they rise
in flight or plant their beaks into the earth.

5.

The coals in the stove glow red
and heat the room. They settle slowly
into themselves and something slips...
You should never stop. The fire

needs making up and I look round
for a way out of the impasse.
Colonnaded in a game of blind man's buff
archways jostle on every side. I am
here. Where are they? Which way
am I beckoned, must I turn to find
sanctuary, the arch which my eyes hide
beyond another arch until I seek it out
at the side or from a distance. I see it now
barred by a line of small red triangles.

6.

I stand before the last arch, which makes
a small enclosure with a rug and
hangings and windows glazed with
crumbling sunlight. The colours are black
and gold and red, evening and dawn
and when I close my eyes against them
I see their pale capillary tracings.
I am there, shaky, overwhelmed by
the sense of it, piece mating to
piece : blood, shit, and pus.

7.

The wind blows around the house
and down the chimney, at night
we are safe from it indoors yet it is
the same wind that briskly blew
the hair into our eyes this afternoon.
Yet it is not the same and never ends
Wisdom and Spirit of the Universe!
Thou Soul that art the Eternity of thought!
And giv'st to forms and images a breath
And everlasting motion! There is never
a last thing while we hold others
to us, this page, this carpet, this
green. You may walk in it until
you know each braided inch or let your eye
dwell on it till it reads itself, it is
as the green still springs up under

foot that you realise how the
illusions and transformations of magic
are different from birth and death.
There is always a page or carpet beyond
the arch, not hidden, green to the touch.

8.

The electric light over the gateway
will show where you are. You
announce yourself on the bell-pull.
No special favour can be revealed here
beneath an arch which breaks off
against the edge of the sky. This is
the ordinary world, naturally incomplete and
in no wise to be verbally separated
from your picture of it. For words
are the wise men's counters, they do but
reckon with them, but they are the money
of fools. What you have come to say
no one can tell, you are wise
                after your own knowledge and
the judgements you make. What wisdom there is
in the way you set it down, what else but
grace taken with you can carry you
back from the desert.

9.

What I know has day by day
been drawn to me, and in my
sleep are drawn the images
which carry me forward to another day.
Vessel and vehicle, around one common model
we take and are taken, green all our
life long. Where we live would be
white in the sunlight, but is hemmed round
by our proper colour, and pressing in on
it too are the sea and the sky.
How can I know anything so grand
but from a postcard, not the tasteful
transcript of some old artifact but

the thing seen for the first time, banal and
awful as any literal image. The fire must
be banked down round a smouldering core
to keep in till morning. The dust beneath my
fingernails is all the wisdom I have
to take with me upstairs to my wife.

THE LIFE CLASS

(for Arthur Berry)

Overhead the sky merges through windows
into neon. I can't make out any black holes
but some puffy white things – impossible to recall
the forms clouds take. Snow on impact
they melt and trickle down the windscreen
in droplets which accumulate and run together.
Events like these have all been noted previously.
Mostly they are subsumed and lead nowhere.

What makes one patch of sky different
from another, or one man from another?
It's possible to prefer the perfection of behaviour
of animals, given the choice.

But the creation of something alive in the cosmos
in which we express our delight, being ourselves
alive, is indeed miraculous, though not a chance
imposition on some bleakly available background.
We are the daily miracle of clouds and snow
with a little extra armature of coal and soot.

Can one deduce from these the just proportion
of qualities in the world, knowing that
whatever sustains the miraculous is not superior
to what spoils and decays what cannot be copied?
A space eight by twelve, for example, painted miraculously
red all over. What impels a man to make this mark
remains as a content of what he has made
which only our common knowledge of the original

impulse allows us to know. Not forgetting oneself
what is seen in the world can't have been put there
something previously not part of it.
We can renounce all privilege, no one
can escape the ordeal of being with everything else
in the world. Nothing is to be the sign
of a separate history. What is read out is the quality
of everyone's personal knowledge.

From PLEATS

Rain totally insistent drizzles
as I walk downhill over the river
back across the new bridge
down by the river walk
where it smells of malt
under an arch where water rattles in
droplets on different kinds of metal
uphill once more and left down
the walled path past the meeting house
then right and up the same hill
another way step inside and out
after two pints into
pelting rain drenching for
200 yards to our house
out of my coat and shoes
sausages in fridge, oranges in bowl
where has this tin full of biscuits
come from?
reading and dozing on the couch
till the phone rings
dreaming of being awake
it's Jean at another station and
Goodness! it's Six already
a few biscuits in a paper bag
slip on my dry shoes
and twenty minutes to what
seems like an assignation
at the Bridge
a quick drink and

take her home
from work after dinner
we split a can of brown ale
and she falls asleep

But such stories persist
like something left behind just as you go through the door
not slowly perceptibly fading but suddenly
just the news of a totally new set

If turning back opened up
alternatives I assert with confidence
you would not have existed
so lacking comparison
variety is real

Revealing what there was or
it can be said to represent
what is missing

The car starts this morning without choke
the battery is dry the plates warped
gaping to be filled

No heavy duty sacks
Next there will be no polythene
Palimpsest

Find a use for these things
renew and re-use

Much rain the wind blew off
my cap turned Jean's umbrella
inside out

A starling flying hard past the window
beak full of bread

Ducks
uninterested at first
bread brought home for another day

Moving on not moving in
today like an extra clarity
love refracted our presences
walking down the street
into the rain still there
an after-image of complement
bodily hypnagogic we were
two but the memory is one

Asleep upstairs
the bedclothes tuck in your body heat
draughts eddy the curtains not a breath
can insinuate down your back

POEM OF THIS POEM

The landing light through our bedroom door
fixes your posture. I create darkness
and enter closing the door behind me
and round the bed skirting the wall
where the window faintly implies spaces
more than I feel. Undressing into the cold
with an apprehension of warmth in
regular low sounds an interval which is
continuous and repetitive as I fall
beneath the bedclothes and roll over
to my side engaging your outline and
rest. Balanced. You return to sleep
diffusing heat and moisture. The other
person I sleep with I am as ever
beside you drawn into the breaths
you take. Not speaking. Hearing such space
that slowly stills into an ambient
jointure of being. Here. Far off.
The world rises into us

Rarely able to sense the pregnancy of cosmos
these days I make a number of local compacts
veiled in desire for whole ground
the non-reductive
smoke from the same chimney and a garden fire
matter rising to its final state
turning along the wind and dispersing
out of sight
no image that I can grasp
more than I hope to
the fires are invisible
tightening painfully on the body to release
the heat rising towards its source
clouds mantle the world's radiance
rain falls in straight off the sea
and gleams on the pavement
inaudible creeping edge
staining each step

        False Spring
was my muse for all this refusal of damage
as the heart rises in unlooked for sunlight
to the frantic activity of animals
within their world
behind the hedgerows

imperceptibly then it is almost over
not false but not authentic either
unlike the punctuation of night

In torchlight to know where you are
and then switch the beam off
to catch a glow at the heart of the fire
charred open at the top
but settling into itself
burning slowly to leave
scarcely any ash

flames interrupt darkness
dried out at inevitable flash point
sparks rise into the air above my head
until they extinguish no longer sparks

I am out to damp the heap down
and it's pre-dawn
                           birds all at once
cut through the air calling out

steam rises off the crying cinders
grey enough to see

but I am unused to this crispness
in the world and walk around the garden
wide awake in space

Colourless like the offering light
the world returns in primary quality
distinct as afternoon but not for me

Needing to wake up yet still dreaming
I return to the house where Jean waits for me sleeping

the horizon is a veil towards which I adapt
in acknowledgement of the sun
about to rise over the houses

the cool air stirs indoors and
the blinds flap at the open window
light pleating through on the floor

(i.m. Rolf Dieter Brinkmann)

Already the ducklings resemble their aunts and uncles
free of all obvious maternal bond
the brood moves in and out of itself
involuted and explosively bobbing
in each other's wake

their movement appears haphazard
and even elegantly natural they all
look the same and know what they want
when we appear under the shadowy leaves
with our bags of bread

it is a sign for them to
come to the edge and when it stops
and the last crumbs are shaken out
into the dirty water they move off
together again while you and I

set off round the pond talking
about ducks and the volume of foliage
on a summer branch which dips
toward the water to be reflected
in words that condense like the image

of each leaf shifting over the others
while unreflected light flickers through
in a web of shining brevity
that glows all night long
as air moves and water rises

within those immense columns
echoing : all language is truth
though a bed of dry leaves when evaporation
ceases and our words turn and fall
flickering with our life upon the earth

LOCAL COLOUR

Flame rather than firelight
where the low rays focus
in dangling metal
and glance across the fields

diffuse light retreats from
the grass embedded in stubble
left closely mottled
from orange to green

the sun vanishes in a bird
scarer in the middle distance
all around the colours flatten
on to the earth like skin

LIGHT IN THE AIR

Light floods the retina
then vanishes along the
optic nerve to reappear
as what we see

a reflected image of the sun
maintaining feelings that
action would transform in time

a bird flies towards me
to disappear through a flaw
in the glass and then emerge
veering easily from my focal plane

only a stone is without memory
and knows only what it is to be stone
worn gradually away

in the early morning the swifts relax in flight

From HIGH ZERO

The advance of happiness
is never an anniversary
nor as the evening light fades
once more and shadows disappear
into the world of objects
should one think of a return
for the light is given back
from its destination and absorbs
the atmosphere of a curtained room
within its swift recoil
and it is abruptly dark indoors
while every rambling rose gleams
like blemished skin in a cleavage
even now last night and tonight
border on resemblance
like the natural twins of an impeccable
bloodline the stock reverts
around them fruitlessly
and uniform like something gone
from memory the date not written
down and the day unobserved
for good slipping past
like thieves of time
escaping to the wilderness.

Then in the smoke
            the extinction of light
whatever follows is masked
by tears that smart the eyes
like blurrings of hot fat:
the picture of this is over-exposed. But
from its opaque depth there emerges
a counterfeit sadness
        tender as regret, wet
as undried tears
a little smudged and reddened
a little rubbed-in message
that'll teach you. The darkness lifts

towards the horizon and stops
at the water's edge
in its deepest tone, over the rim
where all at once the sky lightens
perceptibly out of touch
like a disappearing vessel
dipping its flag conveniently,
Farewell. Whoever else
would see it quite like that
so empty just the place
to sink in out of sight.

Rain drips in the casement
                of an outdoor life
        from day to day bonheur
where condensation clings as though breath
would fly through the window
                still moving slowly
in a gathering wave at the meniscus
        ready to launch itself
in immaculate newness.
                It ripples slowly down
the reeded glass like igniting neon
its reluctance suddenly overcome
before the air can soak it from
the surface down into the lungs
it begins to flow
directly in a current with flat
orderly movement. Beneath
the cill its cruel overflow
picked out in evidence
from the dirt where drops heavily
fell has annulled that contract.
Add your name to the glass
through which you witnessed this
time soon mists over it.

A cloudy night
           lit from beneath
for this is earth-shine
and whatever comes between us
is permeable to our will

And see, spread in that colourless glass
the double image of the garden trees
jerks like an optical toy
you point at the sky
as though the horizon

And you are half-asleep and see less
through such an instrument than while you pointed it

The evolution of the principle optic
fibre is far from complete, we know
enough to admit as much, but
prediction is tentative. You see
intermittently through silhouettes
of trees to where across the valley
the darkness relieved along the crests
of the next hills is streaked
with falling stars.

Don't come any closer
than you are already
that's quite far enough.

Light is in the curtains
like a bright veil of numbers
that rises in folds over and over
and the calculus of persistence
undogmatic and fluent in its changes
draws back with the weave
its light released
in a white rinse.
           Shaken out
like sparks from a bed of embers
dimmer and dimmer to the touch
but there to be drawn back

the shadows fall into the room.

And for ever and a day runs on
without resistance, turned
to a dead stop without a shudder
and starting again without pause
the world takes it all back
reversed.
            Overhead the gears seemed
for ever about to slip
under the strain they bore
but the tension was maintained
in all that measured track of time.

Expensive dried flowers beside
your eyes in a mirror
smooth wet and dry in one light
of present accommodation
looking "as if it were a lamp of earthly flame."
The unfaded everlastings
and the lustre of your irises
hardly resemble one another
do they? The light expires
and with its waning flames
the metered stars go out
like flowers wrenched from the stalk.
Petals litter the carpet
and weave into the design
the hazard of their immaculate lives
settled in the dust
like ungathered nectar. The pupil
flickers in the morning light
like a black insect
dancing towards the sun
in a pattern of flowers.
The colours swarm abundantly
each has its specialist
and I am yours.

Under the umbrella
        of invisible starlight at noon
all the plants come out
        of shelter like new things
but each has a name
        given for the occasion
the visible thing it is
        a naked chance for speech
to flirt in the shrubbery
        reading all the nameplates
aromatically, by sinister touch
        a perfect stranger's sense
of decorum when abroad
        keeping the railings on the right
at arm's length, held with scents
        not straying from the path
and keeping off the grass
        which needs no label
for its name is lawn
        opening among the trees
to let the light down
        to the lowest green thing
which colours gratefully
        all that it surrounds.

Yes that's very good
        more beautiful
and no less true
        than ever before.
                Say it again.
You cannot say it again.
Burn its bright sign on everything
it sheds a
        pallor on the afternoon
as colour disappears under the highlights
in these prints.
                This time last year
was no different
the swifts will home to their nests
like bees to the scabious
beautiful in their kind

the way we remember them.
But beyond recall
for such places to recur
the colours must each revive
in their very locations
rhyming the whole spectrum
in a retained sequence
beginning nowhere.

Begin life again
from day to day bonheur
snorting and sharply rigorous

at the end of a line
let it begin again
it is a dream before birth

The advance of happiness

FORSYTHIA

From there across to there as though
the down-draught from a pigeon's wings
at take-off could unpleat
the limp cloths hung out to dry
on a day like this the air
divides on sunlight and the drifting
shadow of the bird outstrips the
fluttering margin of the hour
where in the angle of light and
shade across the grass
the origin and course of love pursues
and still pursues its flight

UTAMARO VARIATIONS

The colours break out and float
In the appearance of a world
Reflecting the shadows of a boat

As though an inner life unfurled
Like waves and eddying water
In a photograph its edges curled

With age while life still shorter
Yet fluent to its briefest detail
Traces its surface through another quarter

The way it passes covered without fail
Where underneath the sea in one deep note
Falls from the horizon like a veil

Dust coats the leaves with a sultry pallor
Impervious to shadow though shadow
Falls across a field empty of colour

Like a grid crumpled into shallow
Folds or in an unploughed field breaks
Up in the stubble like yellow

Light spread in a ragged sheet and takes
More of the earth than it does of air
Which stiff with glare and distance makes

The far-off hills seem near the bare
Chalk in the cutting meets their fuller
Slope to slide beneath the eyes' unshaded stare

Beneath the surface
Of clear and broken
Colours waves like lace

Fade in unwoken
Substance after all
Nothing has spoken

Forth from the wet pall
That skirts round at eye
Level like a wall

Built along the sky
Until empty space
Breaks where seagulls cry

The sun breaks through the leaves
In a spectral flare and edges
Their turning colours with fringed sleeves

Of smoke risen through clear ledges
In sunlight where greys seem to catch
A shape and substance it alleges

Are contained invisibly in each patch
Of shadow flickering among beams
Along the ground unable to detach

Its clearer outline from a tone which gleams
Beneath so thickened that if light deceives
Smoke ravelling a margin is what it seems

SWOON

Consider waiting, as though not just today
but many days had made it late:
could it be the trains delayed by snow or the slow
twilight of a Victorian romance. There might be
a wall, a meeting place without a point,
the figure placed against it wearing outdoor clothes,
around it what a wall divides. But left alone
patience is visible while the fall of light persists;
the light, unbroken, has its right effect
on monumental detail no sooner has the mind
had enough of that. But how much longer
will the leaves all wear that dappled sunlight
shadows in the air. They remember nothing and invent
nothing but some choice effects
of transience and mood. See, everything
with almost the same clearness
grey twilight poured on sodden woods and grass
all things, at last, stored in myopic fullness
while the dying day is crowned with stars.

WINTER INTIMACIES

Street lights reflected in the wet
On the way back though the rain stopped
Before we went out
The street was empty our voices
Uninterrupted except in the silence
Between sentences
The air was thick with vapour
And almost warm we hadn't long
To keep our hands in our pockets
And step out shoulder to shoulder
Unhurried eager to arrive

And when I close my eyes I see
A vision of my choice
Lights like two shadows fall towards us

Where we were
A married couple walking in the dark

HUMILIATION IN ITS DISGUISES

Don't ask whose face it is when you see me
Being seen in search of your reflection

Scorched earth to the sky stopped with trees and clouds
Dumb reverie recoiled with sightless gaze
Our combat weaves through air and falls with us

Over the fluent nightfall of your rest
The costs of many bargains are exchanged
Moonlight like ice a frozen lake like sleep
Are copies made good as their replicas

The silences of portraits and dumb friends
Turn walls to margins corners sidle round
Start on arrival and shown poised to flee
Still the day lengthens colours mix and fade
A scarlet strip of empire in repose

Rooms contradict the curved weight of fatigue
Repeated details spectral and remote
Turn their straight lines from side to side and down
Where withered beauty turns its head and waits

This sacred place exposed to daily use
Shows by the flames by bare familiar trees
By recognition held back from a glance

Divisions interposed and lost in space
Darkness in layers stunned with eyes and tongue

Rise to the surface both dissolve and set

CLOUDS AND WINDOWS

New curtains darken the room all day
Framing the glassy light of the new year

Depression wrinkles all across the map
We're in a trough, see – this shaded spot
Where the cover breaks is a screen of ice

Windows open like a gap in the clouds
On to a continent wrapped in its shrunken outline
The sky seems frozen over in a sheet
The rippled crests slow at the touch of night

Time dusts the mirror beside our bed
All movement stops at so much emptiness
Your face emerges from the depths of sleep
So suddenly I seem to catch my breath
And artificial shadows fill the air

EVAPORATION OF A DREAM

The morning hovers in a state of panic
Terror and early fear pervade the room
Day feeds on day in starving majesty
The sky drapes heaven across the glass

Clouds drift over like strayed revellers
Fading in the light their frail procession
Crawls with lost shadows on the floor
Festoons the walls with shreds of pleasure
And peters out before it's reached the door

An atmosphere is left which dust congeals
Too thick to breathe out more than once
Cold water drops reflected as they fall

Scorn and regret condense out of the air
Earth's empty case as full as life was full

WHITE LAUNCH

Thick condensation gathers on the glass
Ground soft by light that falls
From the wan moon, over the windows and the floor,
Light deepening the profoundest sleep of shade
Colder than glass it scatters in the air

No starlight surfaces
The shrunken impediment of the sky
A clear perimeter of suppression
Dried to a spectral midnight blue

Houses and trees in flattened outline
Enlarge the screen their interference fringes

The light absorbs its own reflection
Leaving no shadow of itself to shine
With colours of the world beneath its rim

FIFTH VARIATION

Round the margins invisible apertures and leaks
In barriers of retinal pigment level
Out and keep doing so while the end which is
Up goes over the side which is in

Quite like this colour on
This colour or under whichever edge
Is the edge I like them like that too

Behind it thrown in a shadow screen
Before a wall where after
Images fade in front of themselves like gaps
Closing in fog to fill an opaque gleam
The space contained is its own

The light cut in and cut out cut round
And cut back flat to reverse

ROY FISHER

From CITY

Walking through the suburb at night, as I pass the dentist's house I hear a clock chime a quarter, a desolate brassy sound. I know where it stands, on the mantelpiece in the still surgery. The chime falls back into the house, and beyond it, without end. Peace.

I sense the simple nakedness of these tiers of sleeping men and women beneath whose windows I pass. I imagine it in its own setting, a mean bathroom in a house no longer new, a bathroom with plank panelling, painted a peculiar shade of green by an amateur, and badly preserved. It is full of steam, so much as to obscure the yellow light and hide the high, patched ceiling. In this dream, standing quiet, the private image of the householder or his wife, damp and clean.

I see this as it might be floating in the dark, as if the twinkling point of a distant street-lamp had blown in closer, swelling and softening to a foggy oval. I can call up a series of such glimpses that need have no end, for they are all the bodies of strangers. Some are deformed or diseased, some are ashamed, but the peace of humility and weakness is there in them all.

I have often felt myself to be vicious, in living so much by the eye, yet among so many people. I can be afraid that the egg of light through which I see these bodies might present itself as a keyhole. Yet I can find no sadism in the way I see them now. They are warm-fleshed, yet their shapes have the minuscule, remote quality of some mediaeval woodcut of the Expulsion: an eternally startled Adam, a permanently bemused Eve. I see them as homunculi, moving privately each in a softly lit fruit in a noc- turnal tree. I can consider without scorn or envy the well-found bedrooms I pass, walnut and rose-pink, altars of tidy, dark-haired women, bare-backed, wifely. Even in these I can see order.

I come quite often now upon a sort of ecstasy, a rag of light blowing among the things I know, making me feel I am not the one for whom it was intended, that I have inadvertently been looking through another's eyes and have seen what I cannot receive.

I want to believe I live in a single world. That is why I am keeping my eyes at home while I can. The light keeps on separating the world like a table knife: it sweeps across what I see and suggests what I do not. The imaginary comes to me with as much force as the real, the remembered with as much force as the immediate. The countries on the map divide and pile up like ice-floes: what is strange is that I feel no stress, no grating discomfort among the confusion, no loss; only a belief that I should not be here. I see the iron fences and the shallow ditches of the countryside the mild wind has travelled over. I cannot enter that countryside; nor can I escape it. I cannot join together the mild wind and the shallow ditches, I cannot lay the light across the world and then watch it slide away. Each thought is at once translucent and icily capricious. A polytheism without gods.

From INTERIORS WITH VARIOUS FIGURES

THE BILLIARD TABLE

Morning. Eleven. The billiard table has been slept on.
A mess of sheets on the green baize
Suggests a surgery without blood.

Starting the day shakily, you keep glancing at it
Till the tangle looks like abandoned grave-clothes.

And watching it from where I sit
I see it's the actual corpse, the patient dead under the anaesthetic,
A third party playing gooseberry, a pure stooge, the ghost of a
paper bag;

Something that stopped in the night.

Have you ever felt
We've just been issued with each other
Like regulation lockers
And left to get on with it?

Nobody would expect
We'd fetch up in a place like this,
Making unscheduled things like what's on the table.

No longer part of us, it's still ours.

Bring the milk jug, and let's christen it.

AFTER WORKING

I like being tired,
to go downhill from waking
late in the day
when the clay hours
have mostly crossed the town
and sails smack on the reservoir
bright and cold;

I squat there by the reeds
in dusty grass near earth
stamped to a zoo patch
fed with dog dung,
and where swifts
flick sooty feathers along the water
agape for flies.

The thoughts I'm used to meeting
at head-height when I walk or drive
get lost here in the petrol haze
that calms the elm-tops
over the sunset shadows I sit among;

and I watch the sails,
the brick dam,
the far buildings brighten,
pulled into light,
sharp edges and transient,
painful to see:

signal to leave looking and
shaded, to fall away
lower than dulled water reaches,
still breathing the dog odour
of water, new flats, suburb trees,
into the half light of a night garage
without a floor,

then down its concrete stems,
shaded as I go down
past slack and soundless
shores of what might be other
scummed waters,
to oil-marked asphalt
and, in the darkness, to a sort of grass.

FOR REALISM

For 'realism':
the sight of Lucas's
lamp factory on a summer night;
a shift coming off about nine,
pale light, dispersing,
runnels of people chased,
by pavements drying off
quickly after them,
away among the wrinkled brown houses
where there are cracks for them to go;

sometimes, at the corner of Farm and Wheeler Streets,
standing in that stained, half-deserted place

– pale light for staring up
four floors high
through the blind window walls
of a hall of engines,
shady humps left alone,
no lights on in there
except the sky –

there presses in
– and not as a conscience –
what concentrates down in the warm hollow:

plenty of life there still,
the foodshops open late, and people
going about constantly, but not far;
there's a man in a blue suit
facing into a corner,
straddling to keep his shoes dry;
women step, talking, over the stream,
and when the men going by call out, he answers.

Above, dignity. A new precinct
comes over the scraped hill,
flats on the ridge get the last light.

Down Wheeler Street, the lamps
already gone, the windows have
lake stretches of silver
gashed out of tea green shadows,
the after-images of brickwork.

A conscience
builds, late, on the ridge. A realism
tries to record, before they're gone,
what silver filth these drains have run.

FROM AN ENGLISH SENSIBILITY

There's enough wind
to rock the flower-heads
enough sun
to print their shadows
on the creosoted rail.

Already
this light shaking-up
rouses the traffic noise
out of a slurred riverbed

and lifts voices
as of battered aluminium cowls
toppling up;
black
drive chains racking the hot tiles.

Out in the cokehouse
cobweb
a dark mat
draped on the rubble in a corner
muffled
with a fog of glittering dust
that shakes
captive
in the sunlight
over pitted silver-grey
ghost shapes that shine through.

107 POEMS

A scraping in the cokehouse. One red car.
Imperfect science weakens assurances
but swallowing hard brings confidence: fall soft
through to a sunlit verge. Another vision:
stretched out like one expecting autopsy
or showers of sparks across a polished hall.

Swallow all down, to mudstains on the glass;
surmounted by the working, come upon
a sweet for Auntie; for the withdrawn and hurt
something comes sloping upwards, tilts the guard,
then goes across another way: surprise
relaxes from a sideboard in a bottle,
rocks to and fro a while, scores up another –
bottle between the lips – is comforted
into a pointless trip and passes out   .
finally between two stations, wrapped in yellow.

Sepia slippers in a sepia print,
venerable truth again: it comes direct

and broadens as it comes, is beautiful
if truth is what you want; lies in the blood
and lives on without taint. Magnificent
gorges at sunset! They knew how to live.
They draw us in their footsteps, double-tongued.

To drive under the fog again, and to it,
park by red lights along the road gang's ditch;
changes of *Satin Doll* are getting smothered,
two trumpets and a rhythm section working
carelessly through a roof under the ground;
at twenty past the hour they hit the dirt,
go on across the talk, hit it some more;
a silver surface rears up, wonderful;
somebody scared runs in and turns it over.

Squatting resigned among the rest of it
there's cut and come again; eat anything.
Demolished streets make foregrounds to good skies;
warm hands at rubbish fires, or on a keyboard.
But brightness picks out streaks of signal red,
it's morning. Rumpled, nobody can cope.
What leaks through rotted pipes into the gutter
leaves a long stain that tired arms cannot move,
dispirited by sickness and privation
when peaceful hours have coal dumped under them,
a last delivery, ferried in through sleet.

What's newly made gets treated tenderly;
damage is easy while the aconite
first shows under the window's overhang
and looks well. In the cold light is a refuge,
lying back after breakfast to see birds
flash down the pale grey strip beyond the roof;
and it's a lime-green tent where everything
is fugitive and found, and luminous,
with shadows of a dark track off the calendar
into a depth of sky. Hanging there free,
spiralling down, the ink-trails in the water
that reach the floor and spread. To be well-treated –
a café with net curtains where they bring
coffee or coca-cola to the bedridden –
something to recall on a beleaguered common.
Roads open in succession, windows break;

if both your legs get tired, find a good stick;
slow before lunch, but in the afternoons
Olympic stars perform for invalids
and dark brings in harsh winds and roadside breakdowns;
better to hear of rain on other roofs
or technicolour wrongs worked by hard men.

No choice left but to run, and into it
and back again each time, that being where
the way goes anyhow – so, running
brings it round so much faster, the same dream –
daffodil plastic, various laminates,
children released in yards then sucked away
into an unseen hall; enormous tolerance
somewhere about, and for immediate sky,
hand-lotion-coloured plastic overhead,
the first thing in the world; and back again.
Walking across to the cars in the night air,
everyone slows and vanishes. There'll be
familiar movement when the season dives.
Watch ampelopsis redden the tarred wall;
go straight, and not so fast. The inner sky
is coloured plastic – none the worse for it.

Somewhere the copper pipes a pale gasfitter
left unsecured under the floor tread loose.
The new face might look younger were it not
too harried and too sleepy: there's no time.
Old people go so childish you get scared
thinking about it: someone's moving out.
Under the trees, headlands of alyssum
break through a spring where danger without risk
develops to a style and loses body,
loses its ear for trouble. Ride again.
Desolate sunlit foreshores, visited
and photographed, lie doubly far away;
one more red car gets dealt into the pack;
one guest is laid to rest in his own nature,
his to resist if it should overcome him
travelling in the tracks of a clay lorry
or when the powercut lets the dark back in.

Exhausted, by a different route, twice blessed –
they seem like wooden roses, without yield –

draining the glass again, whatever remains,
past all sunrise, repeatedly and strong
though without strength, except to head on out,
surrounded by a street, braced up to feel,
ready for thunder, inescapable change,
the healing of the injured; some idea
of what tradition numbers like these are benched in.

AT ONCE

I say at once there's a light on the slope among the allotment huts. If I leave it a moment unsaid it'll set solid, and that only the beginning. But, said, it has gone.

The wonderful light, clear and pale like a redcurrant, is set off by a comfortable mist of winter afternoon over to one side of it among the allotment gardens.

Appearance of mist. The light in its glass. The witnesses were built in about 1910 in the shapes of houses. The stream crawls past the bottom of the slope, edged with vegetables and crossed by planks. You can approach.

The light is in the earth if anywhere. This is already the place where it was. We've hardly started, and I want to do it again.

SOME LOSS

Being drawn again
through the same moment

helpless, and to find
everything simpler yet:

more things I forgot to remember
have gone; maybe because I forgot.

Instead there is blankness
and there is grace:

the insistence of the essential,
the sublime made lyrical
at the loss of what's forgotten.

From HANDSWORTH LIBERTIES

8

At the end of the familiar,
throwing away the end
of the first energy, regardless;
nothing for getting home with –

if there's more
it rises from under the first
step into the strange
and under the next and goes on
lifting up all the way;

nothing has a history. The most
gnarled things are all new,

mercurial tongues
dart in at the mouth,
in at the ears;

they lick at the joints. It is new,
this moon-sweat; or by day
this walking through groundsel
among cracked concrete foundations
with devil-dung
in the corners.

Newest of all
the loading platform
of a wrecked dairy,
departure point

for a further journey
into the strangest yet –

Getting home – getting home somehow,
late, late and small.

13

Shines coldly away
down into distance
and fades
on the next rise to the mist.

If you live on a slope, the first
fact is that all
falls before everything rises,

and that can be too far away
for what it's worth. I

never went there.

Somebody else did, and
I went with them;
I didn't know why. I remember
coming a long way back
out of the hollow

where there was nothing to see
but immediacy, a long wall.

THE TRACE

Although at first it was single
and silver

it travelled as ink falls
through cold water

and gleamed in a vein
out of a darkness

that turned suddenly on its back
and was dusty instead

letting go forth as it must
a plummet of red wax

from whose course when they lost it
rings of dull steel

like snake ribs in a sidelong curve
twisted away and lifted

to clamp on to a concrete
precipice broken with rust

and with shrubby growths
clustering under it

their leaves
shading and silvering

in the currents of light
draining among the branches

to where it was sodden
full of silky swallowed hair

that dried and was
flying in a fan

air flickering from its ends
collecting silvers

as it twined itself
into the gauze

then scattered as many
mercurial bolts

all through the chamber
darting everywhere

in under the roof-keel
with its infinite brown decline

its warp
unmistakable as it reached

down into the daylight
with a sidelong wooden nose

biased like the set
of a rudder and pulling in

everything that could raise
a bright wave against it

making colours print
themselves on to planes with the effort

one plate of red enamel
dominant and persisting

even through a grey
sleet that scored its face

running away as water
welling downwards

through a raised irregular
static vein

moving only by rills
within itself.

WONDERS OF OBLIGATION

We know that hereabouts
comes into being
the malted-milk brickwork
on its journey past the sun.

The face of its designer
sleeps into a tussocky
field with celandines

and the afternoon
comes on steely and still
under the heat,

with part of the skyline
settling to·a dark slate
frieze of chimneys
stiffened to peel away
off the western edge.

I saw
the mass graves dug
the size of workhouse wards
into the clay

ready for most of the people
the air-raids were going to kill:

still at work, still in the fish-queue;
some will have looked down
into their own graves on Sundays

provided
for the poor of Birmingham
the people of Birmingham,
the working people of Birmingham,
the allotment holders and Mother, of Birmingham.
The poor.

Once the bombs got you
you were a pauper:

clay, faeces, no teeth; on a level
with gas mains,
even more at a loss than before,
down in the terraces between the targets,
between the wagon works
and the moonlight on the canal.

A little old woman
with a pink nose, we knew her,
had to go into the pit, dead of pneumonia,
had to go to the pit with the rest,
it was thought shame.

Suddenly to go
to the school jakes with the rest
in a rush by the clock.
What had been strange and inward
become nothing, a piss-pallor
with gabble. Already they were lost,
taught unguessed silliness,
to squirt and squeal there.
What was wrong? Suddenly
to distrust your own class
and be demoralised
as any public-school boy.

The things we make up out of language
turn into common property.
To feel responsible
I put my poor footprint back in.

I preserve
Saturday's afterglow
arched over the skyline road
out of Scot Hay:

the hare
zig-zagging slowly

like the shadow of a hare
away up the field-path

to where the blue
translucent sky-glass
reared from the upland
and back overhead

paling, paling
to the west
and down to the muffled rim of the plain.

As many skies as you can look at
stretched in a second
the manifest
of more forms than anyone could see

and it alters
every second you watch it,
bulking and smearing the inks
around landlocked light-harbours.

Right overhead, crane back,
blurred grey tufts of cloud
dyeing themselves blue,
never to be in focus, the glass
marred. Choose this sky. It is
a chosen sky.

What lies
in the mound at Cascob?
The church built into the mound.

In the bell-tower
is in the mound.

Stand
in the cold earth with the tower around you
and spy out to the sanctuary
down to whatever lies dead there

under the tiny crimson
lamp of the live corpse of the god.

Later than all that
or at some other great remove
an old gentleman
takes his ease on a shooting stick
by the playground on Wolstanton Marsh.

A sunny afternoon on the grass
and his cheeks are pink,
his teeth are made for a grin; happily
his arms wave free. The two stiff
women he has with him in trousers and anoraks
indicate him. They point
or incline towards him. One
moves a good way along the path, stretching a pattern.
The cars pass
within a yard of him. Even so,
he seems, on his invisible stick, to be sitting
on the far edge of the opposite pavement.
Numerous people
group and regroup as if coldly
on a coarse sheet of green.

Parked here, talking,
I'm pleasurably watchful
of the long
forces angled in.

The first farmyard I ever saw
was mostly midden
a collapse of black
with dung and straw swirls
where the drays swung
past the sagging barn.
Always silent. The house
averted, a poor ailanthus
by its high garden gate and
the lane along the hilltop
a tangle of watery ruts
that shone between holly hedges.
Through the gaps you could see
the ricks glowing yellow.

The other farm I had
was in an old picture book,

deep-tinted idyll with steam
threshers, laughing men,
Bruno the hound with his black muzzle,
and the World's Tabbiest Cat.

Describing Lloyd's farm now
moralizes it; as the other
always was. But I swear
I saw them both then
in all their properties,
and to me, the difference was neutral.

As if from a chimney
the laws of the sky go floating
slowly above the trees.

And now the single creature
makes itself seen,
isolate,
is an apparition.

Near Hartington
in a limestone defile
the barn owl
flaps from an ash
away through the mournful afternoon
misjudging its moment
its omen undelivered.

The hare
dodging towards the skyline at sunset
with a strange goodwill –
he'll do for you and me.

And *mormo maura*
the huge fusty Old Lady moth
rocking its way up
the outside of the dark pane
brandishing all its legs, its

antennae, whirring wings,
zig-zagging upwards, impelled
to be seen coming in from the night.

Now I have come
through obduracy
discomfort and trouble
to recognize it

                    my life keeps
leaking out of my poetry to me
in all directions. It's untidy
ragged and bright
and it's not
used to things

mormo maura
asleep in the curtain
by day.

Scent on the body
inherent or applied
concentrates the mind
holds it from sidelong wandering.
Even when it repels
it pushes directly.

Streaks of life
awkward
showing among straw tussocks
in shallow flood.

Neither living nor saying
has ceremony or bound.

Now I have come
to recognize it, the alder
concentrates my mind
to the water
under its firm green.

Fetching up with
leaf-gloss against
the river-shine.

I want
to remark formally, indeed
stiffly, though not complaining,
that the place where I was raised
had no longer deference for water
and little of it showing. The Rea,
the city's first river,
meagre and under the streets;
and the Tame
wandering waste grounds,
always behind
some factory or fence.

Warstone Pool in the fields
I realized today was a stream dammed
to make way for the colliery.
Handsworth Park lake, again a dam
on the Saxon's
nameless trickle of a stream
under the church bluff. The brook
nearest home, no more than a mile,
ran straight out into the light
from under the cemetery;
and there the caddis-flies would case
themselves in wondrous grit.

I'm obsessed
with cambered tarmacs, concretes,
the washings of rain.

That there can come a sound
as cold as this across the world
on a black summer night,

the moths out there impermeable,
hooded in their crevices
covered in the sound of the rain
breaking from the eaves-gutters
choked with pine needles;

the slippery needles wash everywhere,
they block the down-spouts;
in the shallow pool on the porch roof,
arranged among dashed pine branches
and trails of needles,
I found two ringdove squabs

drowned and picked clean,
dried to black fins.

Fine edge
or deflection
of my feeling towards
anything that behaves or changes,
however slowly; like
my Bryophyllum *Good Luck*,
raised by me from a life-scrap and
now lurching static from its pot,
its leaves winged
with the mouse-ears of its young.
I'm vehemently and steadily
part of its life.

                    Or it slides
sideways and down, under my suspicion –
Now what's it doing?

Suddenly to distrust
the others' mode;
the others. Poinsettias or moths,
or Kenny and Leslie and Leonard,
Edie and Bernard and Dorothy,
the intake of '35; the story of the Wigan pisspot
of about that time, and even
Coleridge's of long before:

I have to set him
to fill it by candlelight
before he transfigures it;

with *mormo maura* the Old Lady moth
beating on the pane to come in.

VERONICA FORREST-THOMSON

PASTORAL

They are our creatures, clover, and they love us
Through the long summer meadows' diesel fumes.
Smooth as their scent and contours clear however
Less than enough to compensate for names.

Jagged are names and not our creatures
Either in kind or movement like the flowers.
Raised voices in a car or by a river
Remind us of the world that is not ours.

Silence in grass and solace in blank verdure
Summon the frightful glare of nouns and nerves.
The gentle foal linguistically wounded
Squeals like a car's brakes
Like our twisted words.

THE LADY OF SHALOTT : ODE

The child in the snow has found her mouth,
And estate-agents must beware;
For if what we are seeking is not the truth
And we've only a lie to share,
The modern conveniences won't last out,
Bear tear flair dare,
And the old ones just don't care.

Back and forth she moves her arms;
Forth and back, her legs.
No one would wish to say:
Her lips are red, her looks are free,
Her locks are yellow as gold,

Whether she's very young or old,
The nightmare life-in-death is she,
Who thicks men's blood with cold.

What of the future is in the past
Channels towards us now.
Present and future perfect past
Makes no tracks in the snow.
Turn the tap and water will come
For five seconds
And then the sand
Flows into our ever-open mouth.
What was it we understand?

She does not stand in the snow; she kneels:
A parody of prayer.
Lucretius said it long ago:
Why think the gods care?
When the telephone goes dead,
The fridge is broken, the light...

Why should we think of knowledge as light;
There is enough to see her.
And, having seen, the message is plain
To those who wish to know
(They are not many):
Run quickly back to darkness again;
We have seen the child in the snow.

THE GARDEN OF PROSERPINE

in memoriam A.C. Swinburne

Th' expense of spirit in a waste of shame
Is lust in action and, till action, lust
Until my last lost taper's end be spent
My sick taper does begin to wink
And, O, many-toned, immortal Aphrodite,
Lend me thy girdle.
You can spare it for an hour or so

Until Zeus has got back his erection.

Here where all trouble seems
Dead winds' and spent waves' riot
In doubtful dreams of dreams.
The moon is sinking, and the Pleiades,
Mid Night; and time runs on she said,
I lie alone. I am aweary, aweary,
I would that I were dead.
Be my partner and you'll never regret it.
Gods and poets ought to stick together;
They make a strong combination.
So just make him love me again,
You good old triple goddess of tight corners.
And leave me to deal with gloomy Dis.

Death never seems a particularly informative topic for poets
Though that doesn't stop them dilating at length upon it.
But then they would dilate on anything.
Love, on the other hand, however trite, is always interesting
At least to those in its clutches
And usually also to their readers.
For, even if the readers be not in its clutches
They think they would like to be
Because they think it is a pleasant experience.
I, however, know better.
And so do Sappho, Shakespeare, Swinburne, Tennyson and Eliot.
Not to mention the Greek dramatists:
Sophocles, Euripedes, Aeschylos, and Eliot.
We all know better.
Love is hellish.
Which is why Aphrodite is also Persphone,
Queen of love and death.
Love kills people and the police can't do anything to stop it.
Love will:
> ravage your beauty
> disrupt your career
> break up your friendships
> squander your energy
> spend every last drop of your self-possession
Even supposing you had such qualities to start with.
The god knows why we bother with it.
It is because it bothers with us.
It won't leave us alone for a minute.

For without us it wouldn't exist.
And that is the secret of all human preoccupation
(As others have said before me)
Love, death, time, beauty, the whole bag of tricks.
All our own work including, of course, the gods.
And we let them ride us like the fools we are.
Of all follies that is the penultimate:
To let our own inventions destroy us,
The ultimate folly, of course, is not to let them destroy us.
To pretend a stoic indifference, mask merely of stupidity.
To become ascetic, superior to the pure pleasures of the senses,
Arrogant and imbecile senecans, unconscious
Of what is going on even in their own bodies
Old whatsisname stuck up on his pillar,
A laughing stock, the ultimate in insensitivity.

The only thing, contrarily, to do with the problem of love –
As with all other problems –
Is to try to solve it.
You won't succeed but you won't make a fool of yourself, trying
Or, at least, not so much of a fool as those who refuse to try.
So here we go for another trip and hold on to your seat-belt,
                                              Persephone.

I loved you and you loved me
And then we made a mess.
We still loved each other but
We loved each other less.

I got a job, I wrote a book,
I turned again to play.
However I found out by then
That you had gone away.

My dignity dictated
A restrained farewell.
But I love you so much
Dignity can go to hell.

I went to hell with dignity,
For by then, we were three.
And whatever I feel about you,
I certainly hate she.

The god knows what will be the end
And he will never tell.
For I love you and you love me
Although we are in hell.

And what death has to do with it
Is always simply this:
If it isn't your arms I'm heading for
It's the arms of gloomy Dis.

CORDELIA or 'A poem should not mean, but be'

To those who kiss in fear that they shall never kiss again
To those that love with fear that they shall never love again
To such I dedicate this rhyme and what it may contain.
None of us will ever take the transiberian train
Which makes a very satisfactory refrain
Especially as I can repeat it over and over again
Which is the main use of the refrain.

I with no middle flight intend the truth to speak out plain
Of honour truth and love gone by that has come back again
The fact is one grows weary of the love that comes again.
I may not know much about gods but I know that
Eros is a strong purple god.
And that there is a point where incest becomes
Tradition. I don't mean that literally;
I don't love my brother or he me.
We have been mutually avoiding each other
For years and will continue to do so.
Even I know about cross words –
Something. The word you want is Dante.
He said he loved Beatrice. Whatever he did
He didn't love Beatrice. At least the
Beatrice Portinari whom history gives.
He knew her and the point about all these
Florentines is that they all were
Killing each other or dying of rapid
Consumption. Beatrice died; Rossetti painted her
Cutting Dante in the street. Botticelli

Painted the rest: Simonetta Vespucci
Died of a rapid consumption (age 23)
Guliano dei Medici murdered by the altar rail (age 19)
Guido Cavalcanti died in exile (age 35)
Dante dei Aligeri died in exile (age 90)

Lorenzo dei Medici who lives for ever
Since he stayed there and commissioned
The paintings and poems and statues
And if he also commissioned the deaths
I don't blame him. He didn't feel
Very magnificent when his brother
Was murdered in sanctuary.
Do you realise whoever did that
Would be excommunicated if, that is, if
He hadn't also murdered the papal legate,
His best friend.
I have lived long enough having seen one thing;
That term has an end.
It was getting dark on the platform of nowhere
When I who was anxious and sad came to you
Out of the rain. Out of the sound of the cold
Wind that blows time before and time after
Even Provence knows.
And as for this line I stole it from T.S. Eliot
And Ezra Pound and A.C. Swinburne. All very good
Poets to steal from since they are all three dead.
The love that is must always just contain
The glory of the love that was whatever be the pain.
We played at mates and mating and stopped up the drain.
Hear me. O Mister Poster I know
You have burnt me too brown you must boil me again
You simply have no notion how delightful it will
Be when they pick us up and throw us with the lobsters out to sea.
It is the lark, my love, and not the nightingale.
None of us will ever take the trans-siberian train.
She wanted to and was collecting people who did
I thought I did but now I know I don't.
It is the lark, my love, and not the nightingale.
In fact I've never heard either bird
But people say they sound very similar.
And what the devil were Romeo and Juliet
About wasting their last moments
Listening to birds. Hah.

I like kicking up larks or
Larking up kicks. So do most poets
Including J.H. Prynne, the memorable poet
Who is happy to say that the U.L.
Has got his middle name wrong.
He claims it stands for Hah
But there is a limit. I know it all.
Riddle me riddle randy ree
Round and round in the snotgreen sea
When they pick us up and throw us
With the Joyces out to sea.
Tell us tale of Troy's downfall
We all would have liked to have been there.
The infernal Odyssos. He it was whose bile
Stirred up by envy and revenge destroyed
The mother of womankind. And Swinburne
Got a kick out of pain but I don't
I just get kicked.
I wish I didn't keep sounding like Richard the third
Except that if I don't I tend to sound
Like Richard the Second. And who wants that.
I suppose I must sound like Richard the first.
What did he do?
Nothing I take it
I get a kick out of larking up nightingales.
Prynne says that if I don't come back
Safe from Sicily by the thirtieth April
They will send a posse.
March is the cruellest station
Taking on bullying men
And were you really afraid they would rape you?
No. I thought there would be grave difficulties.
Not just that I was actively opposed
And so was every other man, woman and child
On that there train.
I was afraid they would kill me.
I may look stupid but I'm not
So simple as to think your name
Is Elizabeth Brown. Well. All right
My name is Veronica Forrest-Thomson.
Agammemnon was King of the Achaians at the time,
Priam, of the Trojans, Theseus, of the Athenians.
And like all Good Kings, they are dead.
In my day it was the done thing to side

With the Trojans for no better reason
Than that they lost. But me I back
Winners every time.
Mary Shelley may go to hell
As she thought she was going to anyway
And take Frankinsense with her.
I want her husband, alive and well.
Who, of course, also got killed.
Hardly surprising if he made a habit
Of reading Aiscylos while sailing.
He wasn't reading Aiscylos when he drowned.
Got cremated like a pagan king.
Not Agammemnon who, as I said, was king at the time
And lost, murderer of his daughter
Killed by his wife and (other) daughter.
Killed by his death killing his life.
Stabbed in the back in his bath.
I think of it every time I have a bath.
Though I have no sympathy at all
For that daughter and son.
I think it is unfair that Helen
Had everything, immortal beauty,
Lovers, cities destroyed and battles
Fought about her. And she just came home
And calmly went around being Menelaus' wife
While her twin sister, Clytemnestra
Was murdered by her son and daughter.
And the Athenians acquitted them.
They would do, a nation of sophists.
Always betraying their allies and torturing
Women and children and enslaving people.
They even killed Socrates, their one good man,
Then Plato tried to be a philosopher king.
And got enslaved for his pains.
I wish they had kept him enslaved.
He escaped, of course, and wrote books
About how he would do it better
If he was in charge. All poets do that.
They are just as incompetent as the rest
If they try to organise things.
As witness my own efforts in that direction
Or those of my avatar, Agammemnon,
Who, as I say came home and was killed in his bath
Killing his wife and his daughter.

And if you don't know about this you ought to.
Read it in the Iliad, read it in the Odyssey,
Do not read it in Freud who is always wrong
Although even Freud didn't deserve a son like Lacan.
But first and last read me, the beloved
Who was killed in the general slaughter.
But rise again like John Donne
(read him too) I, Helen, I Iseult, I Guenevere,
I Clytemnestra and many more to come.
I did it, I myself, Killing the King my father
Killing the King my mother, joining the King my brother.
It is the kick, my love, and not the nightingale
I like larking up kicks myself
But not kicking.
They have power to hurt and do so
Should not be blamed by Shakespeare or anyone else
For hurting though such is the race of poets
That they will blame them anyway.
However it is a pretty productive process
Especially if one may be plumber as well as poet
And thus unstop the drain as well as writing
Poetic Artifice 'Pain stopped play' and
Several other books and poems including
1974 *and All That* (seriously though)
I, Veronica did it, truth-finding, truth-seeking
Muck-raking, bringing victory.
It was a horse, of course, in which the warriors hid
Pretending to bring peace
And they wouldn't speak to me, crouching in the dark
Like a lot of fools, hearing the voice of the goddess
In an alien city, I speak your tongue in my own city
Cambridge or Camelot and you won't listen to me
Advised, of course, by Odyssos, solicitor, betrayer.
And when they had killed all the men, raped all the women etc.
Agammemnon came home and, as I said, was stabbed by his wife
In his bath. Anyway it is the lark, my love
And not the nightingale. I follow the sacred footsteps of
Hippolyta, the blest, the best
That has been said or spoken well in any tongue
Read John Donne – the memorable dun.
Don't read Matthew Arnold; he's a fool
I am not Prince Thomas Aquinas F.H. Eliot
I am not an attendant lord either.
I am the king who lives.

Spring surprised us, running through the market square
And we stopped in Prynne's rooms in a shower of pain
And went on in sunlight into the University Library
And ate yogurt and talked for an hour.
You, You, grab the reins.
Drink as much as you can and love as much as you can
And work as much as you can
For you can't do anything when you are dead.

The motto of this poem heed
And do you it employ:
Waste not and want not while you're here
The possibles of joy.

RICHARD II

The wiring appears to be five years old
and is in satisfactory condition.
The insulation resistance is zero.
This reading would be accounted for by the very damp condition
                                        of the building.
If you come up the stairs on the left side you will see
A band of dense cumulus massed on the banister.
Whatever you do, do not touch the clouds.
Forever again before after and always

In the light of the quiet night and the dark of the quiet noon
I awoke by a day side and I walked in time's room.
To the end of the long wall and the back of the straight floor
I stepped with my years' clutch and the dark of my days' doom.

For the sight of the deep sad and the swell of the short bright
Bid me flee waste of the time web and the long hand
On a life's weft and the grey warp in the year's cloak
For a long shade laps a short stand.

The terms left right front and rear are used
as if one is standing outside the building
facing the front elevation.
Specialists are carrying mirrors to the bedroom.
They are stacked beneath the window three foot deep.

Whatever you do, do not look in the mirror.
Again before forever after and always

The step to and the step back from the still glass in the long wall
Flung the glance wide from the old field and the brown scene.
And the glance broke at the pale horse on the glass turf
While the door swung where the window should have been.

With the ghosts gone and the wall flat as the clock's tick
With a blood stopped and a bone still I squeezed glue from my
                                                            cold glove
And I turned back to my smashed self and the few looks pieced
                                                            my own doll
From the back-lash of the time brick and the last wall of an old love.

In the joinery timbers there is new infestation
And a damp-proof course is urgently needed.
Say a few prayers to the copper wire.
Technicians are placing flowers in the guttering
They are welding the roof to a patch of sky
Whatever you do, do not climb on the roof.
Before forever after again and always.

limpid eyelid

JOHN HALL

COUCH GRASS

You choose the life or the life chooses you
what you have become being that kind of person
you do not owe yourself to the others
how could you
be sure any capitalist notion of the self
has you as the debtor
if you accept the story the part is fixed

                                        (begins as you)

Everybody is laughing

everything at once   (particulars)

a sleek black cat plays with your pen
and rubs her head against yours

beech off-cuts blaze in the fireplace

opposite you a white cat
sleeps in sheepskin

you share the room
with discarded shoes and clothes

somewhere you have a lot of paper
whose blankness excites and appals you
there are the notes of the person you were
you could destroy them without loss
but it's my guess that you don't you wish
you hadn't said some of it but if you don't look
the raggedy files are of the 'past'

just the way that you dream
or the crumbly dark compost is

it has rained a long time
it is March 9th
there is blossom everywhere

it is not that everything has moved

                              (into the key of first person plural)

Take our time and daunce it
for the duration of ecstasy we are
where the tongue folds
                    in folds of time, its tongue
ply for ply on ours

pliant and sweet, don't wait

when I look up there is no ground
there is blue within the curving green
what any of us might come to say

in the rain patience and expectation of survival
it hasn't been said
                    love of the future
of elasticity, of sponge

we may fear what we suspect but love
what we know we don't know
                              the grass
is ignorance

a tumulus of words   cities
of past and future interslung
with mechanisms of human distance
the G.P.O. pole sunk, but not deep enough,
                    into the ground

the seraphic voice of wire

music in airwaves
a vegetable past

speak of the insect on the window
or rain   or spider-wire

listen to what you might say
re-form under the grass
wet, spongey and not quite

if we know the future it can't be

if watery secretions from cells in the tongue
don't continually flush its pits and grooves

A landscape like a photograph
agriculture the least part of it
through the window it is too cold on the skin

how we hear the accompaniment
within *the* truth

that we haven't spoken our misery
landscape is always the distance

green is sometimes a melancholy colour
but hope informs it

the surrounding fields approach
a house is a way of not being in them
we are all somewhere else

from the distance the soil
lies passively under ignorant grass
but again we aren't where we began

couch-grass roots clutch the soil and are
its future
we've been there in an agricultural past

this is a probable order of need

Turning the soil the plough-shares
slice under the turf and
lifting it free from the ground
twist it over

all the grass disappears under the top-soil
it is lost
everyone knows what will happen
it is held together with the root-systems of couch-grass

(and back)

The narrative is given over to time
nothing here will stay the same
if you put your fork into rich soil
you know this
how much do you expect to see
from your window
time is a measure of temperature and light
the potatoes sprouting in your shopping bag
it'll take more than you
to stop the couch-grass
you get up because you are older
and look out of the window
time seems an inadequate agency
for your affairs
how will you succeed
another year comes round and you lose
yourself in beginnings
but the soil won't quite do that
for you   you are more than usually
in the middle of everything   not too sure
how any of it will turn out   lacking
a model of success
listen to the wind
time
blowing through the roof tiles
measure the damage
the lighter blossom of the berberis
survives

First the limed fields
                    then light snow
the water of surface life
                    frozen
as the alkaline dust works

first the lime
                    'like snow'
as though in a photograph
                              going by what we 'see' again
then the grass
                    sweating off biotic warmth
                                        as ice
kills as the frail motor-car
                              glides on the surface
there is an entry to break
                              the layer
of ice on the liquid nettle manure
                              fractured

Chain-harrow : drag the barbed contrivance
over the sliced clods and grass
re-appears :   the area of choppy waste
illusory, of course;   these green slivery dreams
the fields breathe hidden in hunched soil

A sense of incompleteness
keeps you from saying
you have finished and after all
you have now mainly to wait

the germination of barley
takes place without you
as it sprouts you roll it again
a further act superseding the past
the sequence saves you
from the mechanics of pure risk

the hiss of the green tassles of the past
swells your thoughts of a cerealist's livelihood

Spray-drift : applying the chemistry of poison
to the principle of selection; burnt nettles
show where the wind got under the spray jets
carrying somebody else's negative choice
across into your garden of decisions;
in this border zone the language
is particularly problematic: 'weeds' are quite simply
what the single-minded don't want
and poison re-inforces their point of view
persuasively

MEANING INSOMNIA

where the language dreams in derision
sleeping at the felt tip
of the red muscle where the lioness yawns
corpuscles of dream speech into her lungs

& words in an appalling irresolution of
undisclosed destiny need their sleep where

green eyes in the night of peaceful dreams
like the dreams the stars have
flicker in our dark
eyes   points of the life that moves
through the darkness
in the green painting where black
comes to its senses as an outer limit

and lying in the crumpled sheets bound
in the appalling poverty of insomnia
a language tosses fitfully about
its daily affairs in the heavy drapery
of a towel over an empty suitcase

or clings to the pedantic contours
of the ancient wall   asleep three hundred years
the words slip   let them sleep
in the night where their green dreams
already move unwaveringly

REEVES TIMBER YARD

breathe on the mirror
the way the river
breathes on the valley

the heart of the syllable
lying as the one true plain: a litany
sung to the music of Thomas Tallis

so the medium be a good man
that is have a clean tenor voice
and the water be the thin skin
that separates two banks
of images
          where we are

all returns or rises
it is a subtle and moving medium
that repeats piles of timber with its reddened tips

it is a poem   it is a singer   it is the glistening
surface of water   swelling under reflection into the space
between lined piles of images
of timber and its Orphic voyage
into the space behind

where an artful thought might
move subtly and cleanly
across the valley's one true plain
and repeat earthly
things

and erode them

RALPH HAWKINS

"EASTER MONDAY"

in the light like rain
where the fields form
with small birds there is
red and green indoors

just here there is no one
small circles break from where
the craft appear and the waters are starry
I cross check the location

for in an hour or so I will
have forgotten the pockets of
dust where the house is split
the children gather (lower right)

the heart is in a window
flowers and an apple planet bloom
above brown buildings and a vase
all the visitors seem to

have split from English
if only contact could be made
not with them but they with us
like a snowly owl in an embryo China

something rings on the wind
yes they have chosen correctly
this planet does not fit their requirements
now all these days seem first to yawn

and we its ever imprisoned captives lay abed

BUT IT MAY BE SO

it always rains against the front door
thumb latch
west south west
nowhere the world
her fields all green
drum against the changes
looking at it looking

under the carapace
various concerns
your brittle shell
soft blue to a bird
ducklings on a lake
what make
you out

dash in and out
temperature rising
earth sweats now rain
now birds now breath
in a tumble the micro
circuits of communication
trouble in

if you walk
the wind is high
various insects
various colours
take wing or hop
from what you say
from vetch and grass

or earth she is
of other words
from Ezra Pound
of all men light
was in his birth
room and dark and
fragrance from almond

another
quick
rose
your voice
the door
I mean a flower
with thorns

you are lost without trace
but I could trace you
but no longer in that way
as long as the brain I flitter
brings in what it does
an old no
a new yes

smoking an old cigarette
where
do you feel at home
you wander
with things to do
you put off
are tentative

in the distance the still
moving
the news washes over me
as I glance from that to this
why
I shall fabricate a way both
in and out of this

in the middle of now
in the day changing
the wind
constant
bird talk
animal fidget
I itch thought

some plates are in season
how they come and go
balanced by what the eye
sees and the mind's eye
so it isn't a documentary
the way the fields change
and the pollen floats

                    .

you are my slight changes
fully at home and restless
thinking of the electrical
insurgence we are all wires
this month of the longest day
not knowing what to make of
the news, which service

time for a change
heading into the hinterland
got my bags packed ready to unload
and what would you take with you
1 : if you were going to another world
2 : if you were leaving home
3 : if you were going on holiday

pale grey of my moods
maybe not
well, to another world nothing, sweet fuck all
home, the colours of mud, slate of sky
I aint ever got there
all these trees
for birds to perch in

the appearance of food is always important
just dish the stuff up
or Gods
as the big bee bumps into the window
for three I guess a few books
the smell of mint
the red of paprika

still raining
gentle rain last night
and again this morning
their songs never more
various their down
so white their little
ring collars

the words as though
they flake off and
scatter
clinging to a thin
line
sparks fly off
and gel

insular
sleeping under new conditions
I cannot say
you were sticky
but I'm O
it's a song
stuck on you

drift in and out all day
of the light as it shifts
through colour
am I stuck, stranded or moving
and in what
the light shines from a
this lamp

it will not stand still
in such a small place
pictures of the world
imagine what you see and hear
constantly
you will not make sense of it
though you try

break what you say
up into
lemon and herb
the fissure of fracture
the neat and bright speak of
with such surety
give us a light gov

leave the paper in
just in case
and say
I haven't a penchant for mystery
I will try to
path the clear
of nettles

fabric of the warm
materials
yolk swelling to
blood
ducklings and geese
in wind and rain
on water

you dunk yourself in
I hear the water running
the martins over the water
it's boiling for tea
we agree over this surface
the words slide
and are tapped

from the paper
he wanted to play a cultural piano
the way some play with syntax
he didn't know an adjective from an adverb
now you kids listen, chiao
I am not rewriting the Maximus
but learnin to talk proper

wherever you go
your head is full of bumps
then there and now
where would you be without them
is this a temple
no
it's a broken nose

but our luck can change here too
in this sleepy town
of constant or so it seems
wind the flat and few trees
you feel you impose on others
my tongue wobbles my knees shake
why be so silly

then I went
distorting and walking
with indulgence
I should stop this
call myself another
I mean change my name
if this I is I

is this true or false
or too close
what is there to do
you have your own notions
we are entering a thermal
up and rise we go
trying to change

whose voice is this
moving through various waves
caught up and carried
there go the birds
and here comes
there is no place to go
except there (no *t*)

it is all here
skips of the heart
beat of the words
no mention of stars
where in heavens
June days full of
clouds my clear eye

double fault
precise time
date
season of what bird
flower names of grasses
long light
no ball

grasses pollinate
June the 24th
the clouds
wondering what others think
how all these years
your friends are
both come and gone

the last day
warm air and the
world full of news
between friends
in a small way
I wonder with this
rebuffed as I am

full of doubt
oh he wants no more than
what he does want
in this small town
estranged and hello
brittle as a pun you
come from where you've been

shall I measure this room
a number of friends
in a novel of the marshes
in bleak winter wind and grey
in summer blossoms
at night the fields fall short
to encircle the home with stars

NO HEAD FOR HEIGHTS

the heart of the matter is where we know
seeing ourselves from some gantry or mountain lookout post
but it does no good or is not in charge
as we race off on a toboggan down the ice slopes

unhesitant of parental calls or the nagging voice from within
as we tumble over snow-blind and in need of company
even if we become injured along the way
or have swopped roles presuming that certain actions

were called for in the urgency of the present.
Of course nothing dramatic is going to come out of a rut
except a few flower beds
and these are but small adjustments

of our relationship with our environment. Rather, risk
is diminished, placed on a shelf with the *Salz und Pfeffer*
in order that we never put ourselves in a position
to climb mountains, having no head for heights

(this could well be economic like the wish to keep
a leopard or to completely refurbish a wardrobe) neither
are we prepared to risk the snow without knowledge
of our destination. That is, let us make this clear,

we wish our destination to be familiar.
This view we know poses a problem
not only of that which we call the *familiar*
but of the journey itself, be it through glacial mountains

or the rooms of a grand hotel. One
is never in control although of course we say
that something is, usually an engine of some sort
and a driver and crew of the transport of our choice. What

direct action there is, with regard to risk
is in the negative, or however we wish to colour
the sections or join up the dots, something does emerge
to be the overvoice and has banished as in a fairy tale

the loved one or sought after with a fear of heights
and dizzy spells; thus we shy away
from the emotional upset of glue and amphetamine
by avoidance or inaction we avoid harm and aggression.

What one means by avoidance here is removing oneself from
the presence of actual danger or threat (say falling
rocks or racist mobs). Perhaps escape is a more
appropriate term : it is the one adopted by the present author.

JOHN JAMES

EXULTATION

A ton of white rain will overflow my self-shaped sleeping-bag of
                                                                earth.
But today I love what is betrayed
by every indifferent Saesson –
what will be obliterated
from the human view –

                              the curving horizon breathes
over the reclined anatomy of the sphere,
the open lands to the North & West
still sprawl under the windy skies beyond the cities –

& remote mountain plateaus –
                              Eglwysilan
where the shepherd raised his eyebrow
at the question put in English –

The waters of the Taff shine with the blackness of coal.
She gushes like piss
from under a mare's tail
out of the irregular
gap in the mountains, through the Vale
the low parklands barely embank her,
everywhichway discharging herself in
deflected forces of current
over the hidden rocks & the
spewing over at Blackweir
with a smell of dead chub & pit effluent.

The waves ceaselessly lay stress on the shore.

I love all wild rocky beaches –
the smashed boulders under the cliff at Marcross
& the calm pools left behind by the tide,
the smooth grey pebbles as big around as a cricket ball

& the vales & the wailing gulls
& the trailing-haired girls
& even fake Castell Coch with its phoney pinnacles, Disneylike
                              in its half-shroud of dark beech woods

I care for the colliers, squatting on their haunches
on the swept pavements
under the shining windows
– Oh man, how bravely they bear up their spirits under the dark
                              stress of the looming slagheaps –

But ach a fi, I do not care for the oppressive household
& war maintained in the interests of an economy.
I do not care for the offensive sight of uniformed spirits & I regret
the flashing of leather I made
in the mean alleys back of Charles Street
under the skies' dim glow from the foundries

A ton of wintry rain will overwhelm my lichened bed.

A ton of ocean, wicked with dread,
the colour of hoar-frost in its night of coming
curls over us.

Oh man, how far Worcester is from Newcastle –
we drove hard night & day to reach it.

O Earth, give me before my last lonely bed the love of her I love –

Duw! I take off in her élite beauty! –
Though my flesh carry a dark hurt in heart
may I find peace in my last nothingness –

A dark wave hangs over us

... or as we wheel
down over Crickley, chivalrously high on our seats
    you see across the gleaming generous screen
right to the Severn Valley, tawny with the broad
    spread of distant grain, & beyond
            is where I'm going, where the mountains
put up their profiles &, in the moister
air of that higher altitude, the woods & valleys
will be deeply soft & made greenly
vivacious again.
            In a mutual presence
catastrophe may be averted, &,
for myself, new paths of motion are asserted
out of that & the gentleness a lady does
grace me with. So I relax,
sustained by a net of neurones like a hammock
which we cause to dance
& we are regenerated by it &
the soft flicker of myoclonic light
just under the skin. The paroxysm of an embrace is
the intense & complete awareness of one
another as dream for example – either you are my sister
or my brother, or I have known you all my life.
It is the amygdala that gives me being as
an imagined creature & after your remaking
the first thing you do is call my name. – Thus we
recall the moment before, both what
happened to us & what we did
as from the tops of small hills
blackness is eased away
under the green & delicate
leaves of the border hardwoods. They
do not separate from the grey skies
flashing with intermittent sun. It is we who are
threatened by the children of empire at Burrium,
but the Olway is fluid enough to be ours
& the ease of your disposition towards the world
can be & is as lovely as that – we remember; & so
we are aware of ourselves as persons with a
particular history – the circuit
touched off by everything we see or hear
appraise & want to do.

ON LEAVING THE FOOTPATH

The metal of the footpath is
narrow & confined, its walk
short & crooked round
the hideous hangars. But
pausing for an hour or two
resting on corn stubble, that
glossy yielded ripeness
really does take on its curved
quality of extension from us as we
push it out in a wide
hillock-shaped surface, catching
the sun on its skin with the
same aplomb of intention there is
in the cup of a radio telescope. Alive
we hold it all, the signals
separately received are
poised in balance by the achieved
leap we are & the fence of
the footpath is oh a
hundred yards away, warded off
with the same intuited use of magic
or selection that the
corn too has used to give itself
significance & its own chance of survival.

WRITTEN ON BEGINNING GEORG BÜCHNER'S *LENZ* & WHILE WAITING A RETURN

Lost on the outer rim of some
barely perceptible whirling, I float
slowly in toward the other. It is
no longer necessary to look for
lost dreams, the dream is found &
has a tangible & purposeful
content. A hillside breeze
ruffles the hair about
the temples in it. We know it

is a dream we have called into
being of necessity; &, with the joy there is
in returning to a friend or
place we have long craved
to be with or at, we look in
at each other, as though from a
long way off. But the void is
cancelled by our own assertion:
the codings of our senses fuse
into created fulness the apparent
immovability of the clouds as they
caress the turbulence of these hillocks &
valleys, ours, as far as the eye can reach.

SIDE WINDOW

What trees are those, where the low clouds infiltrate
the furthest limits of the fen? We may discover,
sooner or later, should we venture out across
the languid fields. Meanwhile, my position lacks sense –
I'm neither perturbed nor unperturbed. As long as
I know it's either raining or not raining, what can I
know about the weather? That's not to say
there's no place to begin, but you hesitate,
wary of possibility "b": a couple of arrows
departing in opposed directions. Thus,
the contemplative delay cannot be named
indolence; rather a poised inhalation of.. er..
certain powers. But what a pleasure to clean
the petulantly dirty staircase & munch a
sandwich with you, standing at the sink, talking
over our plans as we let the afternoon
recline to its conclusion with as much poise as Manet's
Olympia, but not so bold erotic or passé – just
resting, calm in the assurance of a lack of stasis.

This to be done
              before I do that, like
    drinking the coffee before I can
              look into the morning
light. My brow feels caught inside
              a cap. But what is there
              to speak of else? Perhaps a
      lost delicacy at the
              faint lips might cause me
      tremble as do the uneasy
sycamores before the
              rain, turning their leaves
              pale underside o
              ver what delicacy I can
      not find, likewise my
              spectacles or a
              reason for
                        not keeping still I
              squirt the insects   the trees
                        their metal leaves
                              uneasy go
                        into the harsher
                              light of dusk.

      The merest
      thing we are
              can often falter   is
      utterly otherwise
      as often as
              not a
      fallen pen, no
              declaration to
              the summer if it start
      or draw the cork
              the wine may pour & it
      shine while we
              sleep, divining

      & when I wake, please I
              walk in the
              sunflecked trees of

the grove, for she herself
may be felt to
pass there,
& her hand as a
breath moves out
on a tenuous
breeze that lightens
the ache. My shoulders
have learned to be
tense in the night

---

for the snow
to melt into the earth of mountains

watching for dawn
in an oppressive bedroom
all that water piped away & into fountains
in the municipal squares

wanting the dawn
though a wavering moment in the dark
may hold something at least
that may last, though you can't always see

what it is you appear to want.   Well,

oblivion finally is extended
whether in the occasional insouciance of sleep
or to the sacredly drunken it settles
over the dusty pavements

& then the little birds fall upwards
& across the sky
from chimney to chimney

& among the folds
of clean white table linen
the glasses are poured & waiting redly

so das strömende Wort
the onrushing
may still be granted & holy
remembrance also
nothing'll be forgotten
either tomorrow
or by night

---

a complete innocence
may be given us on completion
like an irrelevant myth
which floats out into language
with a light caressing
urgency, or I may recall
the inviolate, no more disturbing than
the distracting chatter of the little
sparrows, how French you seem
now as a recollection
your face strung out along the beanpoles
a faint wish turning the entire world
into an erotic object:
you are the current name
of a most impossible condition

so near, the cruel uncertainties of love

ROUGH

for Rolf Dieter Brinkmann

if you don't know German
flicking over the pages of *Die Piloten*
again the poems I'd like to translate

so many lovely words   :   Luft   Tod
Büstenhalter   I'd like a pint   it's hot
the clouds are glum

but it's after closing-time
& I haven't a thought in my head that could
sound like a line of Hölderlin

fishing the Old West River
the wind blew hard in my face all day
it does that any time it likes, forever

but it's quieter here in the attic
I don't need to be amused
I can make my own coffee as strong as I like

best to die in summer   /
when everything is bright
& the earth turns over lightly

---

the day writhes in an immense crater
some gleams want to burst out now & then
but further off on the taut horizon
the wind moves hardly at all it becomes
necessary to wait for the voices to return I
put down the pen get up & fasten all the doors

& soon the painted gauze descends once more
it looks like you again but with the centrepiece mislaid
the parti-walls tilt back revealing the greater sky
where a star comes loose & a shadow runs over
everything closes up on itself a
single occasion in the time continually piling up
but when will I be able to come to the moment
when it's possible to finish everything & begin again
you never look at me when will you be able to come back

it's only a game but oh so steadfast we keep on
passing the brink of an elegant nothing though
sometimes something in us makes everything tremble
& then the world doesn't exist anymore
or else we're mistaken & it merely makes a different sound

then it's yourself you see behind the universe
a dancing silhouette in a series of portraits
you fail to recognise any of them
but they're family you're looking at
in the middle of those motionless faces
the only one who's living is apparently the most placid
he leaves never to return

in the room where the walls are beginning to smile
it's only the night which gets up to leave
it's getting cold
your attention rises toward the stars

THE DRAGON HOUSE

her bright green leather high-heeled pumps

draws back the curtains to the sun & coffee in bed
on trays with legs this windscreen of a morning
moving with beech & yew a stewpond full of goldfish

I would wish to attend to nothing more than that
which is the measure of a lack of prayer

how could I be able to propose anything other?

the way the ice melts all along your back
that soft declivity near your tail

the sun warms through the glass
we drank last night
little yellow cups of prunelle & now
what litters today?
a pile of pastoral trousers & an old straw hat
a pale blue notebook bought in Hannover...

discard *The White Stones*
open on the quilt at p.71
finish the coffee
& sniff the smoky November day

which is thrashing about in the poplars
& looking more like poplars in the wind today
though otherwise the life of plants is not so
powerfully bedraggled here, the garden
ordered as a circulating library
soft romance & too much glare
for my watery eyes.
                So here we all are
                & here we all are then
                like a hardy 70-year-old
                stripped to the waist
                all tan & grizzled
                in the gale
& here is the day with its clouds, a Sunday,
& we're writing & reading & checking our oven controls
& wondering if after lunch to become spectators of the unbeatable
base-line-school-of-old, just-get-it
over-the-net-child-or-you'll-spoil-the-game
Diana versus the locals &
Smarden   Bethersden   Appledore
foreign as white clapboard houses
windmills   a curious zeitgeist never very far away
the clouds are getting up from the west
I think it's going to pour with rain, lunch
can't be very far away either as you have this pain
you think is hunger so you eat, you eat too much
& so you are "in pain again"
                    yellow tomatoes
I particularly like
              what is
Wendy doing in the orchard? She has cut
either a cauliflower
or a...!? "your English vegetables are so good, all you need
is to prepare them in an American way..." so I duck
out under the eaves again, hunting for postcards
& send one with love to:
                Master B. MacSweeney,
                90b The High Street,
                Barnet,

                        Herts.
                              Now it's the turn of
the shrivelled roses. Luckily
she doesn't have her towalong basket, her gumboots
riding mac & floppy flowered summer hat the brim
held down & tied at the chin with a chiffon scarf
of blue or green, ahhh, quick, shut the curtains!
this continuous sun! O rum
bustuous machine, redolent of Picabia,
his *Parade Amoureuse*, rattle
the rafters, the wall & quietude of Grandmama
Daubeny Russell-Clarke her grey eternal smile
enthralls me working freely in the morning though the
easing of the light is also good before Britannia
pulls down her shades of a wintry evening, yes
the piano please Diana, *F minor Prelude* pushing it away
like pressing buttons
or small clear bells
that sphere out lighter from themselves
against the indolence of the loggy room

What to those fabulous flying creatures carved & white?

GOOD OLD HARRY

we go to sleep like anybody else
though some awake like bullets
like Romans
munch munch

we aren't Romans
we aren't Americans either
we drink a lot of beer
every nation has its own greatness

we are the English
easy-going & lazy
we sleep pretty well
& when we wake

we are usually pretty thirsty
but not for anything too drastic
you can trust us to be
wooden & quietly proud

of our laver bread
our dumplings
a tomato or two
does no one any harm

& if there did happen to be a bullet amongst us
it would never find anywhere to go
it would just keep travelling through the air
without hitting anything

we have thirty-eight rulers
which is very economical
& they are well protected from
tomatoes on the whole

we call them the cabinet
& cupboard is the name of the land
where everything is in its place again
the natural rulers

behaving like proper gentlemen again
eating a bit of cabbage
& sausage now & then
like the rest of us no doubt

when Edward goes for a walk
we take off our caps & wave them in the air
England is a mature nation
& is not a bit like America

INAUGURAL ADDRESS

Good Day/you're in tune to If You're Going To Do It
Do It Alla Prima Time/

it's a Radio Babylon interference calling
a largesse of Delirius
more fundamental than America
ruddier than Silbury & more abused
greener than Mekonta &
mightier than the Wig in Wigan with a yellow in between/

Dreamier than the Kill in City
shinier than Krypton & more clear
more on top of it than Atlantis a
Blow Out on the Bauhaus
A Roll Over Old New Veau
A Knock Out on a Nico off the DD & D Co
A Granite Against Gropius/Toasting with The Hosting
No Touting for Bruno but
pouting & more tantalising than
Island Three the desiccated orifice of
The Woman with The Three of Everything she say
What on EARTH are Maltesers/what in THE WORLD
is a Power Tower/

A Cruising in a
3rd Century of The Decline
of Industrial Investment I & I for short The
Fantasia of The Plan Voisin Begat The Beaubourg
Glossier than La Ville Radieuse
& Sharper than Arcosanti The Architect
is The Invention of The Masterwork &
couldn't live without it/

Wrecking his Neck-Angle on the EuroStandard
we drift & mooch in the marinade of his metered Overspace
down on the Bogside Jesus & The Redevelopment Corporation
snicker into sight a fault in the beam-out from GPO Tower
back in Finance Capital/
neglected scabs of Venice Florence Rome Glasgow
flake under foot
on the black marble stairs of Milan Station

.

Inside The Riverside
Articulate Trace as Non-material form of Capital
blisters each side of your face with a blush
an intense blush blisters each side of your many faces
in the flux dance slab stance ba
lance of glittering felspar
the straitened moment speeding
in the ruinous curve of vinyl & circular dwelling
a cutting of deliberate gesture
in the passage of indelible act

.

Good-bye Savonarola Brunelleschi Alberti Bramante
Good-bye Dublin The Centre Pompidou The Guggenheim
Ghiberti's doors are the doors to the biggest bank
The Los Angeles County Museum of Modern Art The Hayward
The National Gallery "West" Berlin & Hello Tokyo
Good-bye the Monumental Fault & the Faulty Monumental
Great Fish-Knives of the Future Hello/Good-bye
Good-bye you fully automated cities that keep operating after we
      have all left
Good-bye computers transistors space-probes automation
      miniaturization acid & San Francisco
Good-bye the Marlborough Good-bye Sir Humphrey Gilbert/
not a room to be had in all of Broadacre
though you may get there
on The Old Straight Track
By the Rights of Orthogonal Planning/

Good-bye Auschwitz Hello Angkor Vat Pol
Pot Napoleon III Pinochet Pinocchio of Chairman Hua
Haussmann Mussolini Sant'Elia The God
Father of High Tech & he with no lustre on his
bite in the echo chain of Sardis the thatcher the carter
Teheran the Arc of the Shah
The Biggest McDonald's Advertisement In The World
Whose Cancer spreads easier than butter Kissinger
Rockefeller The Woman With The Three of Everything
Everything Terminates The Wedding
With Frozen InterContinental Rice/
Miniaturization of the Social Body

Into Occasional Table Arrangement
Micro-Explosion of the Thousands Transformer of Millions
peripheralized to the slotted sides of the votive Gold Heap
Market of Commodity Futures Miniaturized orgasm
of little yellow men spray from the planet edges
one by one
we drink & eat the sweat
& muscular steaks of Africa straight from the freezer
on Microwave Alert for The Republic
Sparta Miletus Periclean Athens:
The Acropolis Metropolis Necropolis Death Star Voiding
Hearthstones into 3D Vision Gelatine/

C'mon EveryBody/let me take your little pinkie
point your knees overhear
see me in the Arkle light of me anti-perspective altar back
shift your gear over here
get your fore-quarters into tune
& put them on this here blue plinth
Before your very stereoscopic vision
sky-junction Sky Junction
flux in sky junction Masterwork the flux of/
This is Sky Junction

CRAVEN IMAGES

1

> *"Oy vay!   Oy vay!"*

I like to dance so much & a kind of mania
conspicuously lures me on to your pointed hairless chest
but since here I am engrossed in the reading
of this here copy of *Sounds* & I am not Mechthild
only the punter with his meat on fire
outside the station in the fog I will swear
never to have seen you before in my life
when the Old Bill cruise by on their talking machines
matelots linger at the cab-rank I

carefully flick my second finger over the hard &
shiny folded notes in my shirt pocket
as the lull at the end of a lonely street
in the orange glare of the vast suburban night
holds me to the sluggish rocks of the pavement
your face in the shadowy shopfront at 3:00 a.m.
ain't exactly the ski patrol but then what with this
disaster area called my teeth like a roar of jacks
in a flashing orange search for a burst water-main
among the indeterminate commodities at the corner of the bar
Jackie Petersen dreaming over his amber sleeve of light
one immaculate black hoof over the brass rail
under the falling cloud of resin & chalk
passing from night to desk & desk to night
shoulder to shoulder with an immaculate new fish-tail
Where are the hatters of Luton? American devices
come round again like a thousand Chinese paper inventions
I would have liked to have been to Bucharest with you
Budapest anywhere taken all the boats the wagons-lits
mooch round all the bars gawping at all the young dudes
ate up all the food making for the Man in the Moon
crossing the Park in the soft purr of taxis
ah that sweet viola sound

> her back is arched
> & her breasts are bare
> I feel a rose down
> in her hair

the inimitable life of hotels
a rich display of feminist cactus in the lobby
lingering crows on the steps of Brompton Oratory
the poor animal life of the region we
will try the grand gesture the sag-arsed manner
the sculptors throw cat & rip off cock manner
tails the piece the hands of me manner
& up to a certain point manner
a couple of borzois on a leash manner

> o baby what
> a dog to be
> in the Suck Age
> of the bourgeoisie

perhaps I could finally bring myself to leave
your baleful pluralism my fingers
pause deliciously over sticky keys
as I hover over a faint icy rhythm
straps vibrating under your immortal propositions ideal
pedestrian on the King's Road
enraptured by the stare & cheek of very early Logic
another little Pils & pointless artless & frank
I get drunk without you
until the mixture degenerates & a bad odour
returns us to the Angel the harp player of the age
scraping his knuckles on the rough-cast ceiling
blood on the tambourine I sing
under my breath & my you're nervous
under the snow of a cold algebraic desire
an inkling of a kiss in the foyer

but in the calm of your bed in the late afternoon
there are these agreements of the body
the little pores in your back the gently lifting slats
parts of the outer city are atrocious
hatred of the meagre portion
even the bars are closed when we leave the cinema
it never stops no end in sight
till morning takes you home
here is your bed
be stupid beast & sleep
last of the occupants
who sadly scrape their feet

2

in the lines of the slipstream of an heroic express
coming in on the long curve eastwards into Cardiff
Atlantic rockas make their move a brazen cloud of
fiery smoke is lifting over GKN as we embark

& in the palace of globes a dazzling array of glasses
in various stages of depletion
& the sweet high tenor of the crack

under the rain under the sun & under the starry circus
the green sea rolling like an egg

3

black moleskin
tender pastures juniper & Coke

far from the underworld
green penetrates the sky levels

a glass of Volvic could have made me happy for ever

4

a glass of Aveze held me smiling vaguely in the grass
like a great lost wader
sad to have been a fighter & at what cost what times
& what a summer where are you now my little musics
mind you cowbells
                        make me sick
with misery & pain

                        ".... twenty times I have denied my heart
                        I am no longer able to rest"

I flew far in pursuit of your traces
une peinture une musique qui serait simplement voyou
the insanity of my legs the millions of my thighs
the tang of the pike in the mouth
a piece of chocolate sweating in the sun
like a very rare stamp in the middle of a banal collection
the bosses vacate the City at the hour of the illuminations
thousands of voices lift themselves up to heaven
in a velvet liaison with her boulevards
like love among the ants
the strawberries were ripening my ideas were turning blonde
the sky glazes over the purified volcanoes

5

The west side of the fishpond in the Jardin des Tuileries, looking across it & down the long terrace to the crepuscular distances of the Place du Carrousel. It is a bright sunny day. The usual scatter of public chairs has been cleared so that only three remain & these are placed very formally in a row looking out over the water. The carp or whatever, are jumping about all over the place. It is August 1970. There are two figures sitting quite still their backs & heads quite strikingly neat & similar. But the one on the left is Arthur. The other one is Douglas. The chair to his right is empty. "It's high time I was getting back to England you know, Douglas."

6

I was leaving, love on the platform
possessed of your greatness, o dear Thames
windows all lit up & rosy in the setting sun

This morning at 10:00 the Inter-City 125
will float me to Birmingham Stoke on Trent
but at the eleventh hour you grow sick at the rumour
                                        in the back of the heart

likewise my craving for newsprint the smoke of small cigars
a proper slow burning characteristic of a superb condition
tumblers whirling downwards over shining rows of slate

your ideas were captivating & the wounds superb

as we rush out of Euston I turn & smile at the disappearing
                                                            grass

a dart has pierced to the centre of this alluring folly

Bad Thoughts

"You are unable to imagine that one day it will be possible for you
    to say hello to yourself to recognize yourself as a friend & to
    make a definitive peace of that
you remain surrendered to your alternatives
when it comes to tomorrow you are unable to recognize yesterday

the defunct days lean towards you with their images
from them you read off the inscription of your old outrages
& those yet to come tremble away into distant complaints

the scattered griefs fail to gather in the vicinity of where your
    heart has been
you have forgotten why you are sad
but you will know the hour where your sadness was born

tired of searching the night you will relish the day
she will nourish you with her light orchards
the trees of the night the trees of the day

the seasons turn in their balmy cycle
& you will not know what to say to their mild passage
it's a big chance you think it over

you cease to see yourself as a fit up for what is agreeable
exhausted by the winding distance covered by your staggering days
the lost homelands the rusted autumns

           & a fiery rose in the September sun
you will feel your body give way to its constituent parts
it will bear less resemblance to you than a rose-bush

the spring lies in wait for in order to prune
when the evening twilight falls on the deserted lane
you will not have any dread left in you

you may wish to cut yourself off from certain parts which you
    disapprove of
you would take a slice of this thing or that to offer up as a quarry
but when you rest on the restful breast of your lover

by her let yourself be carried as far as the border
where to be cancelled itself is to revoke all endings
accept yourself & your heritage from which you have been formed
    & passed from age to age

stay mysterious rather than be pure accept your multifariousness
    your pluralism
when you come finally to take leave of your youth
all the fallen dreams born of your very early childhood

shoot beside fresh jasmine
an adorable person comes together in your arms
at the charming little cross-roads where the day slopes

into the flat open country & the little hill expires
the implicit beauty of sacred places will be troubled for you
this restlessness will have put everything in question

& you will be subject to the craziest actions
but the road runs away from under your step the horizon never
    approaches
& you give yourself to this walking life to which the dust of the
    road attaches itself

BYE BYE BLACKBIRD

for Douglas Oliver

over the clay-laden estuary a
soft grey light comes sneaking
my heart away it is the spirit of Colne Spring

& all along the shoreline an oyster-catcher
dips & bobs a splashing blur of black & white
against the easterner

curlews ghosting by a little above the fleet
fly our souls out of perversity

Brightlingsea has grown where it is the sepia
gaff-rigged sails of the smacks manoeuvre away

into the Dutch hinterspace beyond Mersea Island a rich
alluvium gets itself laid over years we mooch along

towards a frith
dreaming of sprats & opals

AFTER CHRISTOPHER WOOD

it would be ordinary enough to live
in a room that balanced above

the sea's implied presence
a soft draught of light taken in

by the half-open lips of pale green shutters
quenching the tender places

left in the flesh of the mouth

caused of a recurring breathlessness
caused of living in low places

& we could relax into that thing
we vaguely call "life" whatever
the shade of dress in which it might present itself

& we could sprawl on a white bedcover
reading the *Lives of the Poets*
provided – & this indeed would be a provision of
our existence – that we brought nothing
mean or sordid into that place by virtue
of our mutually ridiculous appetites
whereby we are able to lose each other up to the last moment
when your fingers catch at my lips in a smile
& we do become dwellers in that glittering place
the towels white with orange borders
a kind of mortal incompatibility

SISTER MIDNIGHT

stuttering rain at the window
early in autumn your breast
loosed from its hold
the caprice of your lifting thighs
the serious depth to your smile
I seem made of insubstantial elements like a leaf
the otherwise silent house occasionally sways
two blocks away the river seeps from lock to lock
the telephone obdurate & yellow against the blue rug
the gale now pulling the whole room apart at the seams
hungover leaves fill up the dusty often
can't do anything at all at other times
you just don't care at all you try it
your own way her face a little blue that shaky
girl with the shaky hand can't hold the pen
too weak for the desk the lower chair
the lower sky hurry by on the pavement outside
everything slipping away with the day
which is closing in on itself at 3:58 the sky
all lit up between a crack in the buildings
& under those clouds lie the chimneys
decorated with a fretwork of little birds
& large grey washes of sky over the gables

the bell rings but I refuse to answer
I might have been a painter but there was an accident
in my life right down the line of a fierce fatigue
replete with overcoats my cherry which is why it is worst
when you have forgotten the mayonnaise remember
I told you there'd be something funny about it she said
like her potatoes of lead, flash flash, alas a
cold pallor has overcome my scrotal sac
in the sharp gusts of autumn in all those places
I said I'd never go again & then did
as if I'd never even forgotten
                              meanwhile
your head my little sweetheart of the steppes
don't hesitate grab the momentum while the going's good
sink to your knees beside the yellow sofa
take him between the folds of my bright magenta wraparound
the bright glossy oval of a knee & remarkable vest

rippling up over my becoming
the casual spectator of hoydens in the sharp grass of the park
steam rises from the coffee cups
the wine splashes into the little glass
a vigorous red in keeping with the tone
of all that battles to be without my arm
oh my arm in this smallest minute where I enter your name
for the aim of the race do you know
there are certain sounds which tear at my liver
like a cat at its matted fur & a certain
absence of detail has for the first time
featured in my life tightening my collar
& lurking near the black marble of Italian headstones
shining back at the bright little windows of the local
do-it-yourself shops in the rising morning
like a sickness that imprisons the heart in a fettered glove
& now I recognize your great talent as a member of the
human race as the peasant offers me the plastic salt-box
& I look around for the snuff of the father
painted in green & embroidered in my vest
as a text for my meditations

outside the window the trees move in the night
your grand desire rises in my throat & my heart
pulses on into its thirty-sixth year like an indifferent
steam-engine while milky tea embalms the organ
a woman feels very cold around the buttocks
once in a while & yet your laugh brings light to me
cause you're the first good man I've found
pressing the glossy black embellishments to the hand
under the gentle curtain imagery of the gasfire & the
dusty smell of old red velvet cinema seats
                              but still this hanging over
                              of the female in the man
                              means maybe
                              rather than
& that's not the end but a beginning like when
you can't turn the key any further in the sardine can
& all along the edge of the skyline
the last green cringe of daylight
drops like a plate to the ground

TIM LONGVILLE

EPITAPH

My grandmother, dying, thought my
uncle Tony, thirty
five and balding then, her favourite
son, rode on
his bicycle, a boy
of ten, beside a
dangerous lake, and called to him.
It is a weakness

in our family
to call to what

cannot reply

and is best loved.

PIGEONS

for my Grandfather

I never knew you but my mother made me
see the scars on your chest and back as what was left
of a life spent in pits and on your pigeons
you seem to have lavished almost everything else
you'd got, although in passing you begot
as many sons and daughters almost
as would fill a pigeon-shed, it is the pigeons
they remember, and your strap; your wife,
their mother, that they hate or love,
and miss. Gossip, this? And yet
what remains of a human, nothing

more than that, irrelevant detail, irrelevant
impact and exit, important only
in its signal lack, the grey-blue pigeons rising
as in my dreams they do in fact, out of the blue
scars on your back, you are for ever
in a world as wild as pigeons
caught in a high wind, losing your grip.

GRAVE STONE

Alone at night, afraid to move
From my father's stone, in a dream, my own
And only father, a stone, seen once
And snapped, on Malta, by my mother.

Never known, by me; or, it may be,
By her either. Gifts: a name, lack
Of a home, at heart, the knack
For being alone : – for pity, stone.

HEAVY AS EVER

I still remember the almost first kiss –
                    forced to it
by all the giggling others – and the hiss
                    she pushed out
as our faces, pressed against the bars, met.
                    Furious,
both of us, yet filled with relief. And yet
                    we ran out,
crying, white. For what? Perhaps the only hurt
                    we had was
we'd been picked, put out, on the spot. For what?
                    For our fat.
That made us. We were special. And were fit
                    for their use,

as emblem and idol, breaker and butt.
                    Oddities.
And so, of course, the first to kiss. Yes that
                    perhaps is
it. And as unwilling-willing now as
                    then I press
to the bars and expect, from behind, the push.
                    And the kiss.

GOING OFF

Your smile that trembles on the edge
of giving in, your walk of such outlandish elegance
that some exotic bird, flamingoes say,
caught half off into space
could hardly match its lack of weight :

impalpable but close : the mind and eye
grip these to pull you back by
but without success, already you are off,
your feet are moving always and your heart is
lost, you promise and expect

so much, but never come to rest
and fail to hold
what you most want, not through a lack
of charm or luck, but through excess,
lost in your own response, you live for ever going off.

POEM OF APOLOGY

*L'amour n'est pas du tout le feu (comme on dit souvent), l'amour
c'est l'air. Sans lui il n'y a pas de souffle. Avec lui on "respire à l'aise".*
V.V. Rozanov, Fallen Leaves, published in a French
version by Gallimard, 1964.

Love is no fire
   despite what people say
it is our air
   the very element
we breathe
   and as unsure
as air and we are
   servants
to its vagrancy

            Half bird afraid
            the current up will stop
               our flailing bodies
            tumble and smash
            half fish of the air possessed
            by thoughts of an airless beach
               wrenched open mouths
                  cries lost

      Else out for
   unknown pure high current
      endless depths

where movement is such ease it is
excess we founder in
   demanding bliss

            Each way love's breezes
               take us as we pass
            fleeing from fear or in pursuit of
               what can take its place
            each separate failing
                  flight has
            crossed and for a moment forced
               such sharp cries out as
            dying off may bring us peace.

AIRS AND DISTANCE

A finer flesh, air's odour
comes to us; distance is something,

almost, we can touch.
                    Behind us, in the field,
like tiny bombs the snails go off

under tractor-wheels, upturning earth
after harvest.
                What we can

touch is always
lost – through airs and distance we

have come to
                    this
comfort beyond us.

MINE

The fields behind the house ascend in a shell
of impossible green to a pure blue sky.

But walk them, press
turf underfoot, throw

head back to savour it and land
will likely fall a hundred

feet away to the pit and once
that substance has been lost and what was "mine"

become what no-one would possess, he'd be a fool,
in land like this, who'd trust to anything much.

STRICT AND PARTICULAR OLD LADY

A world of most particular facts
she moves among, ensuring each
one keeps its place, its station – just
by being there they form a pattern
keeps her also straight, neat, polished
for the least or greatest
vision, visitor – as God is
shadowed in a teacup's cleanliness and death
strikes out with each new leaf, their steady
rhythms even in her breath, pursuing
grace each moment's change and dust.

COMPANY FIGURES

Swallows, on a wire in autumn. Hum. As
        much and in as short
a space. A definition. Even
        the youngest, who have never seen

the land for which they've gathered, know
        what they are called for, how this
lyric crush supports an epic
        space. Our fastest

wires below can't tell
        as much – as what we've
gained and strung up is a reach
        in error for our own place at our own pace.

APPLE AND CLOTH

The apple on the barefaced
cloth. Both eaten up, reduced
to the least pulped fragment, ruined

shred, each gives at
last sheer shape to the meanest
loss, a form that whole they never had.

ONE LEG AND PEERS

The one-legged starling pecks at dust,
drilling and drilling, its wide eyes lost.
    Around and around them the pecking words
    snap up dry truth, the starving

crust – "I live you you live me we
move about, first left,
first right, safe home at the next and if
it doesn't rain the sun will last" – so

pecking and glaring and running about
they stir up dust :
                "*that* we can trust,
in its waste, its filth, to keep them off,
the two-legged flier, the rabid mouth."

EN ATTENDANT

You might on a day like this suspect
a change of heart, expect events
to double up in readiness
for something else, the long-awaited

newness we just squint at, sketch
with blunt pen in the terms of this
intent suspension as we hold our breath.
Our own desires will be our true death.

POEM ON THESE POEMS

Impossible to praise you as
we ought : the new world will
        be named and made for
        you and till that

consummation all our verse is

        what we lack on
        earth of earth
's true nature and your voice
escapes us as we fall to speech.

PROSPECTS

What's under your nose? Immediate distance.
Extended subjects, you suggest, suggest less
picking of nits and less "significance"? I tell you

this : the moral starts
right here, and goes on, either side of your skin.
You start, and stop, by breathing.

PAVANE FOR A DEAD CAT

an die Verwandten

The sign says Public Bridlepath but long ago the tracks through
    Arley Wood died out. It seems that no-one walks for pleasure
      now or
rides and there's no need and will be none for years
    for foresters : these are not the trees to keep
straight, form a fence, a phone pole, serve a purpose, keep us
    out of places or in touch; which makes it difficult
to keep yourself straight, getting through, and I give
    up the details of the map, watch sun and face
what detail comes up : brambles, fern, low brush and trees so thick
    they've made their own fence, my pace and a noon the clear

October sun can barely push through. Sun's heat's less
    than making paths, and when the pair of us
have come across an open space, we take it, with relief,
    appreciate the distance (and believe in it) we
still must cross, to get to spaces which exist
    as settlements not outposts. Though we make it, both
of us are weak and as we cross the meadow, frightening sheep, we
    drag thick shadow with us to the farmhouse door. The face
that fills it when it's opened is as overwhelmed to
    face me as I her, fenced in our wilderness

of doubt, not knowing what we might escape or
    what let out. Her nearest neighbour's
five miles off for instance and it is
    apparent she's too close. *Yes*, she says,
I took a cat last winter out the back
    to bury it and got lost. Yes, I say,
I can believe it. And we laugh. A lost grave's something
    we can share as truth. It's dark now as
I set off down the wide path, though the stars are
    out, the farmhouse bright, inhabiting not sharing light.

BLUE

for Michael Wallace

The slaughterhouse's heart is frost. Among the hung-up
sides of meat, and drowned in the buzzing
fans, the flies, the butcher's heart beats
stutter out, unsteady as his feet – *My head – my head –*
so cold – I'm bursten – in this nowhere place – let's dance –

and straight-faced, bent-kneed, takes to his breast
the side of the lamb the blood at this new heat
begins to run from, and the tears, unnoticed in
his dropping dance, freeze to his face.
                              In sober truth,

next day, he says to his mates, his bloodied hands so tight
the veins stand white against them – *it's the truth – I did – I did –*
and swept up afterwards, along the guttered
white-tiled floor, blood tears and pride, and locked the door.

DOGS

> *for the Queen's Head, Pensnett :*
> *in memoriam Alfred Glyptis*

        Big Alf's on the way out. Every breath he takes
breaks what he holds on – being what he has
become – the Big Man – letting him
                              down slowly,
                              with pain.
        Size is his emblem. Even in
the war when mined and drifting others
sank, big Alf went on, buoyed by his weight – the story of
his life :
              hit by his wife when snoring drunk
in bed with a gallon jug, he woke up long enough
to say *These bloody flies do itch* and swat
the blood off, slept and forgot;

when challenged to
a bout with sledge-hammers across the pit-back, heaved
the hammer and himself as weightless till (one
handed) dented ribs or skull – *like watching a mountain
run*, his mate said;
                            bred as a hobby
terriers, the size of cats, which snapped
at his heels or peeped, bright-eyed, from his enormous
pockets. Why? Because, *if they get hold
they hang on, you can't shift 'em, short of death* – engulfed
in laughter, all four feet across, he bellowed
down at the tiny dog, who yelped and glared back.
Bastard. Gave its ear a friendly scratch.
                                        Suddenly
still, he looks off over the heads of
little people who do not hang on, bleakly and suddenly
still.
        Hey Alf, what's up? an old man natters,
quick for the door, *you lost your tongue in all that
fat?*
        He he the laugh runs round as Alf's small dogs
snarl to be loose.
                        Be quiet all of you – marked
with a fist on the splintered table-top – *you've no more
sense than pigeonshit.*
                            He he's obedient, squashed.
                                                    One
week afterwards the talk is hushed, both sad and – at its
heart – profoundly glad. The heart that's given way is
Alf's. A month before he's said they'd wanted him
at eighteen stone – at thirty four no chance to
cut through fat. *Though what the hell, it's kept
the sea from off me three days, half
a dozen blokes and fifty years of drink, it's earned its
keep*
        – and kept his death within it, whining
pup in his pocket.
                        Stony-faced, the wife he'd chased
stark naked through the undergrowth, his daughters who'd
climbed over him in high-heeled shoes to bed when he had
fallen on the stairs and slept, too big to shift and blocking
all the staircase up (he never noticed it) – each night,
stone-faced, they sit in the bar and wait because he won't
allow them home, stone-faced, he bears it

out, among the dogs who snarl and fight
across his heaving chest.
                              Yes, Alf is – always
has been – more than life-size, one sharp youngster says.
                                                          Oh
yes pigeonshit? Speak for yourself, his daughter snaps, prepared
(and with her father's voice) to rip his eyes out.
                                                    Aye,
says Frank, frail eighty-two who never speaks, *we'll*
miss him when he's gone and that's a fact – he'll
leave a gap. Pause then a snicker, forced
out deep, from everyone, all round the bar.
                                              I tell you
what – the corner speaks – *when we have carried Alf and put*
him in the ground, we'll all have earned our
piss-up.
          Aye, and god knows what they'll do with
all those dogs – though I can guess, a soft
voice says, and silence
follows this, as deep as if big Alf had bellowed for
the last time *Pigeonshit,* and shut them all
up, and himself, in one dark pocket.

GRAPH

I believe in the English sentence not in cries
or outbursts, sudden jumps, but something
loose, enveloping and yet

controlled enough to take in
Heretofore (the only word on the lavatory wall)
and make its nonsense sensible and felt as (as

the onward pressure of the words insists) what was
is was, is is, and what's to come is
aimed at and will find (of course) its own full-stop : **Hereafter**.

It is not the whole of what there is it says
– it says that sense in any sense is not
the whole – of what there is – of what it says – it says it

falling, holding, helping us (as it does) to persist
in the uneasy looseness
what there is and what it is consists of.

HOMAGE TO WILLIAM BRONK

It's like a walk around strange country
where, bewildered by a shape and tone
almost entirely unfamiliar yet arranged by laws
its own in ways which strike us as at once
beguiling as an unknown face across a street
we never meet and as disturbing as that spinal chill
we call our own grave's ghost, we find, in wandering, our
selves at last, at one same moment, lost
and happily at home in loss, ourselves
is loss, abandoned into fear and beauty, peace.

MUSIC TO LIVE BY

T.V. with the sound on, picture off, we titillate
        ourselves by guessing at our own plot, the eternal
retour of the music, in a melody that's strong enough
        to signal what comes next, convincing us conviction
is by nature in an order of events.
                                Here in
        this Lounge for Residents, where no-one lounges,
no-one lives, after you've gone to bed, I turn the picture
        on, the sound off, and two weary uncommitted pugilists
lean on each other's shoulders and stare out, and they as
        well appear to listen, count their heartbeats out
of what is lost in such a life, to all the humming of
        tuned radiators which insist a "constant heat".

In tones like this no sense of time can last.

Sleep,
love; wake up; keep in mind and keep fast what went
on – not
an easy music morning takes the heart of, but in
what we lacked, in all our undertones, unprogrammatic
accidents and turns, was latent : what events
are as they are's a song to – which we – rise to share in.

MELANCHOLY SPEECH OF BLUEBELL
THE BOGOMIL DOG

*They (i.e. the Bogomils) say that everything exists by the will of the
Devil : the sky, the sun, the air . . . . in brief, they consider all that moves
on earth, animate and inanimate, to be of the Devil.*
                                      – Cosmas the Priest, circa A.D. 970

Dreams and fantasies. The world is alive
with blackness. Holes. Forbidden
ecstasies the other side of me. I turn
and turn in my black skin seeking
ways out ways in. Here is not
and not the place I want but what is
otherwise, elseplace? Blossom the kitten
opens her wide eyes wider in a world of
light it looks like. I implore her
not to exist. Pray for her
hard enough perhaps and with enough love
she will vanish. More lost, more found then
would I be? Fear and delight
ravage me. "Would I be"! Nothing
is what is, *is* what *is*, but in dreams
and fantasies of life we call out to the one
who owns us, makes us run. Devil's. Devils
everyone. Sky. Air. Sun. Breathing. Groans
from the holes we move in. Everyone,
Blossom, everyone. To be a saint would be
to name the holes, acknowledge them. "Come in." Blossom, I could
move my black tail as it were "imploringly" and no more, no
more anyone. I could. You could, Blossom. Blossom,

the world we have we have on trust by
trusting. All that I trust in now is
in my death : lighten our darkness, I pray to
it, and make a light of us. Delight is a form of
cheating, Blossom, which you practise
blindly. Blindly I practise sleep, advance my tail
across my face, and enter and am
darkness, knowing it is nothing if not truth.

THE VERGE OF SPEECH

for David and Mary Chaloner

1

Small trees, smaller emotions; the small clear edge
of some longstanding pool.
                              The white dust
flurried as we pass goes back
so close to what it was it is
unnoticed bar the pool's faint smudge.

2

The reservoir below beneath which
corkscrew waters waste
as night falls, out of the headlights' reach,
deep into darkness where
we cannot look, turning and turning, losing touch.

3

Eyeballs ache,
the head turns
purple, a grape
in the slight and
waiting wind as
storm grows thick.

Pulp in the dust.

4

Cutting it back, the wilderness
behind the house, the waisthigh
grasses, stiff blades fret, the cold
glass creaks against your flesh.

No relief.

5

A dark room, dusk; the white blinds plastic bars
across the purple sky lit up
by purple lightning. Wet rot
sweat off the grass. The coffee
sweats. And breathing. Breathing.

6

Train next day, the wheel sounds
half an hour before, your filled head thick with
rain from each lamp-post, falling fast.

A thick dark night that night with
arc upon curve upon twist of
grass, of dust. They tell you you have woken up

screaming, gagging for breath.
At last, at last.

7

These passages, my friends, which blur
the small clear edge by which,
each day, we live and are,
in some small measure, clear
leave us the next day, dust
by the pond's edge, almost
exactly where we were : at least
what moved us to such sudden
unconsidered silence
or to speech, is so far off
it troubles us no more
than, high up, still by the smallest

tree, in cool sun, peacefully,
we tremble at the unforgiving
deep three hundred foot of
water, on the verge of speech.

BETWEEN THE RIVER AND THE SEA

Homage to the memory of Jack B. Yeats;
for John Riley (whose poem is in it) and for C.M.H.

*And in the darkening dusk of the sea a ship's high prow rose before
me and a bowsprit swathed in cables and a girl's chiselled profile and a
Nereid's figure on the ancient prow sailing towards the shore – a reminder
of the infinite wealth of dreams and the power of love.*

*The spirit of distant lands followed in the wake of the Nereid. And it
seemed to me that the heart would not withstand the onslaught of these
intoxicating thoughts, of a happiness as yet unshared with anyone, of
an existence so free and winged, almost unreal and yet quite real, as real
as a stone in the street.*
　　　　　　　　　　　　 – Konstantin Paustovsky, *Southern Adventure*

I

One thing not to do is worry
where we are: where we are

a climate of Georgian songs and water
falling through them as peace is

beside ourselves and a long way off
beginning to make maps

II

Sweating over the cliff-top path
　　　　with campion in the grass
for mixed voice chorus

going where it's never been
     another version and knowing
it is them: astonishment

well-known on open fifths and repetition
     of what was never entirely
white wings in advance of

what has always been
     a dream of spontaneous harmonies
small pink precisions go past

III

We are making real efforts
to make no effort
to make plans

concerning the strand-lines
as to music and water and who
it is that you are

it is that you are
watery (slap
slap lap

lap) music

we keep on tumbling
     harmonies
          no longer astonished

we never were
   where we are
      who are you

going to become

a song sung in a disused cafe by the shore
The Pink And White Fantasy Life Of Art

departing

IV

On dusty shelves of a disused cafe by the shore
the histories of song and shells
of past performances are polished up by tumbling
off the sides of the blue container
everything is carried in

V

We keep on discussing whether we should
keep on
singing Georgian songs in the shower-bath
of historical accident

but the windows steam up and we stop
to let the dream of tonic unison
drift past
unseen on the night-time ebb

we open our books of poems about ships

we never miss

VI

Where we are is sometimes
watching a window
watching a ship

window is filled with ship
and I read a poem
about it by someone else

coming in identified in a poem
it comes to rest and water
re-makes its music

so that it is
itself and something else
distantly moving always

through steamed-up windows
watching it pass
and stay with us

when we shut the book

VII

We are seeking the white clarities
at the foot of the cliff above the strand-lines
of shells already tumbled and rubbed by the sea's
free harmonies to a thick glass in which it is almost
you who is seen singing that moment with the white
wings in the blue sky above holding you up

VIII

It is a question of flowers and again
and again we don't know
the answers but perhaps it is
the proper questions which we don't know
about blue taking off
our nervousness
with spontaneous harmonies
to a presence
stretched from the foot of the cliff
as Georgian song is
selections from the world
of the Organum

IX

The stone is polished by tumbling until it is less
and more than what it was

NOW I SEE MY BELOVED
based on open fifths
sung by a women's chorus
with lowered seventh
degree of the scale
and sometimes with raised
seventh and fifth degrees

the sea moves

the composer has added new
and appropriate harmonies

small blue flowers grow
in the cracks

what sort of description do you want
what sort of description will you accept
what sort of description is adequate

one way of loving you is listening
to forty-year-old songs and other people's poems

as what we hold is always

an invention

X

The song is what do you want and where do you want it

sometimes silence follows this
when you know what you want and you get it
and sometimes silence follows this
when you don't and you don't

we've decided we is a word
we only use in poems
about ships and perhaps
in poems about birds

such as this is

shadows cast by waving our arms for emphasis on windows
in shapes of birds or ships and silence
sends us to sleep
to dream of clean white questions shining
far off in spontaneous Georgian harmony

the answers are there
to hold up the melody

XI

Through drifting wreckages
of catalogues
of The Charmed Life

it turns to a past which never was and continues
in the music of poems addressed to a profile
of all of its various waves and directions

which in this case once again consists of her
combing her hair to a flurry of questions
quotations and blank white

pages waving
"it" which we're part of as we part from

each other and ourselves

repeat from the start
as often as wished

unfinished
"it" is always
a different form
of the music

of the continuous

transformations
following this

no records

exist

XII

"J'arrive du paradis"
the river meets the sea and each
continues itself yet both
are changed by that
unplaceable moment

the ship which someone wrote
a poem about steams past
going out heavy with music
with a clean white pocket-handkerchief
we wave ourselves off

to return to where we've never been but knowing
we'll be there when we get back
to a future of moments
of music free as it always was
to be made a form of

CONVERSATIONS AMONG POEMS

1

To be full
almost
the characters must consist
of the first time
when nobody here
was here
which we all remember

2

Clear air
we come together
in order
to arrange another order
in which something of air singing
plays part of the part
of a hero
otherwise absent

3

He said I want to confess
it is not significance
either
the sky grows dark
as we eat
our speechlessness or else
it was more than he thought
he meant

4

Not enough
for her
pure
distilled water
the poem said
or any one
what language
or the hand can touch
running away from
the truth
suddenly
she stood up and was somebody
somewhere else
it is not continuous

5

High fronts in a trough moving off
the turbulence becoming less
he says she says and they are
agreed
it is unspeakable
also the weather
somebody says
continuing
you bet your life on it

6

Running away from
for ever
those parts of a part of
a character
the weather
talking
I want to confess
I am in love with
else
the sky is consumed by darkness
the poem said
it is not enough

7

Long after this
in the first place
everyone went on breathing
the poems that had not become
in time
they were almost human

THE LANGUAGE OF DELIGHT

in memory of John Riley

A hotel bar. One more compartment
on another train. Desk by the window.
Imagine our speeches, neither here nor there
as the dog's eyes move between puddle and hill.

Leben ist Tod, und Tod ist auch ein Leben.

What is remembered is already changed (so it was
always), the day's work done and undone and done again
and again, suspended but moving, something
hung between those far-off figures and our speaking.

Life is death, and death is also a life.

So puddles wet hill-watchers' feet today as yesterday
the old man's *Doncaster's a nice distance off*
disturbed the heart and what is
the distance of death? You have to believe

in another life to hear yourself : always
the restoration of the beginning, the beginning
of the end, keeping a sideways eye out
for muddy puddles and dogs while

extremely simple
light streams over the hills
from the closed page
goodbye and hallo my friend.

DOUGLAS OLIVER

WHEN I WAS IN BRIDPORT

You know I'm working Jan, you know
I am John. From up here your chairs
scrape oceanically all the time and
birds shriek, sheafs
of first drafts wing from my desk.
These wills I'm writing, don't think of
floating paper darts from a
cliff-face. It can't be
morning though shadows slant that
way and the sea's a blue flat, not
struggling over much sand. The air's
not crystal but orange against
a sandstone fortress
pitted with flaws and it holds an imprisoned
population. My childhood
of a static shoreline: I
craned upwards towards
the dark prison holes where birdmen
sent out gulls thrown
in a flight-line along the face, bruised wing-tips.
I thought then that quality was in
the hardly-seen arm-movements, the wind after
taking a white scrap in its direction, that
others might throw stones to disappear in the sea.
That beach, archaeologically, was
prehistoric. So much
of cliff-flights are layers below
the level of the present-day town.
                                This
is not a plea for more industry, or you could
joke about flights above the town, how there's
always the aeroplane. I'm just precise
about the level I start from.
To go below it is a final prison, a kind of burial.

THE FURNACES

Weak flame zone

still it's soon flame on a gas stove down the city's very
end a weak resort of the pipe network. Lead tube
extending forward has
a house on its tip
and spits light into a dark kitchen. In the tile surround
alternative gold circlets
spin. The enclosed cooker harbour burns with gas across water
beneath
a wide beach, as yet unpopulated. At
its extremities an old port
and the so-called new,
'new' because burning waves make ruins flicker on the sea bottom.
So the flame
hovering on an invisible
moment of change is the least solitary fact of miles of gas
sent to houses, waves of heat rolling
under the tarmac and here
there are three towns:
the apparent is built on another – the one below uninhabitable
owing to corrupt air
the third is still tawny striations in gas vapour from the
ground, its children having golden hair
and clothes of gipsy yellow
materialising
at the gas flare's fiercest point; the invisible distance, before
such colours, remakes
time in its tremulous millimetres and this middle town
is being remade in sulphur, leaden pipes
melt underneath and we are no
longer masters
even of the miniature furnace on a hairbrained linotype machine.
Lead solidifies
into words, apt to quarrel, of all others fit to be assassins. And each
house is remade a furnace too   the lights go on
anxiety gives me again that old heart-
burn. Leonine children
are in the attic of a house ageing downwards to volatile corruption.

ORDNANCE SURVEY MAP 178

I have never been to Woolland, downhill from
Long Wood, the park on our right until Skinner's farm
at the corner. My hands turn you
across the road, we don't take the left fork; it
peters out. The manor house is grey cardigan and needs
unbuttoning. This brussel sprout field is disordered
as we enter, blackbirds disappear
into the leaves and tick about electric
as brain impulses. I've seen too many churches,
enough like that one over the field, so Victorian
and weakened with green light. We define objects
first by symbols, eventually by movements away
from them, as black sparks scud at low level. Not
the steep hill, at least one in seven, up to Bulbarrow.
For each of us a body we now lay down. There's the deepest
green I've known in the sprout foliage cluttering our
heads. Among roots we are disturbed, aroused
by the intelligence of plants. Earth blotches our cheeks,
moulds to finger bones and rises over them. We struggle
on the floor of growth, under the stench of a deciduous
sky. After a while your head between
my palms lolls short-circuited. Your own
loose grip has filled with etheric water, icy rain spots
our clothes. Soaked, filthy, bursting
upright, transitional, we, the black earth fountaining,
detach ourselves from a lost field on the map. Join me
on the road going out; glance back if you like like
Lot's wife, at a family behind us walking towards
Woolland, the parents of an old schoolfriend,
or maybe my parents. The brussel sprouts were
not possible, no one I've met has ever been to
Woolland. I'll check
the rest of these facts tomorrow.

MONGOL IN THE WOODS

(for Tom)

My son's eyes plead for expense I should otherwise
withhold. You're around. I might as well
pay it for you, not to some future man, Testicles,
when the balls descend, but to the unheroic maker
in him. May I use the word imbecile? We're in woods
where no-one can tell me not to. And
if we don't laugh brutally at the mongol's swollen tongue
that's as if everyone were no longer
mysterious. I think of more drawn
into his iris than just vacancy
decorated with a gelid ruff.
                              Get out of this trance,
the internal restraints on muscle, the hooks in the
oily tissue. If we could only
stop his iris contracting in sunlight
we'd move. Never mind. Pick up
all the money standing in the woods and you
take it as if a gift sealing the voodoo. The pretence
opens his lips; some ectoplasm comes out
which doesn't belong to our thinking. He won't
be cured. Besides it's too much like
the food he's eaten. So my
word, love, attaches to the lining of
his oyster mouth; we'll let him
prosper it. Then Tom
will announce, one day: "My father's dead. You're my father."
That's why I'm confident my rebirth lies in his
right to deep feelings. Ours, though, are deeper.
It's a difference in skies because clouds never
change in his pupils and, once out of shade, on hot roads,
he crawls like an animal.

REMEMBER STORTFORD, BIRTHPLACE OF RHODES

Let's keep it all with bankers she said giving a gut welcome
to affairs that order her. Shopkeepers kept up
the supplies   biscuits in tight
wrappers on the restaurant plates.
So to her in this cocktail party financiers
lift glasses above their heavy navy-blues (I want to
play their striped suits like harps). A reminder of her parades out
of all the breast pockets. Mauve chiffon handkerchiefs,
same colour as the pants she's wearing.
Pudgy hands rise with the drinks. Highlights of sunlight
crawl along glass rims in small circles of appetite. Well,
by the time she's buttered him, and buttered him,
in short-lasting collusions carefully temporarily pleasant, and
who's not? By that time even I'm a man of
address. Of an address. Pack.

Another idea of her flung once on the Bishop's
Stortford bed. Just a methylated
impulse opened her legs. The mauve was new. That signal's
not a comrade genre for this present smart room smart
with starched thugs, matching ties and chiffon. We both complain
they're fresh from mahogany tablelands where Rhodes'
successors raised the gavels, brown folders
opened and someone paid for it. Mostly, speaking to such gravamens
she doesn't even enter her own conversation. The blood
gleams like butter on colonist hearts seen in a butcher's tray
in their element.
Days like these her lips hesitate. The purpose
not natural to her
natural to Rhodes to go
behind my back for treaties to take my lip between
her teeth ambiguously, herself half-desperate. At that
we kiss. Her mouth's dry
fringed with crumbs when I have known it an open artery.

Pack. Gone
away. I could not have let the glasses' light
slip down my throat or seen warriors' backs break
like biscuits in a trade communion. Yet crumbs strafe
this battered tray. I'll just leave you
some digestive ones said the landlady. A tirade

will tide me over into night until the parties
pause. My forefinger dabbles at the sweet crumbs.
They diminish resistance to rancid blood and I must
try to keep ideas clear of it. Which is why
I think of Bishop's Stortford and
damn Rhodes.

PICNIC

You've a green comb in your sandy hair. I'm sorry
to have to ask you this, is this your
cut? Was it the glass? Troubled

by pampas grass loose in dunes, two bits of
tumbler in the roots, by your plate
a blade of grass that might

have cut the hand. The saw edge is limply
disinclined now but you stabilised
it originally in

the beak of your fingers. Don't f-
we don't need this airstream
when your sirocco sigh

comes straight out of Woodford County High School
for Girls. The
harmonious sand in two sky

reflections that swing from side to side across tumbler
fragments and the brown
wind moans and is worse

than your lack of schwärmerei. That's not my
child is it? Sitting
under a sandbank. Where

are the other ones? He's so swarthy and has
elastoplast round his Arabian
leg, robes from Belfast

Linen. Some things worth repairing do not include
names or grass thicker
than rippling wigs. I'm sorry

to ask you, have you *known* me? thinking at the moment
of the comb in your black hair
and we start

upwards from our meal when our eyes and the
tumbler reflections stabilise
as, in the jagged mirrors,

your hand is central.

YOU'RE JULIA

Don't bother with hallo
this is Jan
day-dream the next phrase: you're
Julia try to
give it back in two voices the u-
sual one breathlessness, black
ragged wings above ground-voice
calm parterre of
a new imagination we want to live
in. Quick breath and calm reminds
            me of someone larger
            at a dance a copper
            was stabbed. Jackdaws
            and glossy rooks. And here's
what I mean by sky: those stratus
layers way behind moving brown,
stability only
changed by next morning. When
it dawned we both
claimed the mise-
en-scène as emblematic gift. A view
shouldn't be quickly
given away but in gradual barter.
Be wary,

though, of slowing down
the whole thing, if
you sent me notes
less frequently, told me about
the children next
week, wrote staunch 19th
century letters I
found the name, Julia, in, then
we'd take fewer risks with our
identities.
But no more phone
calls please, with
the door half-open, booth-light
flashing, caws from the receiver and
a fight in the corridor
bumps against
the glass. I don't care who's talking
if she'll only ring off.

NOT IN ANOTHER PHOTO

Your photo in a newspaper. The hotel
fire. No. That's a mistake on
the uneasily-stirring vehicle
of day. The paper,
bearing a dead woman's photo
slides over cracks to
lie half in evening. Our child
is safe with us, meanwhile
a burnt female body
soaks in your chest where
children have already drowned. Warm
nightwinds arrive. We hurry our son
out to the car. Your charred body
sits away from me in the corner.
You look as dead as a queen, not
in another photo, I mean a real
queen, waving. The seat between us moves.
This journey will express the
jerkiness of fear, not its passion, to

drive through cold flames, light passing
across your face. The hotels
of conversation are all on fire
under the wheels.

LOVE IN THE DARK VALLEY

Good hats, good novelties, good hair. It's no
hiding the brightness, the snaps and mottoes,
buttons spinning round, until one stops
and descends its thread. Whistle me
the sad tune the radio picked up, as you sew
and can't rejoin the torn places on our clothes.   They
screw up. Doesn't mean a thing. A misprint
like "Herrings or the Communication."

Sunlight on a wall of plaques was wrong to single
out a memorial plaque, one of those
infant deaths. "Why us?" doesn't mean
a thing. If I say everyone experienced the same summer
I also swear it was a mockery
in our garden. We crept among
the flesh in polythene bathing pools and water
swirled with fishy backs. A radio
blazed in grey corn behind our house
but our ears heard grey and I think
it was an effect of the weather to bring
that particular song to us. Nothing happened that
in retrospect doesn't strike me as contrived by a
stranger.

From IN THE CAVE OF SUICESSION

In what cave in the love of love
does swoftness lie as a
melting wax
       a little lava
which the motive motiveless of oracle
infolds in a rock of memory?

The simplest cave whatsoever
with an inquirer at its entrance
a cast-off coca-cola
       can one
light target
of water in the entrance pitch.

His darkening litter trail is of gratitude also
harm follows steeply he distrusts literacy and also
trusts it more illicitly
       his fiction is of wild-he
although a National Trust owns the mouth
of that earthly swallowing-up.

Moves into a lack of weather often raining
no sun remains interminable a few-volt bulb
of war-time torchbeam
       passes by the wet hundred
grounded helmets tenderly
as a footmarker then lifts to the black front.

The beam is absorbed with laughter
of veils in confusion somberly though
the dust of darkness in progress
       no-one waiting
only attacking the solitary inquiry
descending into the mountain to cut the thinnest figure.

The first question narrows
from walk to stoop to the frontways crawl
to the backways crawl
       wriggling
from the grazed surface underground
like a sheep into soot.

Down there hardly worth-while as himself
to receive a dubiously likely motivated answer
not from the lead sulphide sky
            ore lowers to ground
or does the man seat himself either
getting even in a profound cavern.

Across the night his tongue lash scores the limestone
in seconds what the stream of centuries more so
whose direction takes the sediment
            we hear to light
outside this stupid stupid stupid careful questioning
of what no one can tell what we keep telling all the time.

I THE SUICIDE CAVE ORACLE

*On a warm July evening, the inquirer, Q, parked his beige Austin car
on the moorland verges of the road through Winnat's Pass in Derbyshire's
Peak District. Having erected a two-man tent on the verge, he took
various items of equipment across to a small cave whose entrance tunnel
tucks under the steep slopes of the pass. This abandoned lead mine,
generally called Suicide Cave, sometimes Horseshoe Cave, has a secondary entrance at the other end of the horseshoe; that was left unexplored.
The inquirer carried into the main entrance a torch, two fat candles,
typewriter and paper, bottle of beer, bag of crisps, boat oar, length of
rope, pair of binoculars, and a "sacrificial cake" bought at a Derby bakers'
a few hours previously. He conducted several investigations of the terrain
outside and inside, gathering data. A bee flew into the cave. At 10.20
p.m. he re-entered the cave for the last time.*

*His first questions were posed in the entrance chamber, though he
had previously inspected by torchlight the steep pitch of the cave's throat,
hidden in rubble opposite the place where he began typing. Often, questioning proceeded without light. Touch-typing mistakes of apparent
oracular provenance have been left in.*

Q   There were three men...

A   I know.

Q   There were three men and one of them did nothing to help
    the victim of an assault but dithered while his friends coped.

A   You know already that you are hardly worthy to consult my
    shrine.

Q   I am glad and calm to be here, to have crawled through the
    tunnel of daylight and to have reached the chorus of noise
    in this black cavity where at last I am blind. How should I
    reform my life?

A   Be very patient, feel for the guide keys: it is not yet that you
    will know the oracle; it will take many searches, many vigils
    in many caves (though all these caves are one) before even
    the new plot may start fully. You are not fit, the cliffs of
    moving cloud are dark and turbulent, there is still light in
    the cave, a stain of grey pneumonia; you will be very ill, my
    cold breath comes always freshly upon you, but you may
    breathe it and live. There must be no more delay, you must
    convert my ways to the good of others, must make serene
    the weather under which your next footsteps are taken.

Q   In this cave, what are the noises I should listen to?

A   The dripping water is not the prophecy; it is events. Your
    typewriter keys are the prophecy being born: they are some
    representation of my voice, but you do not hear the cool
    air that comes from the heart of my cavern: you do not hear
    your own thoughts either.

Q   (The cake has been sacrificed.) I don't offer you my potato
    crisps or the beer.

(No answer.)

    10.40. The cave is completely dark. A fall of earth covers
    most of the crisps.

(Pause)

A   You are still thinking of those three men, you are not satisfied
    with my answer; you are an addict of your own guilt.

Q   But why am I?

A   Because it saves you from having to take action.
    A,etallic t hud turne was waterdripping on a tin that hat
    been left in the cavern by trippers.
    A ccp, nomayopm pf
    A combination of drips outside in the now dark tunnel
    sounded exactly li m like someone moving belongings out
    of a car.

Q   I feel as though I could consult with the spirits of the three men.

A   They are very near you.

Q   And do they have any comfort for me?

A   They say your thoughts are inches away from the nothing of their deaths.

Q   Will you agree that I have come here with good intentions?

A   Your presence here is a mere whisper: you have come not to the prison you think but to your own point of inanition. This is what I can first tell you. What is more stems from that point. Your strength is always from what you know you do not do.

Now write for me the story of a man who acts so badly that I cannot be his oracle, who lives as with these failures w don continually reminding him of what he cannot do; and then write me the tale of how he yet does something worthy of me.

Q   How shall I write this?

A   By living it; that rule has not changed.

You have children: lose your-self in them. Offer their lives prophetic doexw force. It is not enough to have good will.

Q   I only feel terror if I suspect another human presence, as I suspect it when the water thuds in the entrance tunnel. Is it right for me to imagine another human presence?

A   You are not here to feel terror, but to be good in the sense that new life is good.

Q   I see you will not inspire me unless I rid myself of self; yet I thought to arrive here was to consult with pure self and that this was the terror.

A   Remember the origins of the Pythia and the frenzies of the illiterate peasant women.

Q   Well then, I have no more ambition for this text. I renounce it.

A   Now we are beginning.

Q   I am so hap y that what I find here is not evil but a calm voice speaking from far away, for it means that I cannot in the **near** heart of me wish harm, though in the **very** heart I wish to preserve myself, respecting life and those I love. I bless you that in the last few days I have come mi re and more to realise the worth of my love, and I would ask that you help me to make these moments into turning points.

A   Then ask yourself whether you will censor out the tone of what you have just said. You would wish to extend its point into the misery of,,,what you have perceived in your work but normally you would censor soft backgrounds: beware that because it does not only censor that softness, it also censors the mean hardness you are supposedly countering. By leaving both to be expressed by writing of just a secondary nature, you manage to evade them as central problems.

Q   How long must I stay tonight?
A   Do you not enjoy my company? You are like the rest. Until dawn.

Movement in a room above this cave: that's impossible; it must be a car.

Q   Will you give me some incidents?
A   A worrying noise like a navel tightening or a glowworm winding its horn, a footstep beside the fog, a constant frown that one day disappears for efer, a drop of blood on a typewriter, a door slammed in the cave, a dart of death driving through the blackness into someone's cheek, a hdnhandkerchief covered with yellow stains a heart with white cowardice and a the air just in front of the tongue warm with good intentions, a gulp of disappointment in a sitting room as the "dowdy daughter" utters her ambitions and presents her bespectacled young man before a housewife with blue-rinsed hair but the girl's breath of enthusiasm more real, the moment itself fine because of that. The cave winding its watch. Now you may jump from frog to noun and awaken the humping suitcases in the uncanny boxroom.
Q   I have thought of performing the act of love in your sanctuary.
A   Then you would betray me.
Q   Will Joanne love me if I do not betray you?
A   You may bring her first to the threshold. She is a person of light and you must seek where she may be rediscovered; do not concentrate on how you have damaged her.
Q   I pe²/₃
     I perceive that the third man could enter a new life not quite coping with old mistakes, continuing to commit them in smaller ways until the greater exemplification of them exposes to his eyes yet again those grave flaws.
          Can I bring a young child here? Do you have interest in me?
A   (No answer to the question about the child.) I can no more see you at this moment than you can see or talk to me.
Q   I look at a man on a high ledge. Will he fall?
A   Civilisation will kill him.

Q   Are you really benign?
(No answer.)

Q   Will you give me some more incidents?

A   Scratching his hair from morning to night, the little black-haired man wished himself alone but when he was alone fell to scratching even more. One day he awoke at a desk and saw through the window St. Paul's Cathedral. Pigeons took a rising wind on their breasts as they flew upwards to the top of the columns. It was not a day that changed his life but it was a day in the change of his life.

Q   As I write, I'm scratching my own hair. How large are you?

A   I fill your brain; I empty the cave. I cannot be separated from the voice of a prophetess. Somewhere dwells a sounder brain than mind... weather in responses... old age, to use the baths... you ask me for rest... no, not the furrow of children except in the furrow of old age... engage in hunting other things where settle son who speaks only once and that a moment of danger... your fate to have no son but he is the first person you meet after leaving your sperm in the cave...

Q   (These are my own thoughts?)

A   ...limestone smears for happy lovers and equaboy happy outcome of the coupling at la nature after you have (inaudible) from your high ledge...

(Silence for ¼ hour.)

Q   Your answers have been veru lomd.tp ,e
Your answers have been very kind to me.

A   (Eventually)... farther in... create a work of light.

III SUICESSION

The inquirer went down the throat a little way

Q   Alone, how do I reach the possibility of good here?

A   Singly here, but the sound of bees' wings ahead
where the motifs will be white wax and the hive
and you'll get stung to quickness
beneath new hardening.

Q   What purpose should this work have?

A   Do you suppose yourself living or sent?

Q   Ex officio presumably. From wheel-shaped towns with names
like Wife Wapping. From the elderly
whose advanced maturity does not put these questions.
From the invasion.

A   Your work should purposefully have a near smell
as you bring events that happened in sunlight
along these final alleyways
to redeem the eroticism of ageing politics
the whippy demons of the greying flesh.
No special envoys needed. Only those
who perform the rites and keep
free of blood-guilt. For instance,
don't desire a woman whom you desire
to impose on you mistakes of the past.
With her, your youth dies into an ideal condition
of no consequence. Her kiss sneers, the large eyes
tragic, the throat wasted,
hand of thongs. Sperm must not flood out
of a wo nded body; it deforms children
and it deforms you as still the child you were;
your soul is a mote in her eyes and slips sideways
as you make way for the ideal and at last
she blacks you out in disenchanting ritual
you not yourself in her wheedling admonitions;
and were you, so marred physically, to enter that ideality
you would live only in her dying eyes
and she, ageing to commercial waste, would grow eternal
in relation to the dust of you.
All such women get between you and the past; have
nothing to do with those suicides
for they lack real testimony. Yield
to Joanne, yield to me, in suicession,
rays of self from the honeyed flame outwards
in creation; so you walk in us,
we walk in you, as subtle bodies.

Q   Why do I want her most when she befriends a child, or an
old man or woman, sensually taking them by the arm,
awaking the nicest eyes? Our young names then invoked
within a home for old people: honourable navy blazers,
grey flannel, principles of which we've often talked. Her
heart-rays reach out and bathe old men whose watery eyes
full of longing touch my own desire.

A   These questions... do you call questions what I hear as only cries? Are these your maturities? What is most real in them is exactly what I would have most real in you. Invoked or not invoked, the real name of old men has your name as stem. Make friends of them to bring yourself alive. The first idea is of a grey-haired boy, the one blameless man of his time, a silver sheen on dark fluxion. If you can bring his full name into brightness, you will open to a freedom reflected through prisms painted black only one side.

Q   If I only knew now what I shall say to replace what I'm saying.

A   You construct conversation for others. The grey ideas wrinkle in your skull. Ahead, buzzing. The new hope – a cone of light behind your eyes – is trying to focus into virgin knowing, vivifying what lies forward past walls that glitter in dark-winding. The candle spurts with flame as mild as traditional childhood, a pleasant family, a life transformed into a wig of age. Think at 52 degrees Fahrenheit; then the day itself will flood into your mouth, nose, up anus and penis, and will at last open your ears, appear in your eyes. In that day, a man will fall from a high ledge and you will be responsible. The crowd, which has not so far moved, crammed in the channel between two commercial buildings, will budge and wedge and squeeze your life from you. A wounded man will spring from the pavement and lightly take your arm, though you stagger with bleeding mouth. While you scribble in a notebook, a mother with blue-rinsed hair, whose daughter married her young man but has now taken a drug overdose, will urge you not to break her confidence. In the terraces below the railway embankment, a grandmother will plead with you to tell others about the drowning of her grandson. You will tear up all past events from your notebook but keep the pages as little screwed up as possible in your pocket. All who are feeble and infirm will ask for you. As you hurry past the blazing windows of the new wing for the mentally handicapped, the hospital's medical superintendent will pull you into the foyer, point out the plaque unveiled the day before, and then drag you, protesting, down the corridors and let the patients in the wards kiss you and mumble in your ear.

Q   I know.

From THE DIAGRAM POEMS

[We used to get the Tupamaros stories on the night shift at Agence France-Presse. Reports of urgent, sometimes bloody events would be wired through in Spanish, translated on the French floor, and reach our desk to be retranslated into English. At every step the events moved away from reality. Orchestrated by the Tupamaros for maximum heroic effect, they were transformed into Spanish news rhetoric, into French, into very different English news rhetoric, and then might appear in the columns of *Asahi Shimbum*, in whatever rhetoric the Japanese use.

Uruguay itself, the poverty brought about by the crash of world wool and meat markets and by the exploitation of the indigenous population by Western financial interests... this lay somewhere behind the bravado of exploit you were reporting. Whether the guerrillas were right or wrong – and you were against extremist violence, along with the rhetoric that falsified events at their origin – you might be dreaming quite obliquely, as you tapped the stories out, of how an authentic politics could combine the mildness of a dead baby of yours, dear in memory, with the stern wisdom of elder ministers truly backed by their people.

In Pando the Tupamaros seized the police and fire stations, the telephone exchange and three banks, before trying to escape as the police closed in on them. These movements could be plotted on to paper, already with some inaccuracy. As the diagrams were plotted, they moved farther away from reality into pictures which both reflected the actual events but were also permitted an infection from personal British fantasy, such as the dead son and your worries about political judgment. Poems emerged, more distorting even than journalism. The final job of this deliberately impure art was to recreate emotional urgency out of fantasy.]

CENTRAL

I heard and slowly understood but then I saw
and I saw years ahead in the light of the eye centre
as I'd dimly heard years past in the sound of the earpiece.
I saw our ageing and I could get it. I saw the airman signal

and I got it. I heard Tom's voice as from a distant receiver
and I got it. Seven guerrillas tying up the telephone exchange
expertly. Then Tom's voice said, "Hallo Central,"
from the booth of death.

In the first days of jellyroll, Tom was my son.
Tom, go ahead.
"Ring my mother; it's an emergency. She's with child
again, by herself. Ring her."
I'll get us some eye medicine.
"No. Ring. In a couple of minutes we sever
our links. The guerrillas have
cut the cables. Condition major immediate...
It's the end of the line and here's a..."
(Still Tom's voice, the past ahead of me, but fading. I'd
better put that down to feeling and feeling's
part of my work.) "Yes, it is part...Don't put down
the receiver..." (fading) "...the ear hears with feeling..."
(fading, cut dead).

They'd already neutralised *le standard* by standard procedures
Oh Tom, go ahead.
neutralised the risk by risk, though some raiders will die
Tom, go ahead.
and I'd like to have friends on these streets, friends
who'd look for me in creations of total emergency
in or out of dreams...Cut...A guerrilla command tone:
"Place the pregnant
woman into the temporary prison with the 40
communication functionaries and consumers. Get on with this.
Cut other connections yourself but obey
the voices that come from long distance, obey sound and feeling."

Tom, go ahead.
But my Tom's in a frightener cell
of the night of youth
where old and young eyes shine and are grey
and the ears fold in
to the internal sounds.

U

The lost child's voice breaks in my throat: no time
for it, softness unheard, a gurgle as a third bank's doors
open quietly to receive attackers. Once more
the set up, the planted "customers" at the retreating U
of a magnetic counter. Now, my children,
in the warning world, lying abroad
or playing with a magnet theatre here at home,
now the forces of life are few and precious and this magnetism is one
commandeered by the banking magnates, by the magnet of their will,
pulling at money through their management and managers
in the hierarchies of their laws. They invest
their fields of force with the hardest law of all:
no casualties above the ground: all hoarding likewise
underground. This is the law which sends
directions through the silver, turns it base,
and binds it to the secret selves
which, deep below, increase in value like jewels.

The lost child's voice should speak softly but undyingly
across a land silvery with democracy
and glistening with wheat, trembling at the spoken kindness;
the voice should temper the muttering
of bank clerks across the mica counters
and ring in the money slipping from their fingers.
We know this. Everyone. But we let the voice break in our throats
the laughs, little distinguished from coughs,
echo discreetly across stone floors;
softness unheard;
until a man with a light machine gun this day
springs on to the cash desk and, astride there,
we know this, waves the muzzle where all the arrows
of acquisition, law and management have come and gone.

We know Tom's voice, we now know this, we see
the magnets sunder in half, induced repulsion
in every sense of order, and soon, my children
in the warned world, the street awakes to shots
and enemies and wounds and chivalries
and carelessness, and showdowns, and innocent bystanders
left to bleed behind an arrow pointing to an unseen cemetery.
The voice breaks unheard across a land formerly silvery

but changed to iron law and deep repulsion.
Yes, there was an attack; it cut the magnet's U in half,
I don't need to tell you but I do, softly,
that I am my children;
in me their voice breaks with the ear knowledge.

THE DIAGONAL IS DIAGONAL

Slowness of gaze, the slowness behind fear
perception
calm thoughts staying in the mist
above a waterfall from the left: but what of the speed
of calmness, since it doesn't stay still?
The wavering of lights doesn't
but moves in remote consequence to
foam at its fastest.
Compare sudden crying to the slowness of this funeral
but it's a fake and speeds up
compare that to the speed of capture
to the rush of a diagonal
the arrow of a bad thought pell-mell towards torture
the pool of suffering arrowed in
and the calm grace of courage that coexists
with those speeds and with the sick other face of slowness.
I do not name the incidents
lest I should seem to lay claim to them,
but I little own this poem; it is nothing
without the original movements.
The diagram could again spring a picture
encircling looks like buttocks,
there's a cloaca. Wolves.
But I should say hardly anything else about that,
my right is minimal.
I let a Parisian journalist in me draw the pictures
let him have his head
it was an academic drew the arrows and the loss of hope
letting him
but now the picture transforms no longer; it is the picture.
The place of reassembly in the cemetery
really is the cemetery

prepared for the ashes of human conduct
and the fires of human behaviour so rotten in origin
that animals whose dead are not cremated
have knowledges above the festival here
and every nerve's alive in me
down the swift diagonal
that slants from the cemetery in courage
and takes the poem almost entirely from me.
Almost in humility and loathing I kneel
at the feet of the next account
which is of bestiality and sadism
so mucky it makes the scalp creep.
It is my dead son who always brings me to this point
of innocence in the heart of swift cruelty
and speed of pictorial change won't get to it
and the poetry won't move from it
that innocent point exactly neighbour to that other start
from which team leader became a finger pointing left,
that's audience left: for the teams
the old sinister direction was, from the beginning,
the cemetery. In the known risk then
an airman became a dog
firemen were pegged down as birds of fire
the baby in the womb was old
the pinman strained against the spanner
if you could only believe he'd hold that posture
an arrow filled with gold
the magnet power of money failed
as a magnet power of luck did
as the magnet power of self-control
as a magnet power of being funny
in situations which don't call for wit to *be* funny
all these started in the drawings from the point
neighbour to
the point at which the innocence stays clean
the diagonal does not speed down
to these loaded reversals
police exchange no shots
there's no sequel of bestiality.
And yet we're carried downwards by a foreign courage here
that we have no right to justify
(lest innocence should run that gauntlet too)
no right to borrow it, jig it into shapes,
display it like a wound on our own opening palm.

But, lacking the one innocence, we are driven into this foreign time
into falseness in funerals, rehearsals
leading from the cemetery;
it all turns so really funereal for us
as brave as that and as flawed
just a final diagram almost straight
and a heart on which the diagram is scored
beside the deaths of innocences we have known
and even caused a little in the scarface heart.
We cannot ask the prisoners to forgive
our foreign nations
but we may hope the dead can kiss
for us the face of innocence in the rushing dark
and grace and courage arrive calmly in us.

[This poem, the last, refers to the previous poems and diagrams
in the sequence.]

BONIS AVIBUS
("With favourable auspices")

in memoriam, John Riley

A blight from England's present-day
covers me. I can hardly move my mind.
Is that any way to speak? Why
do we let these bladder tonsils swell and gag
above the hardly-heaving tongue? Is it respectful
to our ancestors? All outside us so encrusted
by the soft internal harms. Like lichen
the self tears dry from crooked eyes; values
within us beat: "keep pure", "keep pure",
as blood courses along with dust on it.
I don't understand it: the inaction of our good.
A gliding, smooth and polished action
is possible – a man sidles out
of a pew in a church of another language, touches
the lovely kiss onto a flat piece of wood.
It is an ending: but a life of glad anyhow,
of steady purgation of poisons in the suburbs,

of bless this nation, even... that whole life
settles like a bird on the gleaming lid
avis beyond species and out of Czargrad.
       A poem. A bird. Where the head
rests. Are scarcely symbolic but are Robert Grosse-
               teste's
version of "truths in contemplation" – all
I believe in. The censer drifts in its chains.
The wood reflects a dream of purified ancestral red.

From THE INFANT AND THE PEARL

I

Lying down in my father's grey dressing gown
its red cuffs over my eyes, I caught sight
of Rosine, my pearl, passing out of my room
one night while a dream passed out of the night
of my nation. What a robe she was wearing! Brown
and sinewy, lion colours in the doorlight;
she turned, Laura-like, on her face a light frown
to be leaving, not reproving but right-
lipped, reddish hair loving the dead
facial centre: virtue could've kept her
had I enough of it, though I dreamt of it.
In my grey gown I would have gladly slept by her.

I was wrangling in my grey gown, full of wrath
as the door closed. And I felt close to me
the paternal cloth quietening, the rough
flannel lie flat in darkness; if even the
diagonal doorlight had been cut off
in the night of my nation, if even the
much-hoped-for Rosine had just had enough
of the dream – a fragment of light finally
dying in the room – well, the realm in my
closed eyes came alive with one colour:
the rosy-red pearl, so rich and womanly.
I shuddered in the grey for I should have slept by her.

Pearl, whose rose-grey gleams
with infant hints in the hinterland
of my dreams, as when any poet dreams
of a lost pearl – some principle refound
only by resting on a gravestone! Rosine's
the mother of policy, priced beyond
our suspect neo-patriotism. She seems
in my nights to radiate reddish beams
as if whatever our actions, she gladdened
our unseen selves, while without her our
conscious selves are immeasurably saddened.
In my grey gown I would have gladly slept with her.

The self that shines in the greying sunshine
of the immediate is actual, though it is
not all that is there. The feminine
is numinous in my masculine: it isn't nonsense
to picture a pearl placed on a shrine
inside my self; on the swirling surface
is Rosine's reflection which, as if she'd been crying,
half turns away, ashamed where her mercy's
judged Socialistic, too soft for true justice.
For the dream isn't Margaret; the pearl's true minister
would be as lustrous as Rosine is...
In my grey gown I would have gladly slept with her.

My thinking greyed; the vision eventually
flickered in half-sleep – then Rosine had fled,
a fastidious foe of the tin pan alley
serious, powdered, severed head
of Margaret, whose self serially
repeated, televised, pearlised, and reported
ten times, tampered with immediacy.
An empty voice in my empty head...
and sexual absence inhabiting my bed...
like a vacuum in a vacuum, except for the
cuffs on my eyes, recall of red...
I shuddered in the grey for I should have slept with her.

[XVII]

In the blind gap between dreaming, my bed
groaned and the grey gown writhed as I tossed
and turned, tormented, since all that I wanted
had waned at the word, "courage". I almost
awoke, feeling empty and isolated,
continuing the debate with a departed ghost.
But the dream survives between dreams in the red
furnace within and the black frost
without, this double denizen lost
but refound when the live heart unfreezes
a country's Conservative night at its coldest
and in politic blindness bloom pearly roses.

Blindness of spirit had beggared my vision;
its duration that night I shall never know.
Finally I felt a hand on the crimson
cuff of my gown. I came to, and although
dreaming was blind in the dream. "Ash on
an old man's sleeve," someone thought; somehow
the phrase was a parody; for my father's cremation
that I'd attended ages ago
left ashes, not this corpse to clutch at me so
by the gown's red cuff which for me I suppose is
like wearing his heart on my sleeve, as though
in the blindness of ashes could bloom pearly roses.

Yet I seemed like a blind man led by another,
stumbling in sand; and I sensed that the Eliot
thought had been my own thought, for my father
now spoke, in death still a typical Scot:
"Please yourself with all this palaver
about Socialism; the cemetery is certainly not
a Tory stronghold. The truth is, I'd rather
your Socialism shone with your past; you're not shot
of that fatherly honesty, walk humbly but
remember your innocent days; who refuses
his childhood's a booby – and I haven't forgot
your politics, with its blindness and pearly roses."

The blindness began to clear but I saw
we were stepping through sand flecked with ash
which clung to my feet as we followed the shoreline of a rapid river. On a rash
impulse, I faced my father before
I was prepared for his pallor and I wish
I had not, for he fainted and fell to the floor.
When I knelt, there was ichor under his eyelash;
he was grey-gowned, red-cuffed, but his sash
was gold. I held him, held him as close as
I could and prayed for his Scottish courage
to place in my blindness a promise of roses.

XVIII

Lightning blinded me; in the thunder I embraced
ash, and would have kissed ash if I could,
for the flesh fell apart into cinders. The past
would not give me kiss for kiss, though the good
in it flurried the ashes into life. Amazed,
for I again wore the gown, I gaped as each cloud
chased after cloud and discharges raced
into the earth where I knelt, I knew that I viewed
swift time from its crystal shore; then I stood,
unharmed, armoured, as it were, in the old
gown but unable to gaze at a new flood
of light from crystalline cliffs flashing gold.

For the littoral was laved with light as a band
of grey-gowned friars gathered by my side
and a company of nuns came along white sand
in processional; I matched them stride for stride
like the past passing, ashen, through the land
of ideals. I faltered, for suddenly I'd
a presentiment that these were post-Falkland-
take-up-the-Task-Force Tories and alongside
Kinnock-clever, clothe-what-you'd-hide-
in-rhetoric Labourites; yet it's lovely to behold
whatever is wise and all were wise-eyed
under light from crystalline cliffs flashing gold.

The women wore veils but once when the light
raked us a face of sisterly reverence
smiled at me. It was my secretary, who in spite
of all that I'd ventured forgave me. Like virgins
entering God's city the nuns crowded tight
together under the glare, grave pilgrims
to a precipice ablaze. Unimaginably bright
a golden axe glanced down from the heavens
and clove the cliffs into two immense
diamantine doors. On that dazzling threshhold
played a mongol baby. Its babbling was *Ignorance*
in light from crystalline cliffs flashing gold.

Light went spiralling sideways through solid
clearways of glass as one great door
opened and all walked humbly ahead;
the pearl that provided so signal an honour
was *Ignorance* – and him just an innocent kid!
I took him in my arms with just as much awe
as Rosine had aroused when young and splendid,
and believed I was the baby, he my progenitor.
He chuckled and a cheerfulness I had never before
experienced now entered my heart as his bold
eyes, so sunny, surprised my deep store
of light. The crystalline cliffs flashed with gold.

In an interval of fulgorous light, in an
instant when the baby gurgled, all the glass
scythed sideways. I had glimpses of spun
barley-sugar passages studded with sapphires,
fit pathways for the now-modest procession
of silent M.P.s; but my own progress was
an arc across the immediate, as again
in an instant I was inside the cliff. And found darkness.
However, a window glowed weakly, about as
scintillating as a cigarette lighter when some old
codger won't get its refill of gas.
The light so much less than those cliffs flashing gold.

PETER PHILPOTT

LIKE AN AEROLITH

Darkness falls from some air inside a slow
suspension: like glass, a film to surround objects
that cut into doesn't fall, won't go
but is present at the division of any facts
that smoking can rise up, higher there
& that's it: what was predicated is replaced,
the deeper castings push others aside, nowhere
does any of these remain; "as the time passed
yes, that's known! As if one thing
& just one could either be then not be, but
fall, like an apple into a stream, sinking
where no one can, its waves will pass without let
forever, each shaking these things down
like an aerolith into the world & then down.

NINE MEN'S MORRIS

At the eye, we say, of a hurricano, a
durable living. Who enters might wish
an introit, pricked out or not, into day;
day filmic, grainy, a rhythm sluggish
to engage what sweet, lights, our own entrails
that are another centre. What's there here:
most common flesh, lovely desire, light curdles
– that that utterance of us, what's there bare
that's unaccommodated – I don't know how that can operate
in this: but despite meteorologies we sing.
Ripened, like our own apples, we are sour, sweet
most common food, the texture grained, hung
in a way I can't say, its delight ours
as our bodies descend most beautifully in pairs.

It's that we're identical
impossible to determine primacy
I can't forget – only cancel

something that's endless – like
a noose when it's ready, good
talking, that gun, the candles

light suspended between us
where there are no questions, there
are nothing but what is felt to be substantial

not even the air but glass:
going into the darkness, forget
that it will hold on you like a woman

making light of what is pleasurable
with a juvenile privilege – novelty
is half of it – then we're back

where we knew we'd come to be
small, not isolate but disregarded
no one here but who we are

the same as what is lost
a ring closed with one twist
free, monotonous & real

like a sheet of glass darkening with your breath
while the ecstasies that we used to know return
coming casually & unquestioned

from a place unimaginably mundane
breaking with light & our prayers

WHAT WAS SHOWN

The world is blue – spring a yellow
rising up straight beneath the vault
& reflected shakily beneath –
while we sit & hold each other's hands
that hardness around will cool
until our flesh is wooed by softness
& the flowers become larger than we are
like a giant fish suddenly enraged
trapped within a plaster grotto.
Where we go is laid out now –
smoothly down like a pint of stout.
Few things last –
                    old age'
ll be a man on a clumsy bicycle
& youth something stranded in the water.
The churchyard is very quiet:
                              now one
object among so very many
                              we're curious
like small creatures
                    – no significance
within the field. The force split.
All the roads led across that region
to where the peasants gather in the harvest.
The palmist could read nothing.
At an oblique angle she saw a skull –
behind everything power was now absolute.
The poet cried:
                  the ambassadors
were unmoved & knowledgeable.
It was left to our friend the Rainbringer
weaving something like a little tapestry
on which the child fed at his mother's breast.
The poet sat back, smoking an ornamental pipe –
in his mind of course only himself.
She is flanked by angels but ignores them.
The castle turns to an inked blueness –
she must watch him pass into the water
& then die. His poems are shattered.
The landscape will become only a painting.
Hold me within this paradise –

or the corrosive air will enter & destroy.
Fortunately we do have a future:
                                        springing out
of this tree, her body a pale moist new wood
we discover hope. Cattle & horses feed together
& the statue in the small square reminds us
pleasure acts at the most as a trap
unless like absolute light it sweeps down
covering the shapes of the land with blue.
The casuarina sprays up a constant green:
& underneath it you are dead, my lovely one.
There is no reflection in the water: we pass like clouds
& the old buildings of an absolute power still dominate
even in the distance at the mouth of the river.
I am small: everything I own now is burning
& no one in the city will understand.
You surround me & pull me into the water –
where the mundane changes shape, flies off.
You don't look at me with love but expect my payment –
I am pulled into the green water
& my grave is lost, or found only in a ruin –
– you gaze outward constantly & all will adore you.
Someone walks to you in the park – it's winter
& a few dead leaves are on the grass, unfocused,
like something really horrible, clothes become sky
the house having no thickness. I am small again
& you freeze. This is your only real picture:
you, blue, against a yellow earth. I don't believe
you are that languid woman:
                                        black
& white conveys better your mode –
                                        to al-
ways look across.
                        Your eyes are empty almonds.
I think there is distortion
                                – everyone is here
& the ice covers everywhere. The house is like flesh
& our love like ink lines upon paper, yellowing
& reflected in matter. The bodies are confused –
there are so many of them that there must be repetition
except where your form is that clear & blue.
The only reflection now of structure – yellow against blue
out of which come grey houses & trees.
You are not moved. You see forwards & all around you

this world splits. Le Rêve – a true dream, re-
veiling the earth with an obvious light. It is winter.
We split into pieces. Each one will redeem us.

From SOME ACTION UPON THE WORLD

14

The love of the world
a metaphor, like a sunrise
for a larger love, a loss
of embarrassment :

or of the sense that's wrong :
we lose nothing, gain
a balancing of oppositions
into something subtle & alive :

a moment of passage
where the emptiness
is small, coloured
stained by this world's gross
sense

      a beautiful red mask
      for its spring.

17

Upon flesh the revenge of flesh
its songs numb us like dew on the
first summer roses, while the sounds
shift like clouds
          occasionally
to give us bodies, hopes or towns which
we inhabit like words in a sentence
             jostling
witty & destructive. The love

                              we ought to bear
for what including us must
be us : our armature, our practice
our enlarged delight
                    & is not
any one genital
                but the mother of us all
the father, we are by constant action.

28

The weather
if it has a poetry
& its movings
& –

                everything we had thought of.
                We are wedded to the world
                our eyes can perform that

                        – simpler, say than anything
                        any little animal
                        whose pleasure is only that, &
                        though whimsical cannot be removed.
                        The cat waits. She'll
                        sit upon my lap.

The space is light.
What is really substantial
a sum more subtle than imagination
more beautiful than any mirror.

And to pass into it –
bathe within it, fluid
incomprehensible
as the rose or the green pool
a moment of desired passage
at the end insupportable.

29

And darkness. All the old figures
gather like sparrows. The evening light
comes on, the world remaining for the moment
smaller, & related more to other things.

The birds settle into the dark.
The diffusions of energy around us
set into patterns, act & decay.
We are their ruin, actor & acted alike.

The light dies & the birds are silent
no longer figures but images
of our own breath, obscurest desires
abraded slowly by friction & lassitude.

43

Digging out the couchgrass
when a thrush came by.
                              It looked at me
very solidly
then hopped around a bit. I
took a small worm from the earth

& then a man came round for the fuel that we'd advertised
looked at it & said
                              "This isn't the Homefire
that we use. That's in small oblong lumps
                                                            about this size."
He's taken a piece to try, & if it burns

Ginie calls me up to her in the bathroom
to see what's been happening. She is a little perturbed
moving the water in the bath with her feet while she talks.
I should have been specific, yes I
always should – precision & clarity
I mean that is what this little job is; &
even if we can't manage any action
let's at least get it, what we're doing
right.

46

My tiger! My clarity! My small
knot of flesh, light, matter! Smallest sum
& most beautiful contingence! I aim
at myself. I know what is about me –
I say what my words say : I produce
rabbitlike, hatlike, magicianlike. No one needs
my service.
                    I leave my little energies
behind, an unwelcome visitor. They are read.

"You're more beautiful & more happy than a tiger –
your clarity is great : filled by the sun. My
image
        my created focal coherence : I know
I am you. You're more than I am : not chance
but a beautiful contingence, a sum a child
can add without digits or experience of this world."

Each word singing ever after, sung by those that follow
: the crowded syllables fill the room like people
only alive awaiting such common dissolution.

J.H. PRYNNE

SKETCH FOR A FINANCIAL THEORY OF THE SELF

1.   The qualities as they continue are the silk
under the hand; because their celestial
progress, across the sky, is so hopeless & so
to be hoped for. I hope for silk, always, and
the strands are not pure though the name
is so. The name is the sidereal display, it
is what we *know* we cannot now have.
The last light is the name it carries,
it is this binds us to our unbroken trust.

2.   So then, we should not trust the hope
that is merely a name for silk, for
purity untouched by any Italian hand.
The celestial routine is begging, & a nasty
toy at that; the stars are names and the
names are *necessarily* false. We choose
to believe in the flotsam, the light glance
passing & innocent because unpriced.

3.   Which is grossly untrue, because we
pay for it well enough, I have squandered
so much life & good nature I could hardly
guess the account.
                The numbers are out
                there in the human
                sky, the pure margin
                which *are* the trust we
                deserve.
                      And we should
                have what the city does need,
                the sky, if we did not so
                want the need.

4.   The name of that is of course money, and
the absurd trust in value is the pattern of

bond and contract and interest – just where
the names are exactly equivalent to the trust
given to them.

> Here then is the purity of
> pragmatic function:
> we give the name of
> our selves to our needs.
> We want what we are.

5.   And not silk, except for ties, or the sky
as even for exchange, the coin of the
face we look up to as a vault ready'
for trust. That much
> is trickery,
> but the *names*,

> > do you not
> > see, are just
> > the tricks we
> > trust, which
> > we choose.

The qualities then are a name, corporately,
for the hope that they will return to us. The
virtue in whose exercise we retain the fiction
of air, silence, fluid round the hub of the week.

6.   How could this be clearer? The items are,
that we are bribed and that silk is a random but
by tradition a costly gift. Quality is habit.

7.   What follows is where we are now, or where
I am. The old cry about chastity, that we are
bound by the parts of our unnatural frames.
The median condition is the city and not the travel
or the remoteness of travel, in sound. Music,
travel, habit and silence are all *money*; purity
is a glissade into the last, most beautiful return.

8.   And how much we hope for it is the primacy
of *count*. This is the shining grudge of numbers,
the name we will not lose to any possible stranger:
the star & silk of my eye, that will not return.

IF THERE IS A STATIONMASTER AT STAMFORD S.D. HARDLY SO

A matter of certain
    essential oils
        volatile
in the prolonged evening
      nor would he allow
    as the light stemmed
    back
    boarded up in the face of
that the line ran swiftly
      and skimming the
    crests only
into the hills of Vietnam

      With so little water
    the land creates a curved &
    muted extension
    the whole power is
just that, fantasy of control
    the dispersion, in such
      level sky
    of each pulse the sliding
      fade-through of hills
      "a noble evasion of privacy"

    This is parkland for
watered souls, the final
      policeman's dream
    that the quanta of wish
and desire, too, can be marched
    off to some goal so distant
      where in the hermitage
    of our last days the
    handcuffs would seem
      an entirely proper
    abstraction:
      the dry and
arid gentleness, to the eye
    with its own confidence
      in the deep wells
      of the spirit

All no more than
      a land in drift
   curled over and dry, but
      buried way under the ice
and as spillway for these
         glacial waters the
scented air
      runs easily into the
      night and while
the public hope is as
   always the
      darkened ward
   the icecap will
      never melt
   again why
   should it

AGAINST HURT

Endowed with so much
suffering, they should be / and that
they are so – the pain in the head
      which applies to me
      and the clouds low over
      the horizon: soon it
      will be dark
We love the brief night, for its
quick passing, the relative ease as
we slide into comfort and
      the trees grow and
      grow. I can hear
      every smallest growth
the expanse is grinding with it,
out on the flats beyond, down by
the sodium street-lights, in the head:
pain, the hurt to these who are all
      companions. Serenity
      is their slender means.
      There is not much time
left. I love them all, severally and in

the largest honour that there is.
Now and with the least hurt, this
                     is for you

LOVE IN THE AIR

We are easily disloyal, again, and the light
touch is so quickly for us, it does permit
what each one would give in the royal
use of that term. Given, settled and
broken, under the day's sun: that's the purpose of the gleam from my eyes, cloud from
the base of the spine. Whose silent
watching was all spent, all foregone –
the silver and wastage could have told you
and allowed the touch to pass. Over the
brow, over the lifting feature of how
slant in the night.
                     That's how we
are disloyal, without constancy to the little
play and hurt in the soul. Being less than
strict in our gaze; the day flickers and
thins and contracts, oh yes and thus does
get smaller, and smaller: the northern
winter is an age for us and the owl of
my right hand is ready for flight. I have
already seen its beating search in the sky,
hateful, I will not look. By our lights
we stand to the sudden pleasure of how
the colour is skimmed to the world, and our
life does lie as a fallen and slanted thing.

If he gives, the even tenor of his open
hands, this is display, the way and through
to a life of soft invasion. Is constancy
such a disloyal thing. With the hurt wish
torn by sentiment and how very gross our
threshold for pain has become. And the
green tufted sight that we pass, to and
from, trees or the grass and so much, still

permitted by how much we ask.
                                    I ask
                    for all of it, being
                    ready to break
                    every constant thing.
                    We are bound and
                    we break, we let loose
                    what we nakedly hold
                                    thus, he turns
                                    she watches, the
                                    hills slip, time
                                    changes hands.

I ask for it all, and the press is the sea
running back up all the conduits, each
door fronting on to the street. What you can
afford is *nothing*: the sediment on which we stand
was *too much*, and unasked for. Who is the
light linked to the forearm, in which play
and raised, up off the ground. I carry you forward, the motion is not constant but may
in this once have been so, loyalty is
regret spread into time, the hurt of how
                    steadily and where
                    it goes. She feels
                    the glimpse over
                    the skin. She is
                    honest: she loves
                                    the steady
                                    fear. The
                                    durable fire.

And what you own, in this erotic furtherance,
is nothing to do with response or that
times do change: the matter is not to go
across, ever, making the royal deceit de nos jours.
As each one slips and descends, you could call
it coming down to the streets and the seedy
broken outskirts
                    of the town.

FROM END TO END

Length is now quite another thing; that is,
waiting or coming right up slap into the sun,
spreading into the land to cross, the smell of
diesel oil on the road. The friends there are,
as if residing in what instantly goes with it,
as if longer than the infinite desire, longer
and across into some other thing. Keeping
the line, running back up into the mountains,
denied. And so, in the actual moment dis-
honest, actually refusing the breakage, and
your instinct for the whole purpose
                        again shows
            how gently it is all broken
            and how lightly, as you
                        would say, to come in.
All the milky quartz of that sky, pink and
retained, into the sun. See such a thing climb
out of the haze, making the bridge straight
down into the face – which way, this way,
length beyond this, crossed. The dawn thing
suddenly isn't tenuous, and the reach back to
the strand is now some odd kind of debris:
                        how strange to
            say this, which abandons of
            course all the joy of not
                        quite going, so far.
I would not have recognised it if the sun
hadn't unexpectedly snapped the usual ride,
and with you a real ironist, your length
run off out into some other place. Not the
mountains, nothing to do with the sacred child.
The continued quality I know is turned down,
pointed into the earth: love is a tremor, in
this respect, this for the world without length.
Desire is the turn to a virtue, of extent
                        without length. How
            I feel is still along this path,
            down the cancelled line and
                        even in the dawn
as almost a last evening, coming back the
day before. Where they all live, and to say

such a thing is as you say it, promptly no
clouds but the sun. How else, in the face
of so much prudence, as the total staff of life;
as the friends, glittering (who would ever have
been ready for that? The sun, the red
                              shift; your hair
              is at the moment copper, a
              bronze mark, and the absurd
                         gift is just some
allowance, a generous move. How would that
ever have been so, the length taken down and
my nervous rental displayed. Not just holding
or drawing the part. You are too ready, since I
know you still want what we've now lost, into
the sun. Without either, the mark of our light
and the shade as you walk without touching
the ground. Lost it, by our joint throw,
and the pleasure, the breakage is no longer, no
more length in which we quickly say
good-bye, each to each at the meridian. As now
each to each good-bye I love you so.

FIRST NOTES ON DAYLIGHT

Patience is truly my device, as we wait
for the past to happen, which is to come into
the open. As I expect it to, daily & the question is really what *size* we're in, how much of
it is the measure, at one time. Patience is
the sum of my inertia, by which the base-line
lays itself out to the touch
              like the flower in
              heaven, each pebble
              graded in ochre. How
to extend, anyway to decline the rhetoric
of *occasion*, by which the sequence back
from some end is clearly predictive. We
owe that in theory to the history of person
as an entire condition of landscape – *that*
kind of extension, for a start. The open

fields we cross, we carry outselves by ritual
observance, even sleeping in the library.
>The laggard, that is,
>whose patience
>is the protective
>shield, of the true
>limit to *size*.
"The ceremonial use of the things described",
the *činar* trees or the white-metal mirror, forms
of patience, oh yes, and each time I even
move, the strophic muscular pattern is *use*, in
no other sense. The common world, how far we
go, the practical limits of daylight. And as I
even think of the base-line the vibration is
strong, the whole sequence of person as his
own history is no *more* than ceremonial,
>the concentration
>of intersect: dis-
>covery back to
>the way over, the
entire crossing an open fabric, which we wear
stand on or carry in the hand. That this could
really be so & of use is my present politics,
burning like smoke, before the setting of fire.

FROST AND SNOW, FALLING

That is, a quality of man and his becoming,
beautiful, or the decoration of some light and
fixed decision, no less fluent than the river
which guards its name. The preservative
of advice, keeping to some kind of order,
within the divine family of ends. The snow
level is where it fell and the limit thus
of a long cadence, the steppe whitening
in the distance and the winter climate.
The fall of snow, as of man in the ice block
and its great cracking roar, is a courtesy;
we don't require the black spiral, being gentle
and of our own kind. We run deeper, cancel

the flood, take to the road or what was before
known as champaign. We stand off the shore
even when turning to our best and most serious
portions of time. I judge that, as a snow level
but equally in seasonal pasture, pleasure or
as the rival comes, with clay on his shoes.
How far have you come and how long was your
journey? Such persons are hungry; the rival
ventures his life in deep water, the reddish gold
glints in the shadows of our lustful solitude.

So that when the snow falls again the earth
becomes lighter and lighter. The surface con-
spires with us, we are its first-born. Even
in this modern age we leave tracks, as we
go. And as we go, walk, stride or climb
out of it, we leave that behind, our own
level contemplation of the world. The monk
Dicuil records that at the summer solstice
in Iceland a man could see right through the
night, as of course he could. That too is a
quality, some generous lightness which we
give to the rival when he comes in. The tracks
are beaten off, all the other things underground.

On 9th May 1247 they set out on the return
journey. "We travelled throughout the winter, often
sleeping in the desert on the snow except when
we were able to clear a place with our feet.
When there were no trees but only open country
we found ourselves many a time completely
covered with snow driven by the wind." That
sounds to me a rare privilege, watching
the descent down over the rim. Each man
has his own corner, that question which
he turns. It's his nature, the quality he
extends into the world, just as his stature is
his "royal dignity". And yet Gregory did not
believe in the pilgrimage of place: Jerusalem,
he says, is too full of rapine and lust to be
a direction of the spirit. The rest is some kind
of flame, the pilgrim is again quality, and
his extension is the way he goes across the crust
that will bear him. The wanderer with his

thick staff: who cares whether he's an illiterate
scrounger – he is our only rival. Without this
the divine family is a simple mockery, the
whole pleistocene exchange will come to
melt like the snow, driven into the ground.

SHADOW SONGS

1

The glorious dead, walking
barefoot on the earth.
Treat them with all you
have: on the black marble
and let Nightingale come
down from the hills.
Only the procession is halted
as this spills down into
the current of the river:
their glorious death, if
such on earth were found.

2

And if the dead know this,
coming down into the dark, why should
they be stopped? We are too gentle
for the blind to see or be heard.
All the force of the spirit lies open
in the day, praise in the clock face
or age: the years, with their most
lovely harm. Leading the gentle
out into the wilds, you know they
are children, the blind ones, and
the dead know this, too.

CONCERNING QUALITY, AGAIN

So that I could mark it; the continuance of
quality could in some way be that, the time
of accord. For us, as beneath the falling water
        we draw breath,
        look at the sky.
Talking to the man hitching a lift back
from the hospital, I was incautious in sympathy:
will she be back soon I was wishing to
encourage his will to suppose. I can hardly
expect her back he said and the water
fell again, there was this sheet, as the time
        lag yawned, and quality
        became the name you have,
like some anthem to the absent forces of nature.
Ethnic loyalty, breathe as you like we in fact
draw it out differently, our breath is gas
in the mind. That awful image of choking.

We *have* no mark for our dependence, I would
not want to add a little red spot to the wrist of
the man in the newsreel, the car passing the lights.
I draw blood whenever I open my stupid mouth,
        and the mark is on *my* hand, I
        can hardly even feel the brass wire
        nailed down into the head.
Paranoid, like the influencing machines; but who
they are, while their needs shine out like flares,
that quality *is* their presence outward to the night
sky: they do ask for that casual aid. The recognition is accident, is an intolerable fall like
water. We whizz on towards the blatant home
and the armies of open practice. His affairs are
electric; they cancel the quality of the air;
        the names are a blankness as
        there are no marks but the wounds.

Even the accord, the current back (for him as for
me outward) has an electric tangent. He could
have flown off just as he was. Simply
moved sideways, in his sitting posture, across the
next hedge and into a field I know but could

not recognise. The mark is Abel's price, the
breath is blood in the ears as I even dare to think
of those instruments. The sky is out there with
the quality of its pathic glow, there is a bright
thread of colour across the dashboard; the accord
is that cheap and we live
with sounds in the ear
which we shall never know.

THE COMMON GAIN, REVERTED

The street is a void in the sequence of man,
as he sleeps by its side, in rows that house
his dreams. Where he lives, which is the
light from windows, all the Victorian grandeur
of steam from a kitchen range. The street
is a void, its surface slips, shines and is
marked with nameless thoughts. If we could
level down into the street! Run across by
the morning traffic, spread like shadows, the
commingling of thoughts with the defeat we
cannot love
Those who walk heavily
carry their needs, or lack
of them, by keeping their
eyes directed at the ground
before their feet. They are
said to trudge when in fact their empty thoughts
unroll like a crimson carpet before their
gentle & delicate pace. In any street the pattern
of inheritance is laid down, the truth is for our
time in cats-eyes, white markings, gravel
left from the last fall of snow. We proceed
down it in dreams, from house to house which
spill nothing on to the track, only light on the
edge of the garden. The way is of course speech
and a tectonic emplacement, as gradient it
moves easily, like a void
It is now at this
time the one presence

of fact, our maze
through which we
tread the shadow or
at mid-day pace
level beneath our own. And in whichever form
we are possessed the surface is sleep again and
we should be thankful. By whatever movement,
I share the anonymous gift, the connivance
in where to go as what I now find myself
to have in the hand. The nomad is perfect
but the pure motion which has no track is
utterly lost; even the Esquimaux look for sled
markings, though on meeting they may not speak.
The street that is the
sequence of man
is the light of his
most familiar need,
to love without being stopped for some immediate bargain, to be warm and tired
without some impossible flame in the heart.
As I walked up the hill this evening and felt
the rise bend up gently against me I knew
that the void was gripped with concentration.
Not mine indeed but the sequence of fact,
the lives spread out, it is a very wild and
distant resort that keeps a man, wandering
at night, more or less in his place.

THOUGHTS ON THE ESTERHÁZY COURT UNIFORM

I walk on up the hill, in the warm
sun and we do not return, the place is
entirely musical. No person can live there
& what is similar is the deeper resource, the
now hidden purpose. I refer directly to my
own need, since to advance in the now fresh &
sprouting world must take on some musical
sense. Literally, the grace & hesitation of
modal descent, the rhyme unbearable, the
coming down through the prepared delay and

once again we are there, beholding the
complete elation of our end.
                              Each move
into the home world is that same loss; we
do mimic the return and the pulse very
slightly quickens, as our motives flare in
the warm hearth. What I have is then already
lost, is so much there I can only come down
to it again, my life slips into music &
increasingly I cannot take much more of this.
The end cadence deferred like breathing, the
birthplace of the poet: all put out their lights
and take their instruments away with them.

How can we sustain such constant loss.
I ask myself this, knowing that the world
is my pretext for this return through it, and
that we go more slowly as we come back
more often to the feeling that rejoins the whole.
Soon one would live in a sovereign point and
still we don't return, not really, we look back
and our motives have more courage in
structure than in what we take them to be.
The sun makes it easier & worse, like the
music late in the evening, but should it start
to rain – the world converges on the idea
of return. To our unspeakable loss; we make
sacred what we cannot see without coming
back to where we were.
                        Again is the sacred
word, the profane sequence suddenly graced, by
coming back. More & more as we go deeper
I realise this aspect of hope, in the sense of
the future cashed in, the letter returned to sender.
How can I straighten the sure fact that
we do *not* do it, as we regret, trust, look
forward to, etc? Since each time what
we have is increasingly the recall, not
the subject to which we come. Our chief
loss is ourselves; that's where I am, the
sacral link in a profane world, we each do
this by the pantheon of hallowed times.
Our music the past tense:
                          if it would only

level out into some complete migration of
sound. I could then leave unnoticed, bring nothing
with me, allow the world free of its displacement. Then I myself would be the
complete stranger, not watching jealously
over names. And yet home is easily our
idea of it, the music of decent and proper
order, it's this we must leave in some quite
specific place if we are not to carry it
everywhere with us.
                                     I know I will go back
down & that it will not be the same though
I shall be sure it is so. And I shall be even
deeper by rhyme and cadence, more held
to what isn't mine. Music is truly the
sound of our time, since it is how we most
deeply recognise the home we may not
have: the loss is trust and you could
reverse that without change.
                                     With such
patience maybe we can listen to the rain
without always thinking about rain, we
trifle with rhyme and again is the
sound of immortality. We think we have
it & we must, for the sacred resides in this;
once more falling into the hour of my birth, going
down the hill and then in at the back door.

A DREAM OF RETAINED COLOUR

We take up with the black branch
in the street, it is our support and
control, what we do with life in
the phase now running on. From here
each time the glitter does settle out,
around some lamp, some fried-up
commercial scene we live in
support of and for. Who is this
that may just do the expected
thing; not the magic silence

of the inward eye you may be quite
positive. TV beams romantically into
the biosphere, plant food is our
daily misery. Mine: light & easy,
the victim-path is so absurd.

Misery is that support & control: the
force of sympathy is a claim no one
can pay for. We are indeed supplanted
and I know the light is all bribery,
daylight, electric, the matching stroke.

Uncertain whether the stars of my
inner canopy are part of this
brittle crust I watch them often.
The moon is still silent, I count that
a favour unpurchased, but the
scintillant clusters are the true test:
　　　　　　how much then *are*
　　　　　　we run, managed by
　　　　　　the biograph & pre-
　　　　　　dictive incision, it
must be possible to set the question
up & have it operational, in time
to restore the eye of fate: Lucifer, without any street lamps or TV. The
branch is rained on, it does nothing,
the event is unresponsive / & attending
to such infantile purchase is the
murderous daily income of sympathy.

　　　　　　The stars then being
　　　　　　ideas without win-
　　　　　　dows, *what* should we
　　　　　　do by watching, is
it true: is it true? Starlight is the
new torture, seraphic host, punishment
of the visionary excess. What else, they
glide with their income intact, how often
they travel. What they do in this
social favour, that and how with, is
　　　　　　it true. The prism
　　　　　　of mere life is un-
　　　　　　bearable, plants and

animals in their
sæcular changes, eaten up with will-power.
Who would believe in the victim, as, in
such general diversion, who would need to.
O you who drive past in my dream-car
of the century, lead me by no still waters,
don't touch me with the needle. I'm watching no one, the torture is immaculate and
conserved, I'd love to go so much it
isn't true it
really isn't true.

ONE WAY AT ANY TIME

Through the steamed-up windows it says
"Thermal Insulation Products" I can't see
where it's come from, as the warm steamy
sound puffs out from the jukebox. The girl
leans over to clear off my plate, hey I've not
finished yet, the man opposite without thinking says must be on piecework and his
regular false teeth gleam like sardines. But
the twist here is that it's all in that yokel
talk they have for the rustics and this man
is in overalls, his boy about nine silent
beside him. The driver opposite looks as
if from some official car, he carries unworn
black leather gloves & wears a black cap,
with a plastic vizor. He has a watch-
chain across his waistcoat and a very
metallic watch on his wrist – he is not
functional in anything but the obvious
way but how will he too speak? Mc-
Cormick International rumbles past
in truly common dialect, diesel in low
gear but the boy is still quiet. His teeth are
the real thing, crooked incisors as he
bites into B & B his father's mate sways
with natural endorsement back and forward
in his chair left by six he says and I don't

know whether a.m. or p.m. The girl shouts
and the young driver in uniform gives
an urban, movie-style flick of a nod as
he pushes back his chair it is Bristol it
is raining I wish I were Greek and could
trust all I hear but suppose anyway
that one of them turned out to be Irish?

LOVE

Noble in the sound which

marks the pale ease

of their dreams, they ride

the bel canto of our

time: the patient en-

circlement of Narcissus &

as he pines I too

am wan with fever,

have fears which set

the vanished child above

reproach. Cry as you

will, take what you

need, the night is young

and limitless our greed.

AS IT WERE AN ATTENDANT

Proceeding still in the westward face, and like
a life underwater: that facade
                    sheer and abrupt,
the face in all that shot towards venus, march
on the pentagon, all the prodigious cycle of ages.
Going on then any person still frequent, fixed by
the sun in that euclidean concept of "day", takes
a pause and at once is the face
                    or some account
of it: *mostly* we are so rushed. Harassment is
not on the switch, playback of the perfect
                    darling
and late again – we can begin with the warmup
about the politics of melody / that one, and
please you say at once, not *again*.
                    By the face
we converse about stars, starlight & their twinkle,
since sweetly it subsides and by proceeding,
a long file above water, single
            laced after this
            jabber we keep it
            all going, at one time
            it is just that,

                    gone: the
                    rest is some
                    pale & cheshire
                    face. Conspicuous
by its rays & terrible and grand this
                    is not our feeling
as blindly I tread to find myself
            out of it, running
on before them, accompanying them and
                    going with them,
there, as I have not known for months,
                    standing by a hedge: "I
love the shipwrecked man who was betrayed
by misfortune." As a cork rammed in the
century's neck, I see at once the faces who have
unsuccessfully dogged my path – the procession
headed by the old woman who walks & does other
things

maybe she
sings, this is
her song:
Blackie, she
calls (her cat free
of sparks), she
treads with her
face, the grave
carried away

        she has stringy hair
        water flows at her feet
        it is often dark there
        nor quick nor neat nor
any thing / along the path leading
up to the Congregational Chapel at
Linton the sepulchral urns mourn
their loss of protein & like its
beautifully fishy stare the frontage
outfaces the morning, the star at evening, like
milk. *Mostly* this is the
end of it, through into something else, as, statement:

        the child is so quiet now
        he has stopped screaming
        the scarlet drains from
        his cheeks he is pale and
        beautiful he will soon be
        asleep I hope he will
        not thus too quickly die
in the sky the face Blackie she calls
him & he is there & without passion.

THE BEE TARGET ON HIS SHOULDER

Gratefully they evade the halflight
rising for me, on the frosty abyss.
Rub your fingers with chalk and
grass, linctus over the ankle, now TV with
the sound off & frame hold in
reason beyond that. Paste. Thereby take

the foretaste of style, going naked
wherever commanded, by
        the father struck
        in the plain. His
        wavy boots glow
        as he matches
        the headboard.
Do not love this man. He makes
Fridays unbearable, with the
ominous dullness of the gateway
to the Spanish garden. His
herb-set teeth are impossible,
tropic to R.E.M. and the white doll.
It's all so prognostic: he wakes in-
clined to say just that. But then he
stretches / beyond / the
        silent floating torpor of
        stupefaction, flesh
        pierced & stripped like
        comb honey.
                Water the
        ground with song, aria
        with cloud, *that's* his
aunt with the brown teapot jammed
into edible, macerated crumpet. So you
shrilled unwittingly in the 3rd chorus.

Oh he wants no more but bright
honour sparkling in his eye, he
flies into pungent happiness.
He insists, rather grandly, that this
is "right" for him. The greedy mule
recoils from Salamanca, still won't eat.
        And after rain the
        mild rushes shoot
        for you and com-
        mand the house
                to be built at once.
        Red and grey as
        they come. In the sheen
of dew his socks are wet and the
tincture stains his instep indeed.
The head film matches the conduit
with banal migraine. Father pokes

about for the gay snuff of Algiers.
Together we love him limb from
limb, walking in the moonlight;
moderate SW gales do nothing but
blandish the same story.
                              Which is
spelled from birdsong anyway,
        say indeed under cumin,
                fetlock, going out and
                    gentle with the
                        prime order
of frost and reason, reason and frost,
the same stormy inconsequence. A patch
of wanting is not singing successfully,
the adverbs of a spate are too like, well,
écriture fatale. The ring is on the other
                        wall of the shop.
            The plaster ceiling is
                    clear and true.
        Say so, as a median
                nature, up the sad trellis.
        Say you do, lighting the
                "sacred squadron",
            flat on their faces.
                            The wall
of the shop has a blue tablet, in
memory of ATV Channel Nine. On this
bonny bank father pauses, to empty
his boots of seedlings and filthy change.
A rash of invasion follows, in
strict order of love; first the new
non-vintage, then casually sitting
out in the garden atop the grass.

Be gentle with his streamy locks until he gets the wrapper off.
Strip pieces of flesh from the animals lying dead in the streets.

Love him, in *le silence des nuits, l'horreur des cimetieres*;

        otherwise the trendy book will slide
        into the bath & linger there,
                            avec le savon
        and the Rose of Texas, toasted marine-style.
        "If he eats the flesh of his hand: his

daughter will die" – that too
is costly, like rime. I mean, day after day
is sunk into the river & washed
like palest blue *Reinheit* into the last
droplet of Kümmel. So
wolf-tallow is
smeared on his
lower lip. It is
dear to be left
calm in face of the house and the night. If
it is dark and cloudless, without stars, some
friendly woman will blunder with the tap.
No news can be less valued, by
derisive acts
of mercy nonetheless; don't come
while I'm away with the sad
touches of sulphur. Rain.

The water is rose-blue also and gentle while
mist curls into his daughter and she
receives it pleasantly, muting the comic scowl.
Bravely she traces
the path of father's boots
on the lawn – little
sister we sob merrily & settle down
by the newest grave: fresh
earth as the clay to see with,
standing by the head,
making the song with shadows set
over the reed-bed. That's
what they're for, seasons and for days and years in
the circle of teeth by the cosy fire. You know if you ask
that the air terminal
is not yet rebuilt.

THE IDEAL STAR-FIGHTER

I

Now a slight meniscus floats on the moral
  pigment of these times, producing
displacement of the body image, the politic
  albino. The faded bird droops in his
cage called fear and yet flight into
  his pectoral shed makes for comic
hysteria, visible hope converted to the
  switchboard of organic providence
at the tiny rate of say 0·25 per cent
  "for the earth as a whole". And why
go on reducing and failing like metal: the
  condition is man and the total crop yield
of fear, from the fixation of danger; in
  how we are gripped in the dark, the
flashes of where we are. It pays to be
  simple, for screaming out, the eye
converts the news image to fear enzyme,
  we are immune to disbelief. "If there
is danger there ought to be fear", trans-
  location of the self to focal alert, "but
if fear is an evil why should there be
  danger?" The meniscus tilts the
water table, the stable end-product is dark
  motion, glints of terror the final inert
residue. Oriental human beings throw off
  their leafy canopies, expire; it is
the unpastured sea hungering for calm.

II

And so we hear daily of the backward
  glance at the planet, the reaction of
sentiment. Exhaust washes tidal flux
  at the crust, the fierce acceleration
of mawkish regard. To be perceived with
  such bounty! To put the ring-main of
fear into printed circuit, so that from the
  distant loop of the hate system the

whole object is lovable, delicious, ingested
    by heroic absorption! We should
shrink from that lethal cupidity; moral
    stand-by is no substitute for 24-inch
reinforced concrete, for the blind certain
    backlash. Yet how can we dream of
the hope to continue, how can the vectors
    of digression not swing into that curve
bounding the translocal, and slip over, so
    that the image of suffered love is
scaled off, shattered to a granulated pathos
    like the dotted pigments of cygnus?

III

What more can be done. We walk
    in beauty down the street, we tread
the dust of our wasted fields. The
    photochemical dispatch is im-
minent, order-paper prepared. We
    cannot support that total of dis-
placed fear, we have already induced
    moral mutation in the species. The
permeated spectra of hatred dominate
    all the wavebands, algal to hominid.
Do not take this as metaphor; thinking to
    finish off the last half-pint of milk,
look at the plants, the entire dark dream outside.

ES LEBE DER KÖNIG

(for Paul Celan, 1920-1970)

Fire and honey oozes from cracks in the earth;
the cloud eases up the Richter scale. Sky divides
as the flag once more becomes technical, the print
divides also: starlight becomes negative. If you
are born to peaks in the wire, purple layers in the
glass format, re-enter the small house with

animals too delicate and cruel. Their throats fur
with human warmth, we too are numbered like
prints in the new snow.

                    It is not possible to
drink this again, the beloved enters the small house.
The house becomes technical, the pool has
copper sides, evaporating by the grassy slopes.
The avenues slant back through the trees; the
double music strokes my hand. Give back the
fringe to the sky now hot with its glare, turning
russet and madder, going over and over to
the landing-stage, where we are. We stand
just long enough to see you,

                         we hear your
fearful groan and choose not to think of it. We
deny the consequence but the outset surrounds us,
we are trustful because only thus is the flame's
abstract review the real poison, oh true the
fish dying in great flashes, the smell comes from
shrivelled hair on my wrist. That silly talk is
our recklessly long absence: the plum exudes its
fanatic resin and is at once forced in, pressed
down and by exotic motive this means the rest,
the respite, we have this long.

                    Only
the alder thrown over the cranial push, the
waged incompleteness, comes with the animals
and their watchful calm. The long-tailed bird
is total awareness, a forced lust, it is that
absolutely. Give us this love of murder and
sacred boredom, you walk in the shade of
the technical house. Take it away and set up
the table ready for white honey, choking the
white cloth spread openly for the most worthless
accident. The whiteness is a patchwork of
revenge too, open the window and white fleecy
clouds sail over the azure;

                         it is true. Over and
over it is so, calm or vehement. You know
the plum is a nick of pain, is so and is also
certainly loved. Forbearance comes into the
stormy sky and the water is not quiet.

From INTO THE DAY

So the seeds are cut, loose and like
the bounce of the crystal
                         dark scouts
we walk blankly in the universe;
oil from the lamp we need for our
calloused ankles. The shades attend
our motions, we hear their thankful
hum.
         Sometimes a tune by Robertino
Loretti protects us, when so as to
then for cut! Or snip your master
the prince of green devices
                         to stir
his felted palm, conjugate effort:
to arise and strut joyfully aside.

The astrology of hunger proposes
a starry bun. The dust of commerce
adds glamour by morning, the trustful
shepherd stops in his track. Arrest
is sprung up, hope holds it, wish
wears its diadem.

And now crowned with sleep who
may flinch from the eye of God
in the spiral organ of Corti.
Who does we reign our royal house
is roofed with fateful slates.

Wishing to love is the sign now
painted with darkness, as the rain
moistens the huddled sheep. The peahen
shouts with fate also and is accepted.
So lowly is the divine body, so
pale the even rib.

Does the bolt in the street mark
the laundry of the future – he inquires
of the smiling attendant boy. The
turn is spread so thin, how can he
eat what there is, the plate is nailed
down; but a railway, he laughs, is
not open to casual debate. So we
fall to agreeing and pick at the bone
of blind yellow contentment. The
fine tweed comes free and bleached
from the fingers, we are slowly rehoused.

It is the rarest thing, the compounded blood
and light makes lustre swerve in the dream.
By the flux moment we meet and in
flight to its
                thermal precinct, serve the
oil to his master. Why then in the heart
by happy smiles and joy on her face

            gaudio in that arc

the wind turning back. You take out
three of the first from the awning;
later they sip honey, refreshed.

TREATMENT IN THE FIELD

Through the window the sky clears
        and in sedate attachment stands the order of battle,
                quiet as a colour chart and bathed
            by threads of hyaline and gold leaf.
The brietal perfusion makes a controlled
            amazement and trustingly we walk there, speak
                fluently on that same level of sound;
white murmur ferries the clauses to the true
                centre of the sleep forum. The river
        glints in harmony, by tribute from the darker

folds of that gutteral landscape which
lie drawn up under our touch. Blue-green to yellow
in memory beyond the gold number: the
tones and sweetness confuse in saline.

We burn by that echo. It is called love like a wren hunt,
crimson ice, basal narcosis. By deep perjury
it is the descent of man. Above him
the dicots flourish their pattern of indefinite growth,
as under cloud now the silent ones "are loath to change
their way of life." The stress lines converge in finite resonance: is this the orchestral
momentum of the seed coat? Our trust selects
the ice cap of the General Staff, rod to
baton to radon seed (snowy hypomania) – thus he
jabs a hysteric wound, H_2O_2 at top strength.

Yet in the tent of holy consternation there are shadows
for each column of fire; in the hedgerow the wren
flits cross-wise from branch to branch. Afferent
signal makes the cantilena of speech
as from the far round of the child-way.
We are bleached in sound as it burns by what
we desire; light darting
over and over, through a clear sky.

OF MOVEMENT TOWARDS A NATURAL PLACE

See him recall the day by moral trace, a squint
to cross-fire shewing fear of hurt at top left; the
bruise is glossed by "nothing much" but drains
to deep excitement. His recall is false but the charge
is still there in neural space, pearly blue with a
touch of crimson. "By this I mean a distribution
of neurons . . . some topologically preserved transform",
upon his lips curious white flakes, like thin snow.
He sees his left wrist rise to tell him the time,
to set damage control at the same white rate.

What mean square error. Remorse is a pathology of
syntax, the expanded time-display depletes the
input of "blame" which patters like scar tissue.
First intentions are cleanest: no paint on the nail
cancels the flux link. Then the sun comes out
(top right) and local numbness starts to spread, still
he is "excited" because in part shadow. *Not will
but chance* the plants claim but tremble, "a
detecting mechanism must integrate across that
population"; it makes sense right at the contre-coup.

So the trace was moral but on both sides, as formerly
the moment of godly suffusion: *anima tota in singulis
membris sui corporis.* The warmth of cognition not
yet neuroleptic but starry and granular. The more
you recall what you call the need for it, she tells
him by a shout down the staircase. You call it
your lost benevolence (little room for charity),
and he rises like a plaque to the sun. Up there the
blood levels of the counter-self come into beat
by immune reflection, by night lines above the cut:

Only at the rim does the day tremble and shine.

AGAIN IN THE BLACK CLOUD

Shouts rise again from the water
surface and flecks of cloud skim over
to storm-light, going up in the stem.
Falling loose with a grateful hold
of the sounds towards purple, the white bees
swarm out from the open voice gap. Such "treasure":
the cells of the child line run back
through hope to the cause of it; the hour
is crazed by fracture. Who can see what he loves,
again or before, as the injury shears
past the curve of recall, the field
double-valued at the divine point.

Air to blood

are the two signs, flushed with the sound:
(a) "tended to refrain from aimless wandering"
(b) "experienced less dizziness"
(c) "learned to smile a little"
(d) "said they felt better and some indeed
    seemed happier" – out in the
        snow-fields the aimless beasts
mean what they do, so completely the shout
    is dichroic in gratitude,
        half-silvered, the
    gain control set for "rescue" at
negative echo line. The clouds now "no longer
giving light but full of it," the entry condition a daze
    tending to mark zero. Shouting and
laughing and intense felicity given over, rises
    under the hill as *tinnitus aurium*, hears the
        child her blue
        coat! his new
        shoes and boat!
    Round and round there is descent through
the leader stroke, flashes of light over slopes, fear
    grips the optic muscle. Damage makes perfect:
"reduced cerebral blood flow and oxygen utilisation
are manifested by an increase in slow frequency waves,
a decrease in alpha-wave activity, an increase in
beta-waves, the appearance of paroxysmal potentials."

    And constantly the
    child line dips into sleep, the
more than countably infinite hierarchy of
    higher degree causality conditions
setting the reverse signs of memory and dream.
    "Totally confused most of the time" – is
        the spending of gain
        or damage mended
        and ended, aged, the
        shouts in the rain: in
        to the way out

Run at 45° to the light cones, this cross-
    matching of impaired attention
feels wet streaking down the tree bark,
    a pure joy at a feeble joke.

From HIGH PINK ON CHROME

Get out of this, dainty blood in
 the box of gloves. Snow on the grass
spills water on the brain, a fine bird
 in a field of parsnips. To admit
is not to enter, the door is not an ikon.
 And take her softly, in fear for
sanity at the open window, light
 slanting in through the limes.

She looks warily at the clock, not
 ready for its classic certainty
in a case bought with green stamps.
 And yet is not yet, oh sacred
mill-stream the vanes are pressed
 to turn
                and shew where
 the journal rests
                        and is content.

What he says they must do is
 actually starve beforehand: *then*
is the fulfilled backwash. If I
 had given less, or given more,
it might have been prudent too. This
 furtive admission of degrees,
the trial of an F_1 hybrid, splits
 our cold lunch into panic.
Give or take another sandwich,
 himself at a glance, sanctus.

Next they climb to the top, to try
 their new flag. Worse than ever
is upside-down, careless brutes. All
 this across a drowsy shaded vale;
triplex zooms ahead in action replay.
 And nasal congestion makes what
you say less warm than what
 you meant. Silver splints
betray the shattered thermos flask.

In the lane the overdrive is shot sideways
   and parched there, the theme of duty not
succulent as ever was. And midnight ploughing
   on the high field, what grandeur
will save us now. Sinter these glancing
   blows: the half pressure is pretty much
absolute. Up on the grass ley the impossible
   is never required and again, more and more,
the calcium defect plays like a spring.

The outcome is negligible. We must be
   quite direct; the meal ticket is not a coloured
title but the main act itself. How do
   they get in if not by straying, where growth
is a kind of success across the open window.
   Above the night sky the atrophy continues,
costing just what it says on the ticket:
   the open question over and under and wasted
as childish carols, ripe well before time.

Too far past the point
                    the seed splits
and saves its line
              from the wake of high
water stress, in
           vited in catchy weather.

That makes a
          tidy run, food is
"money made easy"
            the tiller raises up
a spot payment
        for the last round trip.

And this little biscuit is as much as anyone could ask for and
more than many could take. Aliphatic hydrocarbons are its tacit
basis, the explosive device was placed on a window ledge and
the area sealed off. His attention was more than seemed reasonable at the time. No trace of his earlier helpful manner survived

the event, and yellow rust was not well controlled. The mark-up gave injury a forensic turn: "senseless" was an alternative, decoy stage, at top-level discussions still in progress.

From NEWS OF WARRING CLANS

They brought up some tale about white fox
teeth, flighty talk with the lofty albino trim,
you know the kind. They burned out the flute
stops without even looking (so they said)
and keenly personal were the stares
that came with it. Lit with one match, right
up to scratch, that crew were over the line
before even the flag dropped.
                        Like the dapper
butcher painted in phosphorus, the town planner
prowled round his snap-shots of triumph.
A real lucky break. "All will reveal right out
to the flat truth" say the nasal rangers alongside.

On such orthopaedic skids the day slides
into its dusky slot; neither barren nor reckless
yet but on the run. And the drive gets
to go straight by decision into falling rocks
again, any whole slur in the nap will do it.
The raid is fixed into the spoke and, yes,
chamfered by vocals at "sweeping spring choice",
roughing up the northline.

The plan

was to spread many lies, each quite gross
and polished to the gloss of air-line greetings.
Several coal and marble mines are already
reported to have been seized. The saturation
of what is "solid and durable" is cooled
to a sham-level of *killing frost*: pain is feared,
false danger triggers waste of fear. Since
in an outraged moral system the lying report,
subject to efficient causes, is bound fast
to a truth mostly formal, the efforts
at mendacious gab exceeded all limits. Good
taste was shunted into the slogan vestry and
reconstructed as billboard nostalgia: the purest
central dogma in the history of trash.

Again

"it has not escaped our notice" that, by
song & dance, men cannot live or move out
in the midst of plenty. We munch and munch
along planned parenthood, getting and spending
on the same credit card. False tedium
bids up each braggart by his plea bargain,
to set the motif as if vicious, viz., *takes*
the getting out of wanting, but in fact
the *Kung* out of *Fu*; the final arts are martial.

> You don't always get
> what you want, so
> storage is less
> of a cramp:

You don't always want
what you say, or
say what you
do (do you):

Bashing the cloud cuckoos,
short of street sugar,
what we need
is hot milk:

The rest is allegory linking reserve error,

we make a *roux* to thicken up the money supply

and merely imitate attention. You stamp about

looking for more cheap cuts and square deals.

From DOWN WHERE CHANGED

A limit spark under water
makes you see briefly
how patience is wasted

that deep sadness is a perk
of the iron will; no sound
catches the binding dark

side of this relish, head-on
in thermite lock. Each one
bound to wait, the other

blunders to see it and suffer
the play at choking
or not turning away.

To be at home is no quicker
than far off as a log
the hate blot is steady.

Amy's lurch gives true colour
a career razor-nicked with specks
of astral white. The gadget hums

stunted by snow on a hip rose
and juice spurts; like a dream
dew-draggled exactly you pick

and choose and habit pales
under the tool-rack, back broken
and split right to the frame.

at all
anyway
whatever

even so

rubbish

Think about it we must know
what this means, some hero strokes
the flame with a wet trimming

and the sparks fly up. Before the fall
of the wall there's the loss of sense
in both seeing and being seen

in his end is my beginning
my early morning start
starting to bend and howl.

Is that quite all, the stupid creep
under the stairs and in the gloom
will do their best to fall asleep

and in the shadow of that room
we hear the shallow call to deep
and fail the test, and miss our doom.

From THE OVAL WINDOW

At the onset of the single life
it is joined commonly to what
                is untasted, lettered out
along the oval window's rim.

And casting the eave forward, in
the first delivery you do know
                this talc in breath,
marking the helm wind as it cools.

It fans the rim on the inside
of the purlin itself, the tenon gives back
                exactly your life task
and for the trained level. Grind up

to the hatchment there, they are later
as to the perfect clank. No time
                first-round, first leg, with
dearer love he too could only panic

through the medium. Hold your chin
to the relief coach; I am a woodland fellow,
                sirloin parted formerly
that always loved a great fire.

The window glints now in the lee wave,
fed with light up-ended. Crape put out
                on the hives. Life cover
streams under, the master I speak of

ever keeps a good fire. Give a low
whistle, such country cannot be burnt;
            fit the rebate, but
sure, he is the prince of the world.

We will cast on the half then and find out
the neural crest below, an inquest
            wrought with frost without
snow-marking on the run to try

the spoil and waste in a white suit.
Speak truly along the lip there, let
            his nobility remain in's
court. I am for the house again

and the egg-timer, give the sweet air
back as nipped by the bud of ruin:
            three to one herring.
Arms in sisal with the narrow gate

over-arched, knocking at the septum,
which I take to be too little for pomp
            to enter a pleasant fee,
their faces are part-eaten. This is the place

where, deaf to meaning, the life stands
out in extra blue. Some that humble
            themselves at the songbook
may turn the page enchanted; but

the many will be too chill below
in profile, and tender-limbed
            in the foil wrap.
They'll be for the flow'ry way and draw

a sharp breath by flutter action, do it
quickly, tongue tied. That leads
            to the broad gate
and the great fire, and deaf to the face

soundlessly matched to the summit.
We go over. The dip stands down
            in the oval window, in
the blackened gutter stop of the newly born.

JOHN RILEY

VIEWS OF WHERE ONE IS

Go by train from here in any direction
And the land is flat : but imagination
Like Mount Tabor is above us all to see

As if on the horizon, so distantly

Trees like maps of intricate green continents
Floating in blue oceans : a constant movement
From mechanical habit to consciousness

Distantly, distantly, on the horizon.

PENTECOST

In the night the struggle of men is not heard
And here I am at almost thirty walking in it.

The animals we have not yet managed to banish
Cry and are doubtless lonelier for our lights.

Were they gathered in one room or under sky
When the cloven tongues as of fire descended?

They were all with one accord come in one place.
At any rate they heard the sound as of a

Rushing mighty wind. How far we've walked since then.
I hear a nightjar's crying by the roadside

It cries and my passing doesn't disturb it
So near it makes the moonlit night less lonely.

SECOND FRAGMENT

I put out the light and listen to the rain
Example taken from history – she loved

The rain : but that won't do for she loves it still
And perhaps awake as I she lies at home

And listens to the rain that once beat on Rome
Or fell gently on the Galilean hills

This time of the year is so beautiful
One can almost abandon oneself to it

It is the indifference of believers
That dismays, not the existence of others

We renew ourselves completely how often –
Daily we slit dumb throats and watch the blood run

I put out the light and listened to the rain
Hear how it falls : I wonder if love falls so

AFTER THE MUSIC

After the evening's music comes a storm.
        The lower air so fills with light and thunder
        I wonder the air itself does not catch light.

It's filled by vertical rain and insects crawl
For shelter under night-green leaves : passions fall.

Meanwhile Americans and Russians walk in
Slow motion one hundred and eighty miles up.

A space a world to move in as in music.
        A given time and strict measure to resolve this
        Curious involvement, a dominant species.

From A SEQUENCE

IX : A STORY

Humans are so uneasy
Even in their loving
To be on the safe side
They call it dying

Some habits are acceptable
If acquired with pain
The sky is a pure blue
And the trees are alive

The horror of the grave
And the happiness of bed
Isn't it early
To speak of dying

The days are not long
And never were enough
And yet we all lived ever after.

What kind of stories
Will you tell to your children?

Tell them how easy love is.

I shall not weary you with poems,
With unfading memory : the earth
Shall be made over; this is our corner,
Where this hope is.

Ponies stand head to head,
Sharing their breath in the frosty air.

Even at mid-day,
The mist does not clear, the night
Will be long : it is ten
Past twelve, there is nothing

To fear, we shall live after
This day, this day.

THE WORLD ITSELF, THE LONG POEM FOUNDERED

The beating of my heart ripples the lamp.
Oh this constant expectation of good news.

A daisy grows. A girl passes. A girl passes along
The wet night street, the houses opposite are luminous.

The sky appears colourless but it is not so,
It could be a love, or longing, or both of these.

†

In full voice, in full throat, in full cry, in full
Flight. To trace, round-eyed, the flight of birds,

As a poet said. How to trace longing beyond sight,
Removed beyond sensible reaching? And to give it voice?

Perhaps, high up, the clouds are frozen rain,
And the stars – we read time backwards, watching it go by.

†

You would not believe how the birds sing round our home.
How easy to consider beauty timeless.

I know of no longing to appease this longing, be it even
Your voice, moving me to a celebration of it, love.

†

A stillness encompassing movement.
With enormous beauty still to answer to.

Blackness seeps through the closed door, douses the lamp.
It is a longing for the same world, and a different world.

THE POEM AS LIGHT

1

In imagination a building, moving with the seasons,
Moving on its axis, and in the courtyard a tree,
Revolving with the motion of the planets
And answering each heartbeat in token of the time
When time, with sun and moon, stands still.

And by the courtyard crystal fountains, peonies and Mexicans
And music
        echoing the spheres of silence
Upon an instrument of ten strings, and upon the psaltery;
Upon the harp with a solemn sound.

Rain will fall and not fall : the dream
Of Byzantium interpreted and re-interpreted :
Eternity will swallow time and art
Become what is. Art is the building, moved in, breathed in,
All creatures move in this, and praise the motive, re-inhabiting.

2

The dream of rivers, fig leaves silent on the tree,
      Countryside almost as white as green.
Spirit of river, of tree, tell me, tell me.

Scarcely middle air, in flight between cloud and birdsong
      Immortal spirits of river and tree,
Hurt as we, can rise no higher.

Dream of the spirit, golden birds singing in its branches,
    Golden throne lowered through the ceiling,
Do not blaspheme, my Father is deathless.

It was written over nineteen hundred years ago – it is the last hour,
    Spirit of the dream, imagination,
Air above the leaves on the topmost branches clear and blue.

POEM ON THESE POEMS

Myrtle tree of heaven, white-scented flowers
Of Venus. Look, I will tell you of a dream that I had
When speaking men were sleeping : moisture ran down the
    windows
Like rain. Outside, the full moon, one day old. It seemed
I saw another tree, laden with light, the clearest of crosses.

Love, love, the great love, or the unexpected,
My God my love I cannot see or sing,
There is no part left of me that does not hurt,
Even dreams hurt my eyes, sober mind's image.
Eighteen months ago the seasons

Became seasons and more than seasons, I had not seen
How slow death is, quick life – blossom
As flower, tree I thought we had done and we cannot die.
Days go by and the scent of the flower
Will kill me for ever and ever.

It is cold beyond the reaches of our air,
Our slow time; its trappings are gold and silver.
And poetry a voice, a voiceless eye
A dream from which I do not hope to wake. Love,
We find ourselves at the foot of the tree. We have always been there.

in memoriam

in almost total deprivation we are all
learned survivors, the soft fruit calls, soft rain
a crystal, carried internally, a facet gleams as if
by chance, at the bark of a tree, glows in the atmosphere

when memory is of the future
then we may speak of fear and sharpening
and of love too more than of the fallen fruit
of the form that is calling and to that lovely form

PRELUDE

To live always as on the brink of leaving – but Goethe said
genius is patience – a crow is –

strong smell of wings or burning on the wind. The clouds
run for shelter behind the breakfast things.

> Great patience.
> Passa la nave mia colma d'oblio
> per aspro mare

> on bitter seas a string of images with
> song, care of crow, or sky
> of sky, care or crow

> "The whole concerto is
> one unceasing
> lighthearted warble,
> with no gloom."

Il Cardellino : the Goldfinch.

✝

blind as moles in sunlight, who
consoles us for blindness and sunlight

"Things one tells
to oneself or God."

Yourself
as image

And without
equivalent

What has to be
burnt.

✝

The wine matures, the colour and the scent, towards drinking.
The voices below the words – what might have been yells
with what could be.

But for the mind
to raise itself
a minute
and the falling
back, unsustained
song, sustaining song,
and as at other
times, the changes
constant.

✝

to the air
a sheep's eye
dog dumb to the moon
and you, and you

†

No man, my name is
no one.

Comes into question, is called, friendship and the metalled trumpets
ring. They sound if they sound; I am not and no one is
over-fond of the smell of one's own
housekeeping.

On shore yes on shore from the bitter seas for the mind is free
for image if reading is not a political act

I have spoken and seen my words fall like separate bricks from a
        dynamited tower
in lust or in love that pulls the heart to a new centre
I have and no one has
seen my children die

                                in spring, when the yellow
                                forsythia blooms

        and you are
no one and we both
                exist

more nearly

                so
using singing
to accomplish song
        the truth of song
to pick up the scattered
        pieces the clouds
run for shelter behind the breakfast things.

                †

wind blows

                        spaces

not on the wind, not
on the seas, on the energies

               of love we move

a crow takes off

               time which is death forming
               space which is absence, no
               man but also
               is

is

               the measure

bitter image

               of patience, burning

and of this

        †

at the limit of the known, enlightened / unenlightened

how many other paths unwalked and this
I've walked on twice before with a shiver of the new
each time to the limit, almost, of the known :

a punctuated silence, third time one tree
a mass of green from ground to sky gathers light,
a figure seen a long way off could be, un-

named, the centre of the world and in between
this known and this unknown, the exclusive, the vague,
in these gaps we gather guilt and love, and die :

imperceptibly the woods the sounds that come
from isolated farms scatter curlews
over unknown land, what I know of myself
what I know of this world and others.

POEM

for Rilke in Switzerland

I have brought it to my heart to be a still point
Of praise for the powers which move towards me as I
To them, through the dimensions a tree opens up,

Or a window, or a mirror. Creatures fell
Silent, then returned my stare.
Or a window, or a mirror. The shock of re-

Turning to myself after a long journey,
With music, has made me cry, cry out – angels
And history through the heart's attention grow transparent.

CZARGRAD

I

to get to know the flight of birds, blossoming
of lilac-bush tipped with white flame
see the movement of the wind and try
to reassemble quietness from the creakings of the house at night,
    night
when the blood-red sun leaves the room I'd have written a lot
having lots of thoughts and memories of lots of people
in a book of hours, meaning, hierarchies
an Easter greeting always, uncertainties
of private death dispelled, carried closely, nourished
and protected till the time for it and the Poet
subsumed in the poet
               blue
flowers yellow flowers a garden a dog a stick
and courage
          but God decided differently
strangely unrecognisable almost beyond
where we've been the ferns, far plants, anachronisms

rampant, uncoil, sticky and rain hours on end
this garden, prehistoric landscape
                              dirty public wandering to
        know
all cities to have heard and distinguished the cries
that women make and men in pleasure, in pain
the future stretched out as the past in faces
the god of grace floats high up over the cloud formation
hymns raised and lowered, seemingly not
getting any place, the common god
                              what the sea
has to say, what we : after the blizzard they
jumped on sailors to get them in their coffins the schoolmaster
"consulted the elements" both flags we wave
in view, in view of, somewhat gaily : enough greenery
to get lost in temporarily
                              reaching out, driven
from pillar to post of millennia blood
thickens, thins
                to get to know
the flight of angels "I have not loved
my contemporaries, I've loved their beauty"
"and pitied myself improperly" *cette pourriture*
I think I hear there the whine of receding light
more than in most
                    not much
jasmine scent from the islands
the stink of colossal crime
                              still on West Europe

        2

delicate the wind through silken corn
a life without compromise
hills over hills unseen the sighing of the wind
weighty in the palm
                    wisdom hovers, unheld
tangible, almost, between sense and idea
the cupped hands
                to get to know

and I could not help thinking of the wonders of the brain
that hears that music

the soft moths the soft hills the soft nights the soft breezes
of Asia   .
and the music? gone, gone, but here and the form :
except, save (save) in the music of the line it is not, that's
the trick, mind
stumbles at that, not imitating
nature but man's art we heard
a priest chant vespers to an empty church (save
for us, spectators) God
in the City   .   the brain sticks   .   proposes
formulations :
                    a city
                    of squatters, drum
                    of the dancing bear at morning, past noon
                    both man and bear asleep in ruins, the bear's paw
                    delicate   .   easy
                            a formulation

dome after dome and dome within dome
was   .   is   .   the caves within made
no space made all space having
rhythm and line and necessity
and duty perhaps in the poem one recites by heart
even to no auditors but beauty
a paradox in the very soft breezes
not apparent   for all
that one lives
                    and is grateful
for all that without which
                    and in spite of
in such plenitude the music
                    comes of itself, were we
able   .
            how make you hear is to say
how shall I hear   .   how shall I hear ? say it or how
hear exactly what was heard
                            in the ruins
till the time
                or this :

there is a flower
whose colour I cannot see
of pervasive scent
                    the name

of the end of all things, in all things   .

                     the poem   .   the City   .

                          a flight   .

II

there are those who are prepared for the ruin
of empire and therefore empire endures
after ruin, a fish gliding to deeper water
there are those who are prepared for ruin
the wind a straight line from horizon to horizon
when the candle extinguished in its pool of water
releases the floodgate of moonlight silver
on shelf on bed on books on faces the measure
of our fall upward into night
iconostasis of our common misery
those who increased the measure of our love and left us
stillness : for memory is a contemplation
that rebirth is possible, that the song be established

where are they now, the people?
dispersed   .   the face of the earth   .   why not join with the exile's
recreation of what's gone, or lost, or never was?
                                    this
keeping house, a few precious objects,
clarities, the form of gratitude,
a gathered circle of light, strangeness
or the lifetime of a mind – hard fate

in retentive air legends persist :
songs made dearer when gone than ever they were,
sung by heroes, animal spirits
in what the storm disturbs and in what the storm
can not disturb, sense quickens
a painful building up of joy and love
gathers childhood's customs and the steady fields
sleek or gleaming, sounds border on ventriloquy,
an alien metallic power in this land,
gulls circle, silent, engrossed in the wind,

the composer returning to his people,
earth's face vanishing around him, *poeta
caecus*, this dream blindly dreamed
down to, back to, the face of it
the measure of it

a tiny world, self-reflected into infinity
the wind all the same about the house and words
hissed out in avoidance of error : what we're seeking
has little to do with belief
shadows violently on the window, thrown a hundred feet or more
and behind that between the turning pages a
shadowed space and (even) on the still white page
     a concentration of attention such
deep well of love
      bright cloud is
fixed
   that love
      is never fulfilled
but the ways
    of approaching
        endless

III

  Morning breeze morning breeze murmurs
  on water trembles leaves
young trees above green branches
birds cascade
   sing sweetly the east
   is bright.
   See, already light's white
   the sea a mirror
   to clear sky
   light frost pearled
   the high hills golden.
   Beauty of moving dawn.
The wind's your messenger you the wind's
   the thirsting heart fulfilled

and that the stars them
selves on clear night the black
birds' nests and budding trees un-
fold
     morning breeze morning breeze murmurs
sparrows rise so much together
motionless with intense vibration of wing
          murmurs the breeze
on river flow
       brown, green gradations
            silent
     white-flecked
         sound, outward
curve
     of time, each leaf a kingdom, the wind's
your messenger, you the wind's
ideal audience ideal auditor the song
       accomplishes the singer

     †

shouts from across the valley
raindrops pendant from the trees
the one manner of knowing : to reach out
as a leaf swivels in sunlight
angel's wings to the limits of sky
and still the roar in his mind
towered cloud domes, air cas-
cades, swirls as water
falls, from rock to rock the reverence
due to an icon :
       green of spring in the Carystian stones
       crocus blooming in light of gold
       blue cornflowers in white of snow

and I apologise to the blackbird
that there is higher in nature than him
to sound true note

†

till the stream overflows its banks
overflows its banks and there is a face of waters
and there is a face of waters
and there is a face of waters
and so mirrored back to the known beyond which is
nothing   imagination   levelled
and beauty is residue after the bluebells
lilac   and the stream
                              name your realities
in silence in secrecy or as much
as the Word permits
relate them to earthswing, stars, a very distant
music through the plenitude of what is
to what must be in plenitude of grasses
shooting overnight two feet high obliterating
distance making the immediate vast
submarine rooms in summer foliage trailing
down rippled by currents a hunter
hovers over parkland, wind soft feathers
this day
                tendrils of passion flower vine round the morning star
counterpoints of rigour
clarity of the far white
walls picked out
                        vapour
trails, a routine with variations sun disc
silent   warm enough
for you? all windows
alive with reflections air
cool still though in breeze, in shade so
singing of first rain and
the rain drop by drop makes holes in my song
la pluie, goutte à goutte, the rain the rain drop by drop
the power to be humble and clear forsook me
this world of moods and voices around silence

IV

weak in the light or a weakness in the light
                    and so the caravan approaches
greedy now for Spring, the minutest details
the pageant flight of love's victims;
caught between sun and moon there is disquiet
the age   almost through mouths of dead poets
the angelic song burns with its own bitterness
that the hand turns inward to the light too often
and darkness grows useless, unused the trees
flame higher, proclaim what is, caught
in desire   stillness in the house, delight still
ascent and descent still possible, labour of precision
the crows' thick wings pass overhead; life in-
tensified, held now
as albatross wings are a part of the wind

                    †

that the City exists
                    tints
of autumn brown and yellow, red
scarlets of autumns I shall never see but could not
in imagination better   and love
a willed deficiency of senses
how else could we bear, why else die   denied

no season is tranquil
recession of galaxies in a falling leaf
life blood   but shrinking the day
to insignificant concerns, deserted
leaves like rain

that the past the present and the future have no motion
no wearisome motion, steady thud of acorns
to the earth, information not opinion and
if we have learnt it is
that the hubbub is also texture of song,
the breath of exiles, survivors,
thought of home

†

birds off across November fields   mist
startling confidence tricks   a heron   slim wrists
the people one meets   what's to be done
with love
spread wider   identity   you
are invited we never
knew each other   hardly
for the years and circumstances begin life
naked   phenomena   dark, evenings, mornings
     and
          the
palaces the colonnades the prospects, domes, winter
dreams, rhythms of the world's desire
slanted sun circles to eye's limit
though the City is partly corruption, decay
a world of greys and greens and white under cloud
no nearer no further than fifty thousand years ago
by stems each of which is stable in itself
the City, jewelled in time
               I hear the sky go by
constellations, star seams in a darkening world

†

faithful mirror in a lake and then
wind ruffles the waters and we raise our eyes
and the image   language of transparent love
meditation   formed of exactitude
the City's walls   fail

slight stir of air through grasses
curtains sucked in, out, to the breathing of the wind
the body being anxious, seedlings attentive
Ararat   the smooth-tongued rain

mouths of hills shrouded
bare rock triumphs where water flowed
yellow death   heavy, nothing
keep to the shady the deep paths
rhododendron-flanked, gross rose from clay
out of sun

arc of hand poised before the other
                                   precious
red rose on the pillow, a sea of perfume
its roots intact
                and that the sun sets
blood-red sated with its own weight
below the bleached fields
that all that is done
all day the drone of a harvester
next field

---

waves lap against rock
light shifts in shades of clarity
fastest movement ends in sadness   ,   creation's
epilogue lifts wings of reason   ,
useless wings   ,   imaginary
                           imaginary wings
beat them
and they   ,   to whom we dedicate experience
had substance before it :
                  awash   ,   awash
Greek islands   ,   lucid bones of contention   ,   still
enduring   .   I have the front door open (on which panel
of lead-lighting is the name CLIFTON) birdsong
and traffic noise   .   this cottage ridiculously
expensive   ,   town one way   ,   country the other
and this houselet too hot in summer   ,   intermittently lit
by consciousness   ,   that vacuum waiting to be filled
in the time before time expands   ,   that fear of it   ,
emptiness before and emptiness after   ,   both full   ,   and
changes in rhythm needing pretty sharp attention kept
tendril sways for a foothold   or shell
or hill-curve   emotion held in truth   thick green
dusk comes onto the tongue
fine dark steel well-tempered   ,   listen   ,
don't you remember days like that   ,   days
like that perhaps   ,   or look   ,   pointing :

the moors   ,   rain   ,   cloud caught in trees :
small catchment area really   .   when we
avoid talking about big things in case we put them glibly
and small things in case we make them too complex
so sheep wander along the roadside and water
flows down the gullies at last   ,   down to where we shall be soon
these years of death   .   that history brings death   ,   is death
frost-sharp stars and ripe fruit
wind tries for a clean sweep
and the kernel now opens with desire
sixth sense
                    of the invisible

traffic noise as before
beech-mast pelts down

summer seeming

everything can be grown from seed – only stipulation
is if the seed's diseased   .   this greasy turf   ,   no
bowlers' footholds   ,   how the childless also figure
in the generation game   ,   dark warm words rise
from the mid-day soil cut across by a cool breeze   ,   gratefully
gulp them down   .   summer seeming   ,   endless
search for a rhythmic foothold   ,   a familiar gratefully
accepted   .   provided   .   ask   no   questions   .   answer   no
     questions   .

now what a dawn unfurls   ,   every surface
wet   ,   glistening   .   the armchair just holds my body
though it could seat someone bigger   .
the essential oil of the plants or herbs employed :
a couple of pieces a day   .   a day ! drip   ,   drip   ,
two by two   ,   two by one   ,   a cloud-growling   ,
a green automatic and finally
no play at all today   .

for the rain   ,   you see   ,   a notation dotted
across every chair in the landscape
and perfectly natural what the bloody hell

to do with emotions . birds dive about – dive
into a respectable dive ,   drink given
words gratefully ,   could be worse ,   a breathing space ,
smugness of fair seed-time pounds ,
it pounds and is not satisfied .

compound air

air ,   compound of familiarities
shared surreptitiously ,   urban ,   what a day for
blinding sun on snow-tired eyes ,   give me that old
washed-out feeling ,   stunned at finding myself here –
and not alone in that who's next hello seagull
you're lost ,   scavenger bringing your whiteness inland
well ,   maybe not ,   the variables ,   scarcely
a straight line from them ,   hello non-seasonal nomads
wave after wave ,   motion but not displacement ,
cat mouse ,   cat dog;sun chronicler of cat and dog?
windswept measurements ,   scraps of flesh
still adhering to the ruler ,
faint horizontal cries ,   we figure what shapes us

below today ,   gasfire hisses and creaks ten
feet maybe above some settlement
not a hostile force ,   not an ancestor in sight
what is it then moves the tongue

across this bland blue sky poison spreading as much
as anything ,   the moment though refuses
to be isolate ,   "full in parts" as the sign goes ,
what wall of holes built at the frontier ,
wherever that is

                    the pattern-maker
in the pattern proclaims loyalty in his fashion ,
as it's given to be fashioned : what ,   by definition
is impossible ,   as standing here ,   who'd have
thought it ,   night emptiness bearing down
a grain of meaning on the tongue ,
shaped air ,   fellow citizen

CHRONOGRAPHIA CONTINUATA

The Emperor was not a good one   ,   in fact
he was rotten (I speak with the voice
of my family   ,   class and party   ,   speech
being a political act   ,   a skein of affiliations) :

small economies broke out in open warfare   ,
a certain siphoning of napalm on the barbarians   ,
maladroit and ineffectual : I suspect
also the certainty of deposition unhinged him   ,
blindness or castration at best   ,   he
not adept at civil war   ,   that is   ,
the constitution

            the days of success before disgrace
scarcely seem so now   ,   bound by necessity ;
yet sometimes   ,   suddenly   ,   I'm brought up short
by a landscape or astonished at
what we've managed to create beyond ourselves   ,
the golden age we look back on and the one
that'll be sifted from this darkness   .

I suspect that this also is bound by necessity
(I sit here at this date wombed in snow   ,
flakes still falling   ,   and wonder
if I wouldn't be better off in a brothel
as a matter of praise) and that I fight against it
here to no purpose – even feel relief
in failure – and that sometime   ,   sometime
I shall be broken in slavery and dullness   ,
the texture of the chronicle invading myself

children coming home now from school
use this snow as a weapon ; *the triviality*
of my ancestors I can scarcely hope to surpass   ,
nor their glory ; the idiot speech
of close family ; the mysteries   ,   let them be   ,
let them tear us apart   .

            I'm suspicious
of any conclusion to mimesis   ,   a ringing phrase
even in the correct tongue bothers me   ,   best

whip off to the shops before they shut :
if seventy years of living
mark a face   ,   why shouldn't this be marked and marred
by a form that hides as much as it shows   .
what we stand in need of   .   what we have   .

----

quiet   ,   willows and primulas are growing   .
it rains   .   days lengthen towards Easter   ,
centuries extend themselves to be judged   .

great excitement among footnotes
away from the iron text   ,   for what kind of
insect eye could take it in   ,   this truth
of the world from outside?

                              space   ,   time
to weigh words   ,   plump bellies on the scales :
after all   ,   after all people do have a
conscience   ,   anxiety in calm   ,   calm in anxiety –
it's the nature of language   ,   unlearned man   ,
to create beauty of its own accord   ,   whitebacks
float in middle air   ,   light powdering of snow   ,
a lot and a little

as soon as the weather changes
death can be vanquished

ghostly fingers   ,   gravitatio mundi   ,
clear sun playing on water
ears filled with its sound

anarchy or rigidity   ,   the discoverer
ousts the pedant   thus
the hypothesis should have beauty
and all things are potential

autumn winds are getting a move on –
the seasons likewise, light dark
light : life and death of a daffodil
in a minute, ballet movement of petals.
what have we done with these years?

the evening sky slows down though it's still too early
to run onto the streets, blue hills on the horizon
and the wind still insists : what if the moon this dusk
should show again, silver lettering on a dark green world,
only the meaningless is accidental, the arrogance
of change   .   blue hills
show yellowed harvest fields, insects fly,
birds follow, every door and fitting in the house
rattles toward sunset

across soundways for syllables,
faithful ones

                  dream body in a tidy garden
as if tired in faith, the wastes of Siberia and America
unimagined back again these slow white clouds
can frame misery and isolation, they can
do that, a vaguely disturbing alcohol
straight from the breast, mechanic's breast
the air supporting separate faces

one step away from vacuum so
softly moving, padded, furry
the strange creatures we keep with us

therefore we keep these things in mind
as ocean waves and clash of rock
whilst living the storm
the smallest animal hurrying home
whilst living the storm

---

quiet birds fly
sky spread all over
nothing sweeter in sickness
than the smell of evening
half-powers held
in the luminous and grass
in now half-light
rather more than grass
the unstill the unstill
checked

at the boundary of mind's reach
at the edge of heart's sensing
violence of colour
and the wind rising

PETER RILEY

I am from language and will return to language
    & no one will know
        what else I might have been

storm waves blot out the lights
along the seafront of Hove and Brighton
not the backstreets of Manchester or
network of estate roads south of
Stockport, not there
the same wind curves across the land
tearing thick grass on the
Derbyshire Moors
                I wasn't there:
the centre of all this tumult
this plastic material woven into
the rocks and meteorology
of the continental shelf
a morphosis the colour of blood
and winter sunsets   out of
dreams of limestone   coagulates
                    into
a device capable of speech
and silence that can
blow up the world
in one syllable.
Because it wants to.

---

if it might be possible
to live in the light of truth like the
sea, which is not one truth
but, minute by minute, a vast and shapeless
progression of truths:

the proposition multiplies into
a mark of reality
by becoming shapeless and useless like the
poem itself, becoming something you can't
hide in

And the entire land is voiced
in the presence of the sea along its shores,
permanently,
the island drifts away singing to itself,
spray shoots up round its edges, we are
off, adrift in the Northern Ocean, our last ties
to the continental shelf are severed and we turn our backs
on that faked-up dream of a new world beyond the Atlantic.
We head North, we enter the realm
of pure idea, free to cope with the weather
by our own sense of direction, follow the Drift Current
as long as we need to.
We are powered from within:

our intellectual engines hoot and puff
as we sail into the light.

From ONE DAY,

visiting the university

what we need now above all is a few hints
on how to pass the age of 40 without
becoming a cathedral.
We are so beguiled by the golden youth
into a complete distraction from the processes
of the earth   and the work of the mind
and no longer know how to sustain the music beyond
the first bright hope.

Confucius I think, said something
useful about this –

the wisdom that falls like
            water to its place

                    directio voluntatis

and that isn't in the library, either

                at the cafe

What we want indeed! He comes in
and states exactly what he wants,
a bacon sandwich and a cup of tea.

Tho the actual reason I like to come here
is that it offers that strangulated feeling
I get with places stuck in the back streets
of some obscure &
complex provinciality – a certain lift,
of amazement that people live and
eat their lives out
so far from hope

as if all our needs
could settle themselves aside
from the main course while we
                        whatever's
left, break through alone

and the tea is 5d
                but re-fills
only 3d

being the main substance of desire

in the pub

Our loss of courtly grace cohabits
with a loss of hope in the land, not
just the government, which is a thing
always beneath mention, but living here at all,
or anywhere. It is not a mode I would have
chosen, to be so utterly
separate from all the objects of power, but I
live with it, it's often pleasantly
comical as against
what might have been or was the case.
A glass of beer, the room blazing
with electric light, and I take
little, knowing
again and again
being awake on the ground we
have it all. There is a bird
called the heron of forgetfulness which hovers
over ale-drinkers. I think perhaps
through her I forgot mainly to forget
about all the useless structures
of trade. We are not held
to any of it. My notion of freedom
is one beside which any job
is an instance of criminal oppression
but I eat from the table in front of me, no
other, and the rest is always possible,
anywhere at any time.

going home

the bus goes through the mist

and we shall never have any other place but that
I shall never have any other place but that.
this, my
            whole substance borne off
into the night

(all of it) held in its
earth, a number 19, to Portslade.

though in the mind, now, it seems
a lesser demand, intersecting
with other roads, across from the sea
upland
        than I'd thought:
network, even
along the coast
no tract has any claim

From THE LINEAR JOURNAL

[1]

Someone touches my shoulder and *bang* this
extraordinary thing clapped in my face full of
trees buildings and a river I can't begin
to think about coping with ah these, the
Central Gardens of your presence, your
image, that I hardly know

a fixed-term loan of variegated parklands
known as "continuing to exist"
or all of the past and all of the present
"Have fun," they say, "Goodbye."
Goodbye goodbye. Our home
is totally unmade, we start
departing

and here we all are, sweaty with trust,
clutching our licences on the corner
we flutter we continue to exist we line up
we break our pencils in the car door, the wood
splinters, we are moved, we take up
our memory-bags and away

My regard, of you, takes the form
of a band of adolescents in shorts

setting out on an alpine ramble
overburdened with tents and Calomine Lotion
leaderless and thinking, for the first time
of wine

Out of this scramble no clarity emerges
no government no textbook no friends
though the light is everywhere we go

[2]

O my eyes hurt and the bottle
is cooling in the stream.
The desired condition flattens itself on the wall,
textual erosion at the river-bend
and calcium accretion, we have
madrigals of love and war
set up in a clearing by the road.

Now there is a hard opaque layer
over all that transportation;
the furthest dark nick of cavern
pulsing through the night sky.
Intensely, our madrigals stand in the
gloaming; green and furiously small, they attract
flies and small groups of deviants seeking rest.

O my eyes hurt and a hard opaque layer
is cooling in the sky;
the desired condition fastens itself on my skin –
sexual light on the road and
cancelled glory bring us
crashing to a future state.
We creep into our madrigals and die.

[3]

the simple pulse like a train is all we need
to get up this huge pass
escape route (1943)   over the top
and it comes easily against us at this
intermediary age that pejorocratic machinery
is at it again elaborating without end
the planned failure of intent, in fact practice
moves us right past the top of it
there is nothing *about* social
economy, beside, the single blade / the leaf
turns over / get
back. We go by the old routine,
we know the words of command, they are
thrust right into the mountain
where they stand on quaint platforms facing
west, which is not our line today
and the cave slowly clogged up with calcium carbonate
(crystalline) on and on again the leaf turns a
horse-fly stings my holiday on its
leg o now my
leg hurts too I sometimes think
a little man in the uniform of
a ticket-inspector is peering through
everything I say and desperately trying
to ask someone something but then we hold
special passes and all the hurt piles
up against the cutting / go
home

[4]

please don't tell me about your life,
the hotelier is very pleased to have us here
or rather bemused and the waterfall
does not disturb his rest. Someone
is singing through the ache of
tiny cobbled streets and in the hot dusk
the whole binding of the landscape
folds over, shut; the song

does not disturb his rent. The bottle is half
full I pass it round, we are still here;
they threatened us with cosmic stature
and moral rectitude by turns but
we took the short cut down and settled
grumbling in the clear but thick air round about.
The financial inadequacy of our shoes
made epic excursions a burden hard
to bear and we took our coffee
delicately, in two-handled cups.
For these are honeymoon tents, & the Asian light
is thus authentic; these are the first steps out
from autosexuality into two, the social flare.
Then you fell over.
I laughed. It wasn't drink but
poetry and a state of war.
As a matter of fact I find things
impossible, day by day.

[15]

and it *is* true, that we move across
a whole range of intellectual/erotic paradises
Monday, Tuesday, etc.

"I feel an immense calm in your presence"
or "Your presence fills me with a desperate agitation"

the day is calm, a variety of sea,
the traders waiting for weeks and weeks
in the imaginary harbour
or a slow train across the reddish plains
for days, specks of fire on the far mountains at night

ending in
a summer palace, fantastic traceries
in white stone, the light is inside it
and gardens with fountains and dwarf cedars
we say we "want" that, meaning
it is there, we have heard of such a thing.

We bear it in mind, for hours sometimes,
imprecisely, in corridors and offices
the delicate act of transfer keeps us,
holding out against
further violence of this kind,
the harm it does our
proper knowledge of heat,
that we have it
in the days we move across, the spectrum
held among us.

[22]

So while it seems we're beginning to get somewhere
this is not actually the case
and *another* open-air trade-fair was declared while I
wasn't looking and here they all are again
with their painted figurines and substandard brass bands.
I'm prepared to believe
this was arranged as a personal threat.

Can't we now and then
get a hand in the right place without these structural permissions?

I experience distaste
and wash it down.
I have deserted my country
in its hour of need
I have longed for the key
to the field
I have handed the power
to girl editors

So in this case take the higher track in this case
keep all the secrets close to you as you
head for the dismantled floor.

[23]

I feel terrible. I feel like
the bearded fungus on this conifer
and in this rotting state I suddenly sense
immediate victory, no

ironies attached; it doesn't matter
how I feel, ever. I'm through
permanently with immediacy and victory and
being-born and

feeling-around / acres of vivid colour
run off from my eyes into the luxuriant distances
where two shepherds are calling to each other
the songs of yes and no

and how can so much warm air
draw itself so loosely through the blue-green crystal
what does it want, shaking the strands and banners of decay
or petrify someone's heartaches into amber globules?

Shepherds are calling translucent cries
in the shattered and untrustworthy distances
from which the wind is due to turn
cold any minute now, from its source

through almost infinite gradations of density
we stand and swivel, continents
apart, defiantly ignoring
the whole crust in beckoning array.

[24]

and what *do* we love anyway (here I am coming up to
a mountain) and would it be some kind of vortex
that slowly approaches holding out its hand
across the Persian carpet

　　　like a wolf's tooth out of the woodlands

which is what we are doing? what is it that keeps us at it? is it
the note that with all the terrible alterations the hot and cold
and in and out and however much more-or-less at the mercy at a
loss at the end of the tether, we still have a marked declination
a pulse in the roadline, a vocation towards purpose and probably
capable, of. Or quite simply
you do not become a factor of the destruction of England
because   oh obviously

(stroking the hairy quarters
of some dog, passive on the lawn, who could have known
or warned anyone what the extension of love involved?
that it cannot be had for a song
or a quick distraction in the colours but constant grind
incapable of holiday whatsoever because no one is going
to complete himself in this field where too much
is to be had at too postponed an offer, set forward and
elsewhere, hammered down on the loss borne by those people
not seen or thought of, which the music is raising and
drawing closer at every minute a song is minted
much higher than promissary trellis, and in this hope
I ventured once, groping in the dark, and burnt my hands
on the most amazing things.

[28]

after which to fall howling into life step by step
the secret risks under every stone we have come thus far
and you don't understand and no one ever will how vital it is
that soon this whole table will darken forever and be forgotten
while we sit and walk around elsewhere there is no cause for alarm
kindly get on with your work but nevertheless something is coming
out of the sky into the open air we so rarely inhabit it falls down
across the wooden huts and pine trees across the electric toasters
        half the
radiators in London spring into life once more and thousands of
        people
are being incredibly damaging on carpets. Which of these rooms
is designated hers or how much space is taken
for granted or otherwise how to manage

is what is left of twenty-seven cosmologies whereas
there isn't and I'm far too busy to be important –
call out the dogs, call out the entire office,
forward and upwards to life in the crystal blocks.

BIRTH-PROSPECTUS. THE END OF US.

1

Little spinner, you are too clever
and connect right over. That is
the end of you, lost in ardour.

Because of this (which is natural)
a surplus of meat builds into the
grass and the trees in the forest

elegantly describe themselves as
interim customers, under contract
to the oceanic combine. It stays.

Not particularly as the level light
sinks in strata over the slight curve
of the land the stars edge past us
to shoot off behind and our azimuth
declines to the east of south. In ways
of which I have no understanding it is
an act of beauty to occur at all, the end
of us too.

2

I operate with a lumpen-vocabulary
on a soiled page, clusters of day
to day. There's not an ounce in it,
but the tenacity and stored size
of a wasp trapped in the instep.

The modern produces this buzz, in-
tensed, the wing beats at the object
till the body renounces its extera-
ceptor and shrivels, the known method.

It began late in the alphabet at a
female bridge, and left such a wake
of murderous nothings, hysteric
suds adhering like fury to a denial
of social intercourse, further and
further in to a black unbreachable
doubt, open solitude, and a nob
of congealed blood.

Quietly,
reading the sun.

3

Brought so often to vacuity the mind
trembles on while we shift out of it
and busy ourselves with flannel. Less
than a kind wish away. This whole crevice
of delusion binds back on itself and
no one has any better place than
the details you find inscribed
on your cell.
                    You read the book
you trace the call. All you know
is man, appointed
to the furtherance of love
so there cannot be a decadence
so our loss burns in the yard before us
to a residue of corrosive albumin,
old gold. You tap our distances.
All the innocent prospectors
scrambling on the interface
                         they all love and
justly to be alive, and say so.

4

Gliding onwards, all the difficult
things of the earth, and how we re-
learn to call them. This evening
five crows move over the garden
homeward: to leave it there as
much as to say that the earth
is as a matter of fact adoration
in its slightest hint of length.
Many have borne witness to this
and never known an instruction to
achieve or not make blobs and
scratches, in French écriture.
Designed to omit almost everything
we do if a hand can touch with such
sweeping gentility the upper of
any known thing.
                    Omitting to mention,
Love its ungainliness against
the likely gain.

5

Or only that it is worth writing
for no eyes to see and as dully and
imageless as it comes (like a swallow
between the rustling and complaining
roots of our patience) as
flat as that, that living furthers.

6

Further life, a clear and
darkened horizon, a lens
in operation at the middle
realm and what this lens is
con
ceivable error.

7

Birth prospect blanked, a blood-mist
of overstimulated cell energy, perhaps
a bipolar arc breaking into spasm
which destroys the child, has her
for dinner in the night without
a footfall without a touch of remorse.

And we insist, in spite, that the turn
of the sphere is at worst hopeful.
And still, living in the failure,
metal retakes its charge, foot
down at the bend, no idea what on
earth is going on.

7a

Apparelled in earth we hear the wing
beats behind us and don't turn.
The child dies into what we call birth.
We call it birth and furrow on.

* *

Wing, petal or placenta, construct
of the oceanic tides, emissary
of a luminous world we fringe
in our absence, but in true light cut

off from; which was all to get us here
where is on the ground.

* *

We have two eyes, the bird swoops
over the lawn (black) and is gone.
There is no pathos in this provision,
no seeking in a fold of skin for
recoverable deposit. It hangs
on the dome, the rush and claw
of terrain, where is where we live.

* *

And are securely wrapped from it,
being exactly where we can be;
the rest is a prosperous nation
of its own speech.

* *

And also that we can't, don't,
shan't, and cease. That can only be,
to know everything. And you,
that must be you.

* *

We in our partial and twisted end
to end time have the vulgarity
to debate various degrees of your
expendibility from all sides – while you
live an entire nation of observances
and suffer honestly your coronation
to the furtherest reaches of the globe.
Your wisdom coheres your slightness,

* *

My daughter, you are
still my daughter.

From THE MUSICIANS, THE INSTRUMENTS

FOR LOL COXHILL : AN ESSAY ON ACHIEVEMENT

Somewhere behind this woollen fence is Welwyn Garden City
  and it doesn't really exist, it's a dream, made of nothing, a
  response to pain,
the final home of God's children in the waning light.
Invisible. Firstly because it won't stay still & everytime you think
  of something else and turn aside to take an egg out of your
  rucksack it's no longer there, in front of you, at the end of
  the road, glowing & humming and sending up distress rockets.
  Now it's somewhere else: Luton or the Outer Skerries, nearer
  & further behind you. Also in your rucksack, in your addled,
  plated, paten, egg-head, your head.
We thought it was kept in a cupboard by a group of sharp students
  at Cambridge and then it's in a glass of brown ale held by a
  derelict barfly in Stoke-on-Trent.
That's the way it should be; the method of getting there, solid
  persistence through the door while the guardians with their
  mirrors are looking over their shoulders, deflecting wasps
  off their pre-packed luncheons...
You're only interested in one thing.
Walking the walls of the city, camping on the footbridge, you're
  only interested in one thing.
Not getting-there: being there, humbly paying your due to the
  elders of the city, becoming an item in the tension across the
  sphere; inhabiting the distance, not from-to: the distance
  at.
Watchman on the bridge, you're there.

TOY INSTRUMENTS (A SONG)

We are caught in a commerce
And wring our fingers:
The nurse is terse
And the gypsum lingers.

The examination
Is only a game
That starts at the end
And begins again.

Play with the toys
That reflect the stars
And suffer the noise
That bites at its bars

Like a broken clock
In a school of music,
Smiling back
At whoever views it.

Father has locked
In stone and bricks
The key to the clocks
And covered with sticks

The hole to the heart
Secure from rival.
We're waiting to start.
Method: survival.

From LINES ON THE LIVER

PROCESSIONAL AND MASQUE

There is a particularly bleak part of North Staffordshire near Leek where you can stand on the very edge of the Pennines and watch the illuminated or brick crusted industrial flatlands run away before you towards North Wales or Liverpool. It is the edge of a plateau of high moors of heather bilberry and moorgrass, where denudation and burnt-out atmosphere have changed scrubland into miles and miles of growth-failure. So where "wheat, rye, barley and beans" were growing in 1385, with oats, and pasturage for sheep and cattle, only the sheep survive. This high edge overlooks the Upper Churnet Valley and The Roaches, with Stoke in the first distance to S-W. An unclassified road runs along it. The moorlands behind are about 4 miles wide and part of the gritstone clasp on three sides of the Derbyshire Limestone Dome. To the East they slope down to the green & white hills at Warslow and Ecton, and high land prices start again.

It is an area of empty disregard, brown grey & purple against the faint greens. The convexity of uplands repels the human transmissive-receptive organism and they are felt as the back of something. The only buildings within miles are occasional stone farmhouses tucked into protective folds of the moors, some operative some not, and one former drovers' inn now relying on car custom in the evenings. An army training camp under the edge sometimes sends bands of tender youths in khaki to roam these wastes in single file, with trucks jeeps and flares at night.

And yet by the side of this road along the edge, at a junction where one road dives down the side towards Leek and the other follows the top round, on the west & edgeward side of this road just where the ground begins to fall away, overlooking everything, the G.P.O. decided for some reason to install a public telephone box. It stands there alone in acres of moorgrass heather & peat groughs, precisely 1519 feet above sea level, exposed to the constant wind. Was it put there for the sake of the army, or the sheep farmers, or even weekend hikers? Who could actually have been conceived as requiring it, walking or riding down the vast horizons clutching his few pence? Anyway it does not work now. The 'phone is completely dead and there is no light in it at night. The G.P.O. decided at some stage no longer to keep it in repair.

I used to pass it quite often driving to and from Leek. Whenever the weather was bad John Dooley might be inside it – he used it as a shelter against blizzards and driving rain. John Dooley was virtually the only inhabitant of those wastelands : a shell-shocked derelict who appeared from nowhere after the war and settled there. His single occupation was to walk and walk the moorland roads all the time. He was always somewhere up there – any time you drove over the top there was a good likelihood of passing him on the road, even after dark. He wasn't old, though usually called "old" as a simple dissociative habit; he was about 40 and big, with a large black beard over which his eyes crow-like regarded without comment the passing car. He had a habit of stopping at the approach of a vehicle and turning to look at the driver, the way people do in the more remote villages where visitors are scarce and people expect to know who's abroad. But he was never known to approach anyone, army or sportsman or stopped car, and I believe he found speech very difficult. He was strong : he plodded unfaltering up the steepest hills and walked like a machine the ribbons of tarmac pasted on the moorsides, with the same dark overcoat in all weathers and a large sack over his shoulder, said to contain empty bottles, or by some accounts, old newspapers. He slept in a hollow he had scooped out under Warslow rubbish tip. What was his daily bread, or how he weathered the arctic Februaries, I've no idea.

His presence as denizen of those wastes was nothing to do with the place. I mean I'm sure the only reason he settled there was that no one else had. An unguarded municipal dump in Birmingham would have done just as well. He was not interested in moors, landscapes, views, walking, seasons, highlands, wildness, any of it. Among all that desertion his own milieu was completely industrial : he never stepped off the tarmac and he slept among old tin cans a few feet from a steel skip. Spring up there was a slight and delicate operation which he may or may not have registered specifically or verbally, but he clearly had his own concerns, and was busy.

The only remaining question would be the state of that faculty of him once known as the 'eternal soul', and whether that had a language. And if it had, how humanly inhuman might it be in its demand. How it would speak only of the final pact between the person and his existence, and the final masquerade of truth overmastering silence even in the total image he makes. That it might be the very voice of the not-self.

For the other thing I remembered was one night in thin driving snow and some hill mist my headlights caught him in that telephone box, staring straight out, not at me, as I veered onto the top of the climb. The reversed pierrot mask : white brow and jowls on one of the small windowpanes – the rest, and the beard and eyes, black. And I was past in a flash but he had the receiver to his mouth and ear.

Blackshaw 289 :
THE REPLIES

1. Walking east towards no-more-home –
    Be careful what you think (feel, dream etc.);
    It changes everything.

2. What we could is no doubt inclusive of what we never fancied.
    What happened is (like me) tall, and
    Never still. My trust warp hates it.

3. Out of care,
    I watch the lesser cars shoot past,
    Accusing no one.

4. I am totally unremployable.
    There is no one but me in this statement
    Of error.

5. Resentment is the terminal of our decline.
    I crack it on the edge
    With "Flowing River Song".

6. Speaking as a derelict factory I
    Think my mind requests what my tongue lacks :
    Air! Space! Light! Fire!

7. What greater issue is there
    Than man, tucked into the horizon
    And folded round a stone for luck. Fire!

8. Fzzz. Is there anyone there? Fzzz Fzzz.
    It is difficult enough, to love being dead living
    In a hole in all the rubbish at any age.

9. Someone breathed on the whole window :
    It's pitch outside and I'm not weeping;
    I itch with the ramifications of truth.

10. Every day the light climbs the earth trembling with veracity
    And passes on. And the knowing hand retains
    A speaking coin – your move.

11. If I stick my head out of this miserable little window
    The sky clatters over us preaching fidelity
    And at night a slowly declining suspension of fear.

12. My mother and my father, my children and my wife
    Lie elsewhere calling each to each it's called
    Counterpoint and I spent every last penny.

13. The Day has proved
    Cold, with a thick mist
    In the late hours.

14. Officially I have forgotten history
    But am remembered by officers.
    Actually God howls in the sack.

15. This box is my office. There is
    No remission, no getting through without paying.
    I pay me till there's nought left and stride off again.

16. But we cannot begin to answer until the question is
    Through us. Like a little hooked noise : why
    Does love fall short, who do you think you are?   ·

17. We also are the brutality that sets
    The questions and disposes.
    Nothing, no literature, helps. Now look here.

18. Separate from sky, separate from ground,
    I say humanity is perfect. I have
    Nothing to lose.

19. I have nothing to complain about. I know
    I am not to keep. I have been told. And suddenly
    The light reversed into a lake, underholding creation.

20. They said it was me.
    They said it was me.
    They said it was me.

21. In the morning I arch my back
    And prise my living between the spheres.
    We die from within, uncertainly.

22. I come nightly to my nightly settlement.
    I may be human but my heart is a dry pea
    That hurts a poor princess.

23. There are weak places and dead spots in everything we do.
    Don't worry about them. Don't let them fool you.
    And the lorries go out again in the roads of destruction.

24. What you are doing at this moment (how
    Ever) is what is called Living a Life.
    Not hoping to be, or other. Welcome.

25. There is space, and rain on the grass
    Where a small house once stood,
    No signs of ruin.

26. It is possible to start again so often you
    Never properly get going – writing a life
    And living a writing, of something else.

27. And there are nights with nothing but starlight
    On the steel rubbish bins. I am
    Confused about this, but cannot help admiring the aim.

28. My eyelids hauled up on the pasty nightscape
    My revenge on myself via time and air
    My halt in the scar in the scar.

29. Oh trust your one possession the only bird
    Worth keeping was Charlie Parker you and I
    Never met a happier man in society.

30. (Man in society, try to be more precise
    And also cut out the wist
    If you want to see heaven.)

From TRACKS AND MINESHAFTS

MATERIAL SOUL

GIVEN TO death and life, no choice,
fallen into these terms, borne as the
tide bears the wave to its strike,
cut to bedrock, crest, charge the shore.
Given to this, life carving itself out
of its knowledge and the earth
is like a cup, to which the lip fits,

and the senses' final construct moves
relentlessly through substance to the houses
of light, mutual, devotion

joined to death; danger
specifies its fear, the message forms
its own access or nerve and just behind
the point of contact perception opens
onto a cleared space, a settlement, holding
people of all ages together,
the whole of life, is this shift
back, this rearing

and arrival, which leaves a mark,
a birth documentation or yell echoing
down the unlivable corridors and arcades
of transitional time. Flesh scores lines
in the calcium slag of earth and the spirit
wakes, the needle enters the groove,
polar tension shakes the circuit, which
responds, gapes, tremors, issues
forth into the acts of day, for good.
Peace is nothing without this resistance,
engaging distance beyond any possible
repair, to the end, the inhabited city.

And this is what we see, and live, all
round us the world arrives at its end.
So I wish it, and plunge
into the stone, you never see me again.

From EIGHT PRELUDES

i

Each day some further light each day some farther dark.
Carry on go here there make a note of it what for.
Climb the hill walk down get in the car & drive away.
It is nothing to do with me. Valley stream
meadow waterfall gorge. There is something else there

nothing to do with us, making no difference.
We can go we can stay at home and drink tea, it is
still there. Far reaches of the upper manifold, where
is it, what is it, green chapel if it rains it rains.
Smear of cloud in the distance, book of nothing not
inhabited, ruins of the whole thing. Light on water
quick by blue shale cliffs, thick in fern, light filling,
bearing the vocabulary of a curved lack. Mineral vein
running down the hillside up the other side and away
over the moors, worked or not. Or not worked, unknown,
what difference does that make? Light filling the valley
with not a soul to be seen, dark beams of disappointment
filling the city streets, death shadowing the grass.
What am I then as you which otherwise stays sleeping, or
if we weren't in the dark star's way would our sense
still open beyond the ground whether we knew it or not?
No, the material soul yearns by the day's annoyance for real.
So does love in silver boxes hence despatch our joyful stake
and I turn us again, front to front to front.

ii

Night outside is the theatre of our patience
as you lie beside me in the dark loft;
distant thrust of steam locomotive in some vast
marshalling yard, cold papers blown
across the square.

Night contracts the distances of love and fortune
to a presence, angles filling the dark room
loud with inaudible instructions like an
equestrian statue in the full moon and a far away
telephone rings;

It is me trying to contact a third person
out of the past or lost in the city streets while
night's cover persists – footsteps of the heart agent
passing by ticket office and clock tower
to an abandoned station.

Then false dawn brings a nil invoice and faint lines
near the ceiling, a small child runs down the corridor
holding a toy angel, wings flapping screaming at us
Not to owe – the world is wanted, and full, our full hearts
crack at it.

And famine of the earth in pictorial wars, false
tensions, monetarization of time whereas the emptiness
is real and there is no return, no restitution
oh keep intact the underwing starts, the
cup through it.

vi

Willing also to be remembered, lost
in fairest lovetask scholarships such
as bring sight to its own predilection
where the broken edges catch the light
at a sharpness, a tract where sense
and love fuse in the energy of script
holding the world together at that point.

And there is immense wastage, entirely ours
as we humanise the world and then resent it,
objectify it and wonder where it's gone
and place such limits in our speaking that
most of the people become figments of something
shot past like an aggregate plum too late for
winter, complete immersion in crust.

But I also think of you as fairest before sight
in a vocabulary which is generally considered
nonsense out of a 13th Century context and still
fairer dark by the light that glims beyond.
Well, it is night at the crossroads and many years
since a dignitary came this way. The faces
of the houses are silent. Time suddenly rusts.

8

IF YOU want messages you must provide an orifice.
But to really want messages is in itself an orifice,
a lesion, an interruption of the diurnal pact. The future
ferments in this cleft, packed with honour and disdain,
drawing us ever larger and further on, to this self-
same world, that listens; the rest is vein stuff.

Surely it is this whole particular, this action we
are that draws our sight into the funnel, opening
and closing as the light wing flutters, back
and forth, back and forth, wisdom and rubbish – poetry
remains the flight. And now if I can just get out
of this notional claw I'll find out exactly where I am.

I'm in the dining shed again exactly up and about
my morning task I crawl at this morning through
the floss of dream. In a wink I fill the kettle
and forget it. I shake the radio. I wince.
The light outside is clearer than any hypothesis.
The edge resounds in light because we don't linger.

And off to work I go. I enter a solid block
of morning light scored with branch lines;
I close the door before you even wake, check
ignition and brakes and turn again to the book,
to the page shewn, the passage marked before.
Fate, it says, is a professional improvisor.

I hunch under the brow as the overtakers
glide past in their dream wagons : Monday
Tuesday and Wednesday, fleeces thick in oil.
Feeling "rushed" (like "crowded") mounts to
a signal. I turn into a lay-by with herbage. Rain
clouds the stream. The entire landscape is verbal.

I lean on the parapet while the police matrons
check my documentation, and listen to the story
of the water vole, his home under the bridge, the pain
of his extended incisors. He breathes under Saturn
and scurries along the bank. He eats or is taken – he
knows that. His duties end at his honour to himself.

We have considerable doubts, but raise a song
of this inadequacy the thrush couldn't fault.
And we keep it, chuck it over the shoulder for
luck and resume direction. A mended stone.
Nothing any longer bears on us that isn't ours;
nothing any longer wears us that isn't love.

Hell in some century's language is where no one
makes his life any more. We have the key to it, fast
to the wrist under the sleeve, the misplaced heart.
And we mine into light in a way no office can
endure or regulate save the office of delight,
past and future safe in a timed shell

> Or we have no power at all
> and are in anyone's hell at
> the flick of a card, no longer us.
> We return, the cloud retires,
> the demonstration thins out but
> love's farther still.

PURE DREAD

Green & white valley and the river
fast, double, manifold, always
full when most empty, bright threads
on the land, spring grass and
history it doesn't mean a thing
if you're sure to go.

Nightscape cast in space, patches of
white rock glowing in the fuzzy darkness,
questionless, clouded eyes turned aside
Why not when we get what we are in the
end anyway, always, end up with what
we are bound to.

Duple creature, quick river every summer
vanishing into the earth, to secret courses
and underground lakes, empty bed blazed up
the valley centre, pebbles hot to the hand –
Carry them up to the summit caves,
the ox-head wake.

Now constant rush and throb of water against stone,
arch of sound, sides of night forming,
our eyelids are stapled to the earth –
we are guardless and empty without you,
plodding simply back to an unnoticed room,
eyelids stapled to the earth.

THE LIGHT alternates, comes and goes
in days and years and yet remains
the perfection of constancy held in
the length of terrain by human sight.
The buildings mark stations of hope across
the land as the sun's face is cast in
the streams, that broaden and deepen,
playing gently back to the side walls
of terraced houses, brick shed deep in
bracken and willowherb – lasting constructs,
signs that we are here to stay, all of us,
a context, whose weathering is on record,
and anchors the language to a history
of completions.

Then there is nothing trustworthy in this world
except the heartfold, the construct that endures
beyond our means. Human promises are worth less
than the cheapest fastener on the market
and the earth falls away at a touch.

                                    The city –
the plastic spoon, the double bed, the book.
Nothing else holds us, no crusty trellis athwart
the race meaning a trust we don't actually
perform – of course it breaks – we know perfectly
well what social good "is" but can't reach it
without the journey, the making quest.

And deep in a diurnal faulting, wedged
into a space making day and night seem wide,
someone is working, scratching away,
and the lamplight of a den persists undimmed
for weeks, burning brighter and sinking deeper
into the gap between two identities where man
in total solitude delves at the bases of love,
the weight and stability of the transcript itself.

THE CITY'S surface and perimeter swollen
with lights, command of feeling as extended
and productive biological need, 5 police cars
and an ambulance, the slightest immediate
kindly act and the very gaucheness to say it.

The catalogues of favour slowly accumulate
in right acts of any scale, etymologies and
histories of musical instruments, whether in
rage or cheer we burn through the night of thought
until the flags descend on us.

All the work is directed to this grace
whereby in a moment's turn as in a year's
bulletin we are rehumoured, and cast
resentment adrift like a fishing line
in the earth's blackness behind our home

Oh lightly as if not bothered, to justify
being this forward transaction between soil & sky
that sharpens its claws on the city walls
and laughs at the tortuous blinds of earth,
knows them to a T and adores the green patina.

Then as the candle burns lower the spoils
of chaos are set in a wicker basket and brought
to market, bearing his fatherly self for smelting,
and courage is care, care is purpose, the weight
of earth falls off.

JOHN SEED

LINDISFARNE : DOLE

England's coast a shadow
over the grey water. Morning
Rain dripping from everything.
Far from the village,
Faces stone, stung by wind, we
Trudge the shore. Kelp
Knee-deep, a cormorant
Low over the bay below the
Castle. In silence
Walking, dreamless for hours.
Everything
We need but forced
To leave as if we wanted to.

AFTER TIME

in the night the night
wind   voices
echo
        in the small street
                            shadows
moving   carried along I think

"... the absolute projection of an object
of the origin of which no account can
be given with the result that the space
between projection and thing projected
is dark and void..."

unknown
       the
unknown
       footsteps fade

INTO WHAT DEPTH THOU SEEST
FROM WHAT HEIGHT FALLEN

Walking   in darkness

Between the trees

As already we'd
Dreamed   a stone path
Curves along the shore   We
Step over the thick roots

In the shadow of leaves
Watch the nightworld

What offered no alternative   up
Turned   brilliant on the dark water all
The distances of sky the
Nothingness at the centre

Here at our feet

Opposite within opposite the

Spaces in the heart

LINES IN WASDALE HEAD

                horizontal on rough grass
For an hour or more
Sleepless I dreamt you here across the spaces the

Silent presence of another discourse
Impenetrable as the limitless
Sky the sky's lights in meaningless pattern the
Whole structure swivels on an axis
Inserted in the earth somewhere
In these dark fields   nightwind whispers of
It whispers of you.

NIGHTSHIFT

Far out in the estuary all night
A boat's foghorn   hour
After hour   like a stone in a
Stream at the centre of consciousness

        ...dark water the haze

Impenetrable   England's coast this
Alien place

Ragged clouds in the wind
Over Holland before dawn

Saltwater foaming on shingle along Spurn

Alien powers

In the mind but in space I

Stand at the window   image
Thrown back on glass against blackness

Far out in the estuary all night
The boat's foghorn   intelligible sphere

External to everything

DURING WAR, THE TIMELESS AIR

the sea shone
and we walked in danger
To the cliff-edge

Soft grass   immensity of cloudless
Space

gulls guillemots   a dark bird
Whose name we never knew

Everywhere
their sound among the white rocks . . .

But we are dumb

Powerless   now totally exposed . . .

Shivering naked into space the

Solitary mind flickers among elements

In silence

For a moment almost free

At the nation's edge
Bede's image of
Was it?   a sparrow
Swooping through the bright hall

England May 1982

"HISTORY TEACHES, BUT IT HAS NO PUPILS"

(Gramsci)

I

we inherited dreams

Woke up in a strange place alone among shadows
Rain blowing in from the North Sea in
Soft blue twilight the lamps come on

Relation   absence of relation
Imagining the real   unimagined contradictions

. . . to make poetry of these streets
Hours and days
                    contemplating a page a line a word

                pale children in broken shoes
                unteachable and silent
            in the mad tangle of languages

Shimmer of streetlamps on the glazed roads
Rain falling through darkness

. . . a place different from this

II

Locked within a human matrix the
Park is quiet
                ducks drift dreaming on the murky pool
Then converge towards us
                    we have no bread no message

Rooted in history   the nightshift begins again

Perfect sky first star   in a tangle of branches
Incoherent
            tangle of
                    moments

... street after street and between   the
Masts of the trawlers

   shed for the waiting taxis
      chalk on the crumbling brick

Beneath amber lamps through confusion
Who could I have been who
Could have changed this...

                irrelevant

          as irrelevant as meaning perhaps

IN THE SWEET DARK

          between statements I
Walk among the trees
Along a dark lane   alone no longer
Relating discourse to experience?
Tracks   criss-crossing
Bare black wet branches
Fracturing into the chill air like breath...

Returning, again and again

What was it I left behind last night?
On the train rattling through the black fields
Till I woke before dawn

         ... mist over the fields the worn footpath
A dog barking
        stupidly insistent

IAIN SINCLAIR

WE ARE GREEN, THEN GREY, THEN NOTHING IN THIS WORLD

*"I had underestimated his reasoning power &
the length of his arms"*

but the morning does not renew, this city
daylong drives and the streets
the blocked victorian heights
*"the key is in the window, the key
is in the sunlight at the window"*

looking at the framed glass, sun gas behind
then turning away closing the lids
receiving a perfect negative print
window bars
the same this morning
with the outline of the painting
no renewal here, nothing to
draw you out of me

the sealed envelope of dust particles
bed rugs carpet, will not be opened

candles are a temporary measure
to light us down from the trees

OAK CHROME

I dream the dream
my father's father dreamt, after he died

an oak tree
bark skin, green with lichen

the walls of the garden were not old;
he crossed his legs

the dream my father's father dreamt
in death sleep, in loss
his parrot crashing against the bars
the bell of the cage

my father in the garden holding up seed cake
for his dog the terrier, to jump

the dream of family of history
of garden patch
which is old hill, stoned over
burnt, cut, fenced, rolled, planted

the oak tree, being part of the other,
was his dream, tube & substance

MOTHER GLACIER

the tree as dream as family

glimpse of fires in the forest
two thousand years
in black, unshaped wood

the dream precedes consciousness
as lights on a motorway in rain
the car ahead
the whole insect tapestry shimmering

memory precedes event, hence melancholy

black glass of ancestor time
scratched with a needle

great grandfather, bird-eye
watching from the tree's beard

I do not receive your message
cannot break the codes of death
am wheeled, day from day
watching the river, keeping score

implausible connectives
the page fills, the issue is clouded

BOOK OF INVADER

"Now, the City, impoverisht, swollen, dreams again"
(Duncan)

1

The Invader carries a soft pack
of leaking consciousness, an undiscovered axe;
his mind's eye rehearses violence
among these strangers,
the traders with their pouches & quick tongues.

He walks his sweat
through dry grasses and dead leaves;
a morbid exhaustion fells him,
hillsman short of patience.

The killings are hard to remember:
the unprotected cold, the raised stone,
mashing of brain cake,
long rusting in river silt.

His eye, sleeping, wakes on industry:
a tall bridge, a death
beyond fading, a closing of all pores,
a mud halt, a blockage.

2

outside the black surgery window
the rope of stars threads a profile

not projected, but recognised
this ancestor

: the clues strung in light

broken necks, locked in bone
perhaps sawed-out on metal studio tables;
dreamed in salt, precipitate left
when the blood has been washed free
has emphasised the eye of the drain

ancestor profile
          mask of torches
slung outside the window night

found among these
          are lobster lion
                    scorpion & crab
the scales the fish

long, kinship assumptions

3

who does the work becomes his own father

he chose the bluegrey paper
in advance of thunder
which he assumed for the white
landscape box
that he had constructed
and walled in bitumen

at this moment all syllables have to be shaken loose
I am a savage, crusted with words
syntax random, stutter of a pelican

he also assumed a half-profile
at the window (his pipe)
the washed-out green of the garden
already cut with lightning strokes

a pile of dirty handkerchiefs witnessed hay fevers
smoked glass stopped down the light

streaks (implosions) suggested
that chain of burning stars

once more he guessed at a mirror trick
casting his anima
onto the screen of space

inside the room the patient
crawled out of his head
and halfway across the floor

the bandaged dog

4

This is the quick of it, that though he watched,
he was what he saw; a cut shape, struggling.

He was what he felt, the awkward blood
thudding in his tub, the glass
that slid through his hand, & smashed;
the treacherous splinters.

Aloof, he cultivated several poses,
changes of shoes,
hats worn at a jaunty angle,
a gold topped cane:
but still they bled, his eyes.

Cataracts, blindness,
the waxy torment in the ear,
the unmanning lusts & secret images.

This goatface, horn-bearer,
could not escape the gastric bolt.

Weight of language food stalls flight
he became what he beheld.

5

Painting with a knife the Invader
creates another Whitechapel impasto

drawn by lines of force from schoolyard railings
he follows a girl in black
down ditch-streets & bollarded laneways

listens to the rivertalk
of vinegar-grey zombies
huddled around cardboard fires

later there is a room a bed
the dissection of time
meat decor, exorcism in blood
the carving of forbidden words
on clean flesh pages

fulfilled his red & bleeding feasts

the machine in Invader's sleep
grinds its teeth.

6

Invader had Victorian early-kodak membranes:
beard-wire, dark hats, thick waistcoat –
this element travelled deep vegetations,
iron on water, steam fire, newspaper.
The confidence in metal construction
kept him rigid & held down

steppe-fears, dane-facing landscapes.
Church-heart scrubbed out
in cigar smoke, the looping of seawave.

Invader posed among pygmies,
sketched in black ink, brought back specimens.
His journals discolour / the skin of our memory.

Looking for (drawn towards)
    off-shore islands,
the body of his life on the tea-estates:
a fortune lost, gold prospecting
in Tasmania, son born at sea

the alchemical shadows then cast
have still to be drunk:
his source remains obscure.

Lima was one message.
Maps drawn, graves robbed, collapse on the Andes.
Spectre of white gorilla
hides in suburban outhouses, waits.

7

Invader's father, dispatched by family, to Ceylon
tea-estates, a possible destiny,
if not a trade, chooses the overland route:
snubs P&O, a horror of sitting still.

Arrived at Damascus on foot, naked,
his horse dead and eaten;
lashed into vision, the city walls
shredding in invisible rainstorm.

Desolation meets desolation, he wrote,
enchanted, of Assyria:
these huge mounds.

Ceylon, he never reached. The worm
crawled out of him

and through cuneiform inscriptions:
crossed the mountain of Pontus
the great steppes of Usum Yilak

An unknown language! *Sa nagba imurur*
(He who saw everything).

They tear up the earth, searching for their fathers.

From LUD HEAT

BIG MEAL

her legs go upwards into eternity & well
out of focus
the red buttons
are stages distinct as f-stops

look how the full
moon becomes an area strongly linked
with the horn antennae of this snail
crossing our path, Keats Grove

sublime bedroom preserved
the tiles of lung blood
confirming the pure status
of his quotable formulations

the cases of sustained emotion

we can gaze
with a whole body of lust
across the table the libidinous plates
the Upmann cigar & german wine
the lies
shield a condition of secrecy
that needs all his five-litre cunning

& is the holiest mood he can summon
in the heat of the matter between them

they wait on a cold platform

it does not chill
the truce of love the modular
basket they share

watching fish in an air-hosed tank
spending money free

as the bubbles break
the longing between them
of the ancient dead generations

to mate again & be born

IN THE SURGERY OF THE SUN

His guard is dropped. He is at ease with the rhythm of the days. Joe has his week's holiday. He drinks the calm restraint of Arthur's routine across the tired grass. The pollen dance is broken. We bend towards the equinox and work the patch named "St Philip Howard". The sky is sheeted, grey-mauve. He feels the weakness enter the plates of his feet. The charge in his bone marrow sustains a field of deformed mushrooms. He can scarcely climb this humble calvary & trim the toes of the wooden Christ.

This day's alfresco lunch pushes his confidence to the point of risk: to rest with his back on the pyramid, St Anne's. The buried brain. The power socket. To swallow the can of mud water is difficult. The greasy fish twitches in his throat. Salmon Lane flickers into white fade as they return.

By the end of the afternoon he is done. And can scarcely get the bike home. Feels/understands the true distance of this journey, the pain trail. Cut-out mechanisms are inoperative. He sees every yard. So the idea of viewing Murnau's *Sunrise* is shelved. As is the scheme, already in motion, of walking the flare-path of Hawksmoor's churches by night, in company with two others; taking drinks in the appropriate cellars & rat-holes (Old Horns, Balls Brothers, Carpenter's Arms, Seven Stars, Ten Bells, Blade Bone); flash-bulb photographs to burn a dark halo around the necklace of shrines. This outing projected for the ninth day, Sumerian time of sackcloth & ashes. This was the overload.

And what occurs is seen as sunstroke. A total collapse. Water stomach. Weak head. Fever. For two days, sleepless; his body his bed, vertebrae a cage of burning wasps.

Then the dry thunder, the club shaken, & he can climb out of the nest. It is the ultraviolet knife that forces him to confront the part of him that is Robert Louis Stevenson: "thin-legged, thin-chested...light in ragged luck." Consumptive skin flares. Unnatural fires glowing beneath the cheek. The whole horror colour range – as with that night of chocolate-cake cannabis, when cosmic ironies stretched into coffin draperies, & his companion vomited – ritual death-mask. The Jacobite left-handed ahrimanic gruel-water magicks of Caithness are upon him. He crawls out, on the third day, shaded in straw, a photograph of the last months of D.H. Lawrence.

On return to the work sheds the men laugh – sunstroke in London in August? But the magnetic storm does confirm that ultraviolet diagnosis. The sunspot code has been activated, the radio message of the Ripper. A time of open wounds, when the clouds of protection are pierced, & the gas blanket wears thin, when "one lifts a flap of paper to discover both the human entrails & the starry heavens."

August 1885 found R.L. Stevenson in Dorchester, aiming at Dartmoor, for health, renewal from stone source – but collapsing in Exeter (New London Hotel). August 1887, his health again in balance, Stevenson shipped out, Tilbury, on a freighter (the Ludgate Hill) for America. The last instinctive search, on a Sunday, was for a copy of Hardy's *The Woodlanders*, to carry with him. The narrator discovers these facts in Dorset. He has one book by Hardy in his cupboard. It is *The Woodlanders*.

The whole fever condition is stained with the pus of the Stevenson figure. Stevenson is insomnia; the wall-prints of an exhausted brain. Hollow words echo, dream quotations: that he has to "swallow the world." Dreams suffused by "a peculiar shade of brown, something like that of a sealskin." "Afraid of the clay soil."

What does he think is the governing process here? It is a total sun surgery. He is now post-operative, convalescent. With a taste of metal in his mouth, the iron of Los. He blinks from the daze & illumination of shock treatment. There are brilliant images on the borders of consciousness, but they cannot be replayed. The spine shivers from the electric couch, sensitive to the unspoken word. A confusion of tongues & radio voices from deep space-time: the dead speak too fast. A sense of genetic bombardment. As if the pattern of chromosomes had been re-made; the DNA dial spun recklessly. This is a lasar lobotomy – actual major character assassinations worked by sun knife. Jekyll dreams, Limehouse nightmares. The germicidal push. All the bacteria of body light have been boiled in malarial blood heat ((the Swedenborgian distinction between the spiritual sun – LOVE – & the material sun – HEAT: Blake's "sulphur sun")). The conviction that death is the cure. That life is a disease, living is disease, is active. Death is a bath of ice. Is the water he now wants, so indiscriminately, to drink. The cure is a piece of death. Death cures the body; its furious nerve pulse. The pages of skin are dried upon hedges. This is cosmogonic surgery: way beyond his control. The patients are not individual, are a strata that curves through the alternating times of the earth. They are beyond the simplistic butcheries of tower block hospitals, secret hotels. The thing is Mayan. Connected to the shape of the essential building, the star tower. Executions (release) are multiple. Each heart torn free from the body case is re-united in the sun. That the great tribal heart should beat. That the sun continue to burn. So we 'volunteer', are generous victims, with Divine Light grins; placing ourselves in the open air, bare-necked under naked skies, away from the safety of the enclosure. We offer ourselves to the equinoctial sunbeast; so that it does not fade, or turn away from us. That its potency is held. That it climbs from the thawing earth into the heavens. Risen arch. Light maker. Promised feast of gold.

Surgery takes effect, what remains? We stumble into the realisation of a doppel-gänger principle. The feeling was already present, of a secondary personality developing, Ka assertion, inhabiting this body shell. "Not quite myself today"; I am host to motivations that cannot be understood. Stevenson again: ". . . & now suffering from what was loosely diagnosed as malaria, he had convinced himself that he had ALTOGETHER CHANGED INTO ANOTHER CHARACTER."

As the ego breaks I am host to another being, who pushes through & not with the pink tenderness of new skin – but with old flesh, hard as wood. The earlier "I-do-not-know-who-I-am" virus is confirmed, as this terminal caricature eases out of my face. His disease ratio is speedier. He is further down the slipway. He offers suicide cassettes, seductive quest routes, film clips of Orkney death rituals: the whole horn pouch. He packages ancient horrors in mute jackets.

The wind is aroused to push back the hairline. So there is that shock, *Performance* re-take, of seeing this thing in the bothy mirror, as he washes the earth from his hands at the end of the day.

And worse is to follow. Another of Anna's casually recounted, but vital dreams: that there are two creatures, one is her husband, the supposed protector, who is sitting upstairs in a wicker chair, while the other, also with my face, kicks down the door. Hyde is straining his collar.

He thinks of the churches as instruments of surgery, himself as golem, invaded by the planetary beams focused by these pyramids. *Invasion of The Body Snatchers* formula. Disease is the means of inter-galactic mutation. The germ is Martian. We are invaded by a virus bearing the message of the stars. Cancer is star memory, misunderstood or opposed. Involuntary sacrifices are the hardest to make. These white conversations rip open the sluggish condition. Talk is faster than light. In the wake, the fouled wash, come the abortions: Scientology, Manson Hole Visions, the Process, Roger Corman. It is too ripe, too ferocious & sudden. He wants to bury himself in a peat bog, to sink in limestone caves for a thousand years, meditating on Conan the Freebooter.

But he has to consider the pyramid, as cause. He attributes

this church to Selkis (   ) one of the canopic guardians, scorpion-goddess, identified with the scorching heat of the sun; shown as a woman with a scorpion on her head. And this is illustrated later – September 4 – at Stepney Green School, when old Bill Gates, the tea-maker with the ruined feet, came out, for the first time, with the school-gang & actually spotted (or caused) a scorpion on the path. We were sitting, dimly, on the grass verge, "taking a blow", gazing with dead eye at the talismanic arachnid as it crawled towards us. Bill was the instructor: "that's a scorpion, you watch when I touch 'is tail." Which he did, the prong arching fiercely back. And we accept this verdict, do not struggle with its meaning.

One of my proposed companions for the night walk did not escape the word of the pyramid either; was opened to receive the appropriate message. He got a varicose vein on the male member.

The sun tho' must be the final agent in this parable; must be given, even here, its fee. Remember that "Cleopatra's Needle" is, in fact, the obelisk set up by Thothmes III in front of the Temple of the Sun at Heliopolis. Consider its relation with Hawksmoor's twin obelisks: St Luke's, Old Street (church decayed, obelisk standing) & St John, Horselydown (reduced to a mere rim of brick).

We are standing, in this cantref, on the path of the procession of the sun as narrated in the journey of Los. Los/Sol works that reversal into the infinity of mirror space: west to east, from druid burial heights at Highgate, beyond the Parliament Hill tumulus, to the Isle of Dogs (Anubis/Leutha). Blake himself suffered when he took his outings upon these local hills: pain begins at the Angel. He crossed the river to the groves of Lambeth. We honour his route.

Los works his surgeries upon Urizen, the calculating intelligence, harnessing the dance of sunspots, "...till a Form / Was completed, a Human Illusion / In darkness and deep clouds involv'd." That Reason be cut into, bound, re-forged, charged with wild light, ionized. Our mummer shadows recall this great archetype pageant. It is all there in the book of visions.

"...*pale stood Albion at his eastern gate,*

Leaning against the pillars, & his disease rose...
Upon the Precipice he stood, ready to fall into Non-Entity.

Los was all astonishment & terror, he trembled sitting on the Stone Of London; but the interiors of Albion's fibres & nerves were hidden..."

DEATH IS

Death is the fuel we are using up; its smell not
unlike petroleum. Sickness. The tree plug
drains. Sky: colour of vein tissue. Too much
melodrama, churchyard lunches. Picnic against
the pyramid at your risk.
The absurd latenight horror film is oracular:
puppet theatre truths. Charlie asks for the
names of the trees. The woman in this game
remains "on the side of life". But she's gone.
The plans to view F.W. Murnau's *Sunrise* are
shelved in hollow body collapse. Swallow the
            commercial maggot &
            acknowledge the respons
            ibility is Mayan.
            Feeling his heart
            under a red shirt,
            sunstroke spews up
            a snakeshead. It
            stares from his
            mouth. The black
            plans are shelved
            also. Acknowledge
            the heart's enlarge
            ment. The screech
            of unclassified gulls.
Heart does sing to be part of the fire chorus.
  Consumed, standing on its legs. A spider
    in the cave. A blue plastic bowl is
      at the bedside, he will not be
        sick. Work is a telephone
        call away. Obey the war
          ning in your teeth
           Trust your inst
            inct if you
             can find
              it.

From SUICIDE BRIDGE

BENEATH BRASS, BONE: the prophecy of Slade,
the Fate of England

*"Thus to burst Death's membrane through – slog beyond –
not float in appalling distances"*

A man's head in a plastic bag. The enclosing darkness confirmed
by the further wrapping of a woollen balaclava. At rest. The cold
floor of a urinal stall. Placed, & by his own volition; facing West.
It is the prophetic, the head of Slade. Thin hair, slicked with
sugar-water, caps the skull. The cranial folds licked into order,
sweetness seeps through as slow energy poison, domestic syrups
strangling the sources of fire. What word is left, what impulse,
what charge towards light, what plant opening on the tongue:
whatever is left in this island, among the moistures of the dead,
the distilled wisdoms, finds entrance in this cave of darkness,
this bone machine sealed into its glassy skin.

Climbing with the sun, at choice, out along the rim of Isla's
Dune: Penton St, Barnsbury Rd, to where Richmond Avenue
dips & surges to the West. The redshift into haze, cold Highgate,
woods filtered blue, retreating, distance enlarging, the folding
of morning, place chosen, witness to this confession. Slade has
no place, all curvature, smooth everywhere, one circumference
of thought meeting itself. The agreed location allows us to
describe, to put limits on infinite extensions of rhetoric. This is
the chosen exterior. The hutment, wayside shrine. Among trees:
'the public lavatory'. But the interior will not serve. Too surgical,
tight. Slade chooses instead the setting of the Islington High
Street dugout with its fine brass, its water-tanks, its length. The
sound of water running over weathered marble, drip of green
silurian swamp, glass too cold to touch, aquarium silence inducing
the urge towards pious confession. It is here that the final effort
must be made.

The head must make a communication necessary beyond
torso. It is charged & live, hot, with the grey electric tortures of
garages, nails in the tongue, genital spark, scored skin, bruises
spreading & bursting, cosmetic preparation for the death of the
body. The swallowed teeth & pains, tyre manufacturer's name
appended to spread beaver & satin pin'd-up flesh, bubble the
high pink into his mouth, the chainsaw hacks through his arteries,

he is released, bone burns to charcoal, fat spatters their varnished boots. The corpse could now be scattered, his finites, definitively, split. Found floating. The torso sinks into river mud. The legs hang white in local tides, adhering to the pole of fish totems, the raw mush. But the head is free to speak: all muddy obstructions cleared. Garrulous in this new freedom. The mouth is all word, the lips quiver. This marvellous trophy is exhibited, secretly, behind the closed doors of East End pubs: the Crown & Dolphin, the Carpenter's Arms, the Old Horns, the Seven Stars. Moves on to the South Coast, back into Essex. A triumph, a tribal score paid. Smoked pink in the flame of igniting Panatellas, Whiffs, Wintermans. The scattered limbs, & knuckles, fingers rap out accusations at low tide, in shale graves & fox-holes, in urban woodland, in concrete, in refuse, across horizons the fragments connect. The word is forged, the wisdoms focused.

The episode that is & was Slade he is reluctant to conclude, to close down, until the word, whose ghost he is, has been spoken; a word as substantial as that ghost of a flea, & gleaming, now, in pristine urgency. He is the victim of his own finality. Now & forever. Advancing entropy. Incapable of expressing his essence or escaping from it.

He is immune to the touch of the wind that destroyed him, though if he comes physically into contact with even the shadow of a dog he is gone. Scarcely there. His conviction less than a rumour. A low glimmer, a star burnt in lime.

His notion of the universe is moving backwards, snail-like, into the cave of origin, the only possible instigation or source of energy, the explosion, the drama, the moment of death. Energy that was the destruction of his previous self. So his birth is out of willed suicide. He died in a mirror, funnelling through, as time reversed, made way for him. Slade realises that he is infinitely attached to that point of extinction, all his motive force, before & after, comes from this fountain. The conic section is smooth, allows for irregularities, singularities, bends, shifts, faults. All that he has, & is, flattens, tubes out, into wire, elongates. The words stretch into colours, streaming back into his eyes. Implosion reversed, as on film. The severed head is lit by this knowledge. For there to be Time there must be Event, & someone using it, no other description possible: without action, no time. No forward.

Seizure. The knuckles of his lost hand make this the eternally repeating moment. The one place is stressed into a fan of frozen sequences. Place is never the same. The moment is enacted, over & over, in invisibly varied locations. An imagined Wall of Brass, an urge to protect this island, is being forged from Slade's knuckles.

The pins pulse red. The charge runs into his creased fingers where they are hidden in a deepfreeze storage unit – in Loughton, where the great east-moving ley crosses the old forest; Shelley's Hill, Debden Slade ("Deadman's Slade"), with Genesis Slade half a mile to the north, the scald marks of his mother's tartan rug. His name precedes him into the map, his death; cold wind streaming into his nostril.

The dead, frozen at their event horizon, strike, like vipers, through the ring of frost, the same crimes not quite completed; leer from behind the protection of their elders, the oak, the beech, the hornbeam, birch, maple, blackthorn & common crab, bird cherry, goat willow & butcher's broom.

And postulated, in eternal opposition, is the Head of Brass, the fate of the island, buried with Bran at the White Mount, lost. The head manufactured by Friar Bacon, whose climax was the sole imperative, "Time Is" – unable to reach beyond naked description. A man-made industrial thing, metal worked, mined, purified, animated by female secretions; back of the skull reson- ant to Europe's cargo, interior fed with local knowledge.

The process of this new oracle is mummification, out of time, the leather'd scalp of Slade. Behind him, & through the forest, the fen, the coast, is that ancient miracle, the Wall, the unseen guardian of value. It is pegged & gated by those high conscious- nesses situated in the East of England, those wills, those animators of the actual, hidden in Cambridge, Brightlingsea, London, curving through to Sussex. They are set into the wall. The wall is their stance, & the connection between them, the spread. They concen- trate their attention on the skull & urge it to speech, articulation. The dried lips move. Its own impulse is another, & opposing, thing. It speaks out of the corruption of the city. It breaks language out of wound & curse.

Slade's aborted syllabic urge has its analogue in the spasms of graffiti-scribblers. It boils too fast for his mouth, is a solar dictate, shafting from the loins, where no loins are. The way they hurl those frantic messages onto the brick. Slade suffers it, no means of writing; he erupts in adrenalin skin colour change, muscles twitch in his cheek. No sound to be heard. The excess spills, mixes with, the voices of Borley, slogans on the walls of bunkers, begging letters in urinals. No blood travels to his eye.

He is romantic & reactionary as are all the spiritually ambiti- ous souls. His point-of-view, curiously, remains almost six feet from the ground & does not fall to his new sack-in-the-corner position. The merciless & predatory ear of Joe Orton flaps in his face, damp, like a bat, unsatisfied, haunting these tiles for a short eternity, furry with blood mat hair, sharp with splinters of bone. He reads on the brickwork: "NF FUCKS MEN." And is not displeased. Belief in visionary release through action, any action that breaks the chain of inertia. Sodomy. Fascism. The Heroes do not want to keep everything as it is – but to make it as it was in Myth Time, which never happened, but which is happening now as they strike the first surrogate blow.

Feet tread down the dead faces into the yielding earth, the leaves, crisp skins flattened, nothing feels. Only aware of a limb as the pain climbs through it, mind among the high trees, the gathering clouds. He treads, with a satisfaction like tobacco, on these mounds & herbal plains. He crushes.

The skull rolls, polarised, caught between opposing magnetic fields. Did it have hair? It did. Each hair a thought, a spine, an action, blazing upright from its alien seed-bed.

He is indifferent to the bright wind optimism of these October streets. He drives his antler into the clouds. Pulling away from the site that he has chosen for his last stand, away from the human debris that came to him with the bricks.

In Slade's acoustic chamber the hawk-nosed man of the west, launched on the Powers, lolls, staggers, his song of plaint, his nasal accusations, rise & shake the polished tiles, the thick brass pipes, the venereal plaques. A Kerry man whose song is a challenge, to the City & the Moment, a disembodied purity, as he pisses onto his cuffs, causing the old tweed to steam, onto his unlaced boots. Nothing drips from his slack member. Though it remains held out over the fresh water that rushes into the trough. A newspaper bulges in his overcoat pocket. His companion two stalls clear, is silent, dehydrated on a sour binge, all fires gone, in Angel exile, in No-Man's Islington.

Darkness of the Nebula closes about the dugout; the urinal is wheeled out among the stars. The song of the old Republican spills thinly between the dust of comets; into the great trench of blackness, into the absence of warm animal light. The head is sucked across the floor, itches into numbers, into marked insects, scarabs, marble chips. Each with its sigil, each impulse has a value: a reason for existence, a motive, a reason for movement. The head of Slade still looks like a head, rings hollow, an elegant lattice of numbers in treaty, in alliance, re-entering the ionized dust cloud, mating with silica, iron, false carbon. The cloud thickens, all voices, all numbers, radial velocities, become the galactic motive, into the arms of the Nebula, bone embrace, stress factors, Slade's purpose served, what he thought

if consciousness
keeps the clouds afloat, the ribs – then the unconscious is forced
down into the darkness where it is active: the unconscious is
made out of darkness, the dust cloud is woven from the shape
of Slade's head, forced wide, travelling beyond the west, there
is no west – into that envelope, travelling plains of nothingness
where the compass loses itself

speech

SLADE'S INVECTIVE

all life is star .
the shadow cannot of its own volition leave the ground
all energy is war .
opposites united, stitch the flux
the weapon discharges the need to reply
the head, cut, floats on its arteries
like a kite
watered in dust, the plant of bone .
life is evil, & its mirror

surface repels (hyper-space / emptied mind)
repulsion like attraction
speeds through the barrier

zones describe, & do not limit

the stars abandon the human strategy
like "Star Wars" operate in archetype

the stars foreclose

every nerve is star born
the dust comes out of our faces
reforming the marvellous
the child of galaxies
the old fire emotions writ large
Keats – holiness of the heart
is modular entrance
is shape of star, essence

the heart floats
cut free of its strings

alone endures,
without actors to clothe the word
gravities to contain the light
shapes where the light clusters
as it comes through glass
as light breaks to this pattern
as we reach across, blood erected into bone
as the skin dreams of folding
enclosing, about the coin
legs into cups
as the beasts rise up & walk like men
face to face, the thought crackles
blue beam for hero, blood jet for power
clamped together in sickle

the hooded core strikes

the assembled fragments
join to illude a new world, globe
of spittle shot into a snake's eye

time is what we cut out of the reptile's belly

Slade faces them. His audience is not posterity, but the dead. In
this alone – like Baudelaire. Not truth itself, the abstraction, but
the truth of his own instinct brought out, set down. All he was.
Facing the raised half-circle, the expectant galleried masks, sterile
planets lifting above the wooden tiers, the sawdust, the table.
His peers, set-faced hierarchies of the dead, non-critical, without
irony, returning his effort, untouched; but subtly altered. The
ecstasy of silence, cunningly, denied.

*"To make it worth while to destroy myself, there is not enough of myself
to do it with"*

LOCALE

The snow is glass
a punched-out window

taking the light, sharply angled

the trees infested with the bones
the essential skeletons of fish :
acid has been introduced
to colour the nerves of transit

feet travelling the sky,
peg'd to half-
dry winds ; nocturne

returning by the same marks to
an unaltered fate

I stay within the power of
calling these vowels,
along the outer casing of the tree
a single ink vein
accepted in the bark

naming this season: "foreign"

lid's off, Apocalypse
re-entering
the gilded capital

a treaty, a division with solitude

CROSSING THE MORNING

Climbing sun boulders the hill crest

between the stones the cat appears
ingratiating, or merely tactical, completing

the arc & arrow of low-rolled desire

chopped pillars making altars or anvils

here the feather, the ant
does its work,
versing & reversing, willing its will,
a system of hair-fine lines;
by its direct movements, abrupt to the eye
by its blade, its balance
making this place whole

all those branches, windows, archways
water chest open to air
leaf-drenched dark pools, unmeditated
folding back to the river & the hills

the Kingstone set apart
on ground that pulses like a warning

that stands because the rest has fallen

SPIRIT LEVELS

"The wish comes/ to write about the places/ I have come to"

on the hills above Port Glasgow
the most impressive, the dead
hierarchies of Azrael
not yet hoarded & ash-scattered
in Cricklewood: the unrisen sons,
& the air . . . rich as bovril

on Hillhead the buildings:
its the broken English aristos who
need the malt, Jimmie,
& the lamb-knuckle tikka
is dished in accents
of Jock Stein: they're pillaging
the stored dust, Voltaire & Rousseau

whose mouth opens to the ice
ocean: Polaris,
grounded, the Resurrection blasts locks
from the monuments, multitudes
of vertical corpses, capital of dolour:
under the rain stones
the dead sleep, face downwards

the beauty of
slums
built to last a thousand years,
a Reich of grey-blue blocks;
no better skyline in Europe
no better place to view
than from under

o lovely gash/ of truth

FLESH EGGS

white herm :
a cyclone of sticky dusts
expressing no relief

the rods in their circuit
grind small wind;
waterwheel set into baked earth

censor the actions, not the words

the magnetic west
weakens the stomach & the prose

allowing in too much "nature"

grateful then for the timidity of sheep
but nevertheless surprised when one

rips your flesh with his
pastry-cutting teeth; never trust a herbivor

"what kind are the rocks?"

no kind at all, a shattering
drench of spray as the resolved waves
unscrew themselves, a bravado

like genocide, too baroque a rhetoric
for the old maestro, the deaf one

the losers say: "SHUT UP & DEAL"

.

A HAT THROWN IN THE AIR, A LEG THAT'S LOST

" an honest woman breaks her leg at home "

trust is a meadow, the light in my eyes,
a peculiar opacity, fearing blindness
and surprise itself, the source of fear

honouring the mortar, the ditch
in photographs that remain potential

the whistle of an arrow or the bark of a dog
hearing in images, the ear has a greater
depth of field, and what it cannot form
goes back into the border of darkness

better to exercise your fingers across the tabletop
than mutilate a sonata

the dream is serial, lke the Vengeance of Fu Manchu,
not episodic each sequence having
the same weight & structure: a pornography
of gesture, not action

asleep in the chair, but not yet become it

alone, this solitude crystallises

AUTISTIC POSES

"alive, but past recall"

her heels worn raw
two bacon-colour'd patches
: dollar sized

black crombie,
collar turned up &
covered in white dog hairs

"I haven't been well"

damp snuffling ahead,
dry rasping cough behind

the shopping precinct
disappears into a glass screen

"THIS SAFE HAS A TIME DELAYING LOCK"

our official, no brahmin,
low caste as an umpire
shovels out the reluctant benefits

on his wall a map of London
cut off at the Thames

so that
the south is not merely unknown

it doesn't exist

SERPENT TO ZYMURGY

more diseases than textbooks

I had thought St Vitus's dance as
much of a back number as the cakewalk:
it's stomping here in full fig,
velveteen jacket worn to flesh, pocket
torn out, like a split cheekbone

try & lift from the coop
of Old Holborn, phlegm, twitchy
parrot moods: they've even
picked up on bird diseases & foul pests

the lolling sheepheaded beaten
men, the form-filling
dole scratching, ill-tempered lumpen
mess of what we are become

this post-office has more patients
than a surgery, sliding
up to the taped window across
a gob-spattered stone floor

on the low wall of the flats
a girl perfectly imitates
the "Ka-aar" of the shit-eating seagull

"Ka-aar, Ka-aar, Ka-aar"

wait long enough:
it will be the other way around

KRISTALLNACHT

"when Soutine finally consulted an ear specialist about this terrible earache, in the canal of the painter's ear the doctor discovered, not an abscess but a nest of bedbugs"

escape with the children but
escape them we cannot, will not
draw up beyond this breath:

beeswax burning in an old tin cup

break the ring with
a child's soft head before
it is too late, it is

already, the fear

is a glove turned, wax smoke;
burning honey evoking
a woman's blood, does not arouse

it terrifies us & the protection
which is this room, marked
with its posts, becomes

a place of torment: the children
we discover in ourselves are

drained, stars only
on the outside of their lids

& the unfractured night runs
wild as a scalded dog

NICK TOTTON

ARMS WHICH ARTICULATE NOTHING

the page's satin that I turn deliberate moulds a fancy bell
lolls on the bed not contemplating this woman sadly
sounds as if speaking to her – "not daring to allow such beauty"
that's going to savour pricelessness.
this woman passes imperceptibly into brutal flowers
sometimes she returns in unprinted seasons
& asks the time or beams at encores (she's making a mine to see
    the jewels face to face)
come, real creature, don't faint
or the world will die in a rapture produced in the annulled air
a croak in the neighbourhood of the heart, whose
morning journeys carry singers
        whose voice is the colour of sable, of tender and
    dangerous rivers
and perfect silken seeds... who read the passage in which all the
    young girls
        leading beasts on chains –
but the most beautiful is the uncertainty, letters
of hands more white than the scorn of stars at midday
ravaging the white nightingale
because it rains all the time
& simpers so basely that the wings can no longer melt
into hands rising up to arms lighter than vapour
        from prayer in such gracious interlacings, undecided
    stares
        in that imperfect mirror
or *arms which articulate nothing other than the exceptional danger*
       of a body made for love
whose belly calls for supper   detached from full bosoms
    famined veins;
which has no terrestial cue but icy vertigo detached
    from the regard of the white sten-gun
which I don't see again
because of the marvellous bandolier
which is mine in the marching column of wounds

            (with regards to André Breton)

IF I HAD TO DO IT ALL OVER AGAIN, I'D DO IT ALL OVER YOU

when now & often I begin to grieve
a white hat defends my fortune.
when I make a triangle to dishearten you
it spreads its arms into a square to greet you.

passion of the terraces:
hot breath, cold comfort
as the rain scare comes in curling
on aromatic breezes from the west.

you leave the country and a hill puckers
sail away   sunny day
& the guarantee of full-time living I ask for
the wages of intensity

are unwavering presence;
personally I trust those laugh lines
my knowledgeable sucker waving
in the gentle warm currents of the north –

& when the intensity began to falter
strung out along all the wire from
here to *here*; it was the mutual question
we didn't try to answer; crying and
exploding through the middle air

THE CONTOURS OF INDIFFERENCE

As mundane effect of the incendiary veil,
purposeful, direct, men of gulps,
you cannot deny you are here.

Melting ice, grimaces collecting in beggars' bowls,
the yawn of mistakes beneath our feet –
it's empty, that's all, debate and judge;
not for having solid muscle, graceful and moist,
not for having entered the sea of scales,

is he who thinks and walks finished.
No plural tone caked with jade.

From the eastern sky, intrinsic east of stars,
digital, in which stars enter, lubricated –
wakers of a foot, marchers in topaz,
passers-by abrased by my arms,
you cannot deny you are here.

Nothing delights or dismays the judge;
nothing has absorbed or destroyed the cruel key of the skeleton.
Only emptiness; as the bravest thing.
And man, so dumb, resists, sad with coloured juices.

Tiny scabs on the trunk, the extremities:
tiny sips and a long-subdued metastasis on a plate.
Powers come a-visiting from on high
and wash themselves with care caressing their solid palms.
You cannot deny you are here.

My tribal refusal, my sensational involuted arm
glacial and a bastard, from the flame
friend of the depths, a rabbi of form
no plural tone caked with jade.

For certain these men complete years in their dangers;
each a whole front to his salutations.
With such men arranged, meat to meat, the arm reenters florally;
they ready themselves by hand for hasty steps to the sky,
and man, so dumb, resists, sad with coloured juices.
You cannot deny you are here.

INFLUENCING MACHINES

for Petra Meier

It's a dreamy party, & wired for sound
on every channel : come as you are
    (and bring a bucket)
        come as you are

"a Reflex man, a Co-Walker"
a clean machine. Clear
        split image
        right down the middle
at the point of impact; clear
               split second
of the unrequited heart, apple of the
mind's eye swallowed whole;
we all survived the crash, only the
        journey died.
Insoluble demands
        in the neighbouring bedroom
turn the sun blind like a solid body;
        a damp passport to
           a rainy country.
The burning breath passes from mouth to mouth
and just when you're ready to die
      – THE SQUEEZE TECHNIQUE –
under their own steam and breathing heavily
excitable machines ascend
        through the downpour
        the wired jaw falls to pieces
it's wonderful what they won't think of next.
We'll have to take our chances, the cards all
      reversed and grinning faintly, & all in that
         sacred half-light, all packaged
           all sewn up; so a call
goes out for the scissors which
calloused your forefinger last night
before you pointed right between my eyes and called
        some name, half-intelligible
         partly mine.
    Abandon, indifference, trust,
surrender, nakedness : I swallow it all
    and still can't get enough.
I'm eternally in love with your productions, the machine whispers;
    tender mouths   tender moths
circling the glowing fringe
        now stripped down
    to rough breathing naturally I
        won't admit the damage
      or ask for the return
of the keys; preferring to tip the waiter,
    tip my hat, & tip-toe

out into the rain. But when the motor coughs
                    when the light goes out
            when the rain and bleeding stop
all that remains will be the names we have chosen
calling to each other across the soaking field.

NOT SLIPPING INTO SOMETHING MORE COMFORTABLE

for J.H. Prynne

*My proposal is, therefore, surely the mildest possible.
Oh, it is so weak! My proposal is that at least we should
make the true state of affairs known.*
                                    – Kierkegaard

1

Through the voice barrier, and formulaic atrophy
            doubling in the blank cistern
is brought to display by surgery
            at first light; cold as brass, striated
throughout the cluster, bat-winged polygons
            of frustrated jerk that beats darkly by interference.
This will butter no solutions to the red
            quadratic, humming and tapping at the
lunar grid; but offers a soft answer
            of minerals to the glare of appetite
serrating the skyline beyond which,
            darkness. Each spectral probe hits pay
dirt. Pain bubbles up like
            black gold from the laminated strata
until the bit snaps or sequence
interrupted bites back on us – all survivors
            fed and blanketed by a team of specialists
homing in on the bone bleep, the snore
            of terminal exchange you can't count
on your fingers. You can't count on
            anything but the matrix and its habits;
it is red hot and looks it; its movements random
            and meaningful as our own.

2

So the tap is installed across the grid,
    leaking in bits out of the system; tremors
announce rapid energy transactions
    on bound and unbound levels, honey and
fire, brilliant spasms dispersed
    by correct use of the cream. Every number
begs for treatment; octaves of drone
    under the ghost dome of regard
offer the shivering victims total cover
    by the method of exhaustion. *Garbage in,*
garbage out, and the imperishable goods
    press down on us like a metal invitation
printing out time, place and purpose
    as back-brain rubric, as horoscope. The matrix
stands square and magic in the somber
    light of earth, old war-wound
transposed into landscape, the lie
    of the land. And yet something burns fretless
at the very tip of sense – a phantom tanker
    in enharmonic shift into the visible :
vessel at which we cling and suck,
    full and sleepy-smiling with the milk of that.

3

Override the cut-off and the stops
    will block; but once unjammed,
the set replays each transit
    in fat flashback on the golden screen,
jolts of pulpy astonishment disturbing
    its even scan. With a clash and beat
of harmonics, the last diesis
    is lost in the wash, and all proceed
to bashing the joanna : panchromatic glut
    across the board, rainbow intercalations
that save appearances and seal the wounds
    of time. Refinery. The smooth lunar fluid
cracks and bleeds off its fractions; returns
    as hands at the throat choking off the progression
before you can say cheese. If you'd rather
    stop now, say the word – but the word sticks

in the inter- intra- innards;
    a clear second ahead at the
tape, squeals and falls, before this double
    movement leaps the year and slips away like nothing
so much as *actual behaviour*, smoky
    oscillations in the final chamber
that every interval reveals. Written out of
    the program, it runs off smoothly
and vanishes over the next crest.

THIS SONG IS DEDICATED TO THE ONE EYE LOVE
A Sonnet Sequence

for Lindsey Clark

1

There isn't a word for what I want from you.
I try Crystal Radio, I try Silence
    I try Meet My Gaze
None of them will answer.
.... Radioactive love
        comes on in a rush
Melting the flesh off the bone
The gold out of the rocks, Mutate! Mutate!
If you can't beat it, join it!
Those weren't the words either.

And you have to go on through all this.
And you have to go on through all this.

An appetite
        without moving parts
That won't take No for an answer

I want it from You and I want it Now

2

I want it from You and I want it Now.
There's a piece missing from the heart
        a gap between things
I can't get through.
                        Love is like
Brain damage, that something missing
And you cannot remember what it is
And you try to tell someone
And you cannot remember the words.

You invent codes
                When you're damaged
To remind you what things are; table, razor,
Comb, hippocampus, anterior lobe,
Part-object, mirror, starlight.

You invent codes.
And then you cannot remember the codes.

3

That You was not the previous You.
That You was me. This is me, now, talking,
Large as life and twice as natural.
This is one of poetry's illusory functions
Which makes it akin to love.

It shares with love also a hunted look around the eyes,
As if afraid it had forgotten something,
Like what day of the week or its own name.

Poetry is also damaged.
Liable to be hospitalised at any moment.
Still on its feet. A miracle.

I want to tell you how miraculously I love
(That You was the original You.
That You was the real thing.)

4

That You was the real thing.
Wow. That time the earth really moved.
I haven't had a You like that since....I don't know when.

I am surrounded by
                    faulty memories.
Like unrequited ghosts – all wanting me to speak for them.
I tell them I am on serious business.

There is a line missing here.

The text resumes :
.... till father's blood is quite transfused;
All the best and hoping to hear from you,
All the best and hoping to hear from you,
All the best and hoping to hear from you,

In bands of alternating colour
Running between the lines.

5

Running between the lines
Or sometimes directly across them
Nimbly avoiding oncoming traffic
Escaped from the hospital *again* –

Perhaps the damage is identical
With what we are, what we are best at, our reaching out
Beyond and beyond any possible help, recourse,
Accommodation, reaching out beyond – ?

Heartbreak is a condition of love.
I just now went downstairs to see you.
You said I could drink your whisky if I replaced it.
I couldn't love you if you weren't heartbroken.

I came back upstairs with your whisky.
There isn't a word for what I want from you.

6

And then you cannot remember the code
And the dialling tone is wrong.
This must be another country. Don't worry, STD
Is international. There must be a way.

But I don't speak the language.
Don't worry. I told you, don't worry.
But we're halfway through already!
                                    – Telegram sonnet nightmare,
Don't worry, I've seen this kind of thing before,
This anxious behaviour syndrome. In a movie or something.

(The sonnet is a good form for love poetry
By its edgy sense of an ending approaching,
Like a last train or vein or phoning abroad –
Like trying to speak very quickly and clearly to someone you love
      who is distant.
The haiku is not so good. For the same reason.)

7

Please don't take this personally.
I mean it personally, but please don't take it personally.
I should explain that this poem may make you immortal,
Or at any rate change your relationship with time.
But not *personally* immortal –
And always the chance of textual emendation –

As it seems I become everyone I love.

Faulty memories; none of them will answer.

So the bell has beaten us again
Still on our feet. A miracle.
Sheer fluke. This flukiness of love,
And poetry : like brain damage :
You never know what's wired up to what.
It just might, you never know.

8

If you count up the different senses of "you" in the text
(Including those two)
You may reach some interesting conclusions
But you will discover nothing about poetry or love.
Discuss.
Heartbreak is a condition of love.
Discuss.
I write poetry because I am so inarticulate;
I still want to tell you how miraculously I love
Here in front of an audience
No cuts, no splices, no editing at all
No script, no rehearsals, no playback, no feedback
No information retrieval systems whatsoever
In a condition of total miraculous instantaneous damaged love.

Bibliography

Anthony Barnett. *Blood Flow*, Nothing Doing (formally in London): London 1975; *Titular I-VI*, Grosseteste Press: Pensnett 1975; *Fear and Misadventure & Mud Settles*, Ferry Press: London 1977; *Blues that Must Not Try to Imitate the Sky*, Lobby Press: Cambridge 1978; *Report to the Working Party. Asylum. Otiose (preceded by) After*, Nothing Doing (formally in London): London 1979; *A White Mess*, Nothing Doing (formally in London): London 1981; *North, North, I said, No, Wait a Minute, South, Oh, I don't Know (148 Political Poems)*, distributed by Allardyce, Barnett: London & Berkeley 1985; *The Resting Bell*, Allardyce, Barnett: London, Lewes & Berkeley 1987.

David Chaloner. *Year of Meteors*, Arc Publications: Gillingham 1972; *Chocolate Sauce*, Ferry Press: London 1973; *Projections*, Burning Deck: Providence, R.I., 1977; *Today Backwards*, The Many Press: London 1977; *Fading into Brilliance*, Oasis Books: London 1978; *Hotel Zingo*, Grosseteste Press: Wirksworth & Leeds 1981.

Andrew Crozier. *Walking on Grass*, Ferry Press: London 1969; *The Veil Poem*, Burning Deck, Providence, R.I., 1974; *Pleats*, Great Works Editions: Bishops Stortford 1975; *Residing*, Aggie Weston's: Belper 1976; *High Zero*, Street Editions: Cambridge 1978; *Were There*, The Many Press: London 1978; *Utamaro Variations* (with Ian Tyson), Tetrad: London 1982; *All Where Each Is*, Allardyce, Barnett: London & Berkeley 1985.

Roy Fisher. *City*, Migrant Press: Worcester & Ventura 1961; *Ten Interiors with Various Figures*, Tarasque Press: Nottingham 1966; *Collected Poems 1968: The Ghost of a Paper Bag*, Fulcrum Press: London 1969; *Nineteen Poems and an Interview*, Grosseteste Press: Pensnett 1975; *The Thing About Joe Sullivan*, Carcanet Press: Manchester 1978; *Wonders of Obligation*, Braad Editions: Loubressac 1979; *Poems 1955-1980*, Oxford University Press: Oxford 1980.

Veronica Forrest-Thomson. *Cordelia*, Omens: Leicester [n.d.], *On the Periphery*, Street Editions: Cambridge 1976.

John Hall. *Couch Grass*, Great Works Editions: Bishops Stortford 1978; *Meaning Insomnia*, Grosseteste Press: Wirksworth 1978.

Ralph Hawkins. *The Word from the One*, Galloping Dog Press: Newcastle upon Tyne 1980; *Tell Me No More and Tell Me*, Grosseteste Press: Wirksworth & Leeds 1981.

John James. *The Welsh Poems*, Grosseteste Press: Lincoln 1967; *The Small Henderson Room*, Ferry Press: London 1969; *Striking the Pavilion of Zero*, Ian McKelvie: London 1975; *Berlin Return*, Délires, Ferry Press, Grosseteste Press: Liverpool, London & Matlock 1983.

Tim Longville. *Familiarities*, Grosseteste Press: Lincoln 1967; *Pigs with Wings*, Grosseteste Press: Lincoln 1970; *Spectacles, Testicles, Wallet & Watch*, Grosseteste Press: Pensnett 1973; *Between the River and the Sea*, Grosseteste Press: Leeds 1976, Island Writing Series: Lantzville, B.C., 1981; *Seven Elephants and One Eye*, Grosseteste Press: Matlock 1978.

Douglas Oliver. *Oppo Hectic*, Ferry Press: London 1969; *The Harmless Building*, Ferry Press & Grosseteste Press: London & Pensnett 1973; *In the Cave of Suicession*, Street Editions: Cambridge 1974; *The Diagram Poems*, Ferry Press: London 1979; *The Infant and the Pearl*, Ferry Press (for Silver Hounds): London 1985; *Kind*, Allardyce, Barnett: London, Lewes & Berkeley 1987.

Peter Philpott. *What Was Shown*, Ferry Press: London 1980; *Some Action Upon the World*, Grosseteste Press: Matlock 1982.

J.H. Prynne. *Kitchen Poems*, Cape Goliard Press: London and Grossman Publishers Inc.: NY 1968; *The White Stones*, Grosseteste Press: Lincoln 1969; *Brass*, Ferry Press: London 1971; *Into the Day*, privately printed: Cambridge 1972; *Wound Response*, Street Editions: Cambridge 1974; *High Pink on Chrome*, privately printed: Cambridge 1975; *News of Warring Clans*, Trigram Press: London 1977; *Down where changed*, Ferry Press: London 1979; *Poems*, Agneau 2: London & Berkeley, 1982; *The Oval Window*, privately printed: Cambridge 1983.

John Riley. *Ancient and Modern*, Grosseteste Press: Lincoln 1967; *What Reason Was*, Grosseteste Press: Pensnett 1973; *That is Today*, Pig Press: Newcastle upon Tyne 1978; *The Collected Works*, Grosseteste Press, Wirksworth & Leeds 1980.

Peter Riley. *Love-Strife Machine*, Ferry Press: London 1969; *The Linear Journal*, Grosseteste Press: Lincoln 1970; *Ways of Approaching*, Grosseteste Press: Pensnett 1973; *The Musicians the Instruments*, Many Press: London 1978; *Lines on the Liver*, Ferry Press: London 1981; *Tracks and Mineshafts*, Grosseteste Press: Matlock 1983.

John Seed. *Spaces In*, Pig Press: Newcastle upon Tyne 1976; *History Labour Night*, Pig Press: Durham 1984.

Iain Sinclair. *Muscat's Würm*, Albion Village Press: London 1972; *The Birth Rug*, Albion Village Press: London 1973; *Lud Heat*, Albion Village Press: London 1975; *Suicide Bridge*, Albion Village Press: London 1979; *Fluxions*, Albion Drive Chapbooks: London 1983; *Flesh Eggs and Scalp Metal*, Hoarse Commerce: London 1983; *Autistic Poses*, Hoarse Commerce: London 1985.

Nick Totton. *Making a Meal of It*, Curiously Strong: London 1976; *Radio Times*, Grosseteste Press: Matlock 1983.